Contents

The Responsible Workplace
The redesign of work and offices

Francis Duffy, Andrew Laing and Vic Crisp

DEGW and the Building Research Establishment

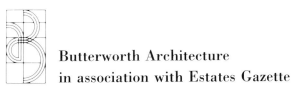

Butterworth Architecture
in association with Estates Gazette

Butterworth Architecture
An imprint of Butterworth-Heinemann Ltd
Linacre House, Jordan Hill, Oxford OX2 8DP

 A member of the Reed Elsevier group

OXFORD   LONDON   BOSTON
MUNICH   NEW DELHI   SINGAPORE   SYDNEY
TOKYO   TORONTO   WELLINGTON

First published 1993
Reprinted 1994

British Library Cataloguing in Publication Data
Responsible Workplace: Redesign of Work
and Offices
  I. Duffy, Francis
  725
ISBN 0 7506 0802 1

Library of Congress Cataloguing in Publication Data
Duffy, Francis, 1940–
  The responsible workplace: the redesign of work and
  offices/Francis Duffy, Andrew Laing and Vic Crisp.
  p.   cm.
  "The Responsible Workplace research study was
  undertaken by DEGW London Limited with the
  Building Research Establishment." – CIP data sheet
  Includes bibliographical references and index.
  ISBN 0 7506 0802 1
  1. Office layout. I. Laing, Andrew. II. Crisp, Vic.
  III. DEGW London Limited. IV. Building Research
  Establishment. V. Title.
  HF5547.2.D84 1993
  658.23–dc20   92-37496
                                         CIP

Composition by Genesis Typesetting, Laser Quay,
Rochester, Kent
Printed and bound in Great Britain

Sponsors

The Responsible Workplace research study was undertaken by DEGW London Limited with the Building Research Establishment and was funded by the following Sponsors:

Founder sponsors

BICC Technologies – Haden
British Gas
Conder M & E
Formwood Group Limited
ICL
Land Securities
MEPC plc
Steelcase Strafor
The Wellcome Foundation

Sponsors

EPAD, France
Norwich Union
Plan Construction & Architecture, France
The Rutland Group
Unifor, Italy

Contributors

Dr Francis Duffy, Founder and Chairman of the international architectural practice DEGW is one of the leading thinkers and practitioners in the science of workplace design.

Dr Andrew Laing, is an Associate Director of DEGW London Limited, where he has specialised in research into changing users' needs and their impact on the office workplace.

Dr Vic Crisp, Director of the Environment and Energy Group, Building Research Establishment is responsible for research programmes concerned with the technical, economic and social factors affecting the environmental and energy performance of buildings. The work provides advice and technical inputs to UK government policies relating to building and construction.

George Atkinson, Consultant to the Building Research Establishment.

Iain Borden, Consultant at Building Use Studies and lecturer in architectural history at The Bartlett, University College London.

William Bordass, Principal in William Bordass Associates.

Alan Flatman, Manager of Local Network Strategy, ICL.

Andrew Harrison, Associate Director of DEGW London Limited.

Simon Hodgkinson, Senior Consultant at Touche Ross Management Consultants.

Adrian Leaman, Managing Director of Building Use Studies.

Bruce Lloyd, Head of The Management Centre, South Bank University.

Brian McDougall, Partner of EAL Property Research Consultants.

Acknowledgements

The Responsible Workplace research project was made possible by financial support from Sponsors who directly participated in reviewing the progress of the study. Their interest was a great stimulus to the research effort. Our thanks are due to:

Founder sponsors

BICC Technologies – Haden: Gio Lusignani and John Deal
British Gas: Derek Chisholm and Clive Taylor
Conder M & E: Graham Farnfield
Formwood Group Limited: Gavin Barlas
ICL: Andy Mawson
Land Securities: Graham Field
MEPC plc: David Parkinson
Steelcase Strafor: Paul Godfrey and Christine Lawson
The Wellcome Foundation: Anthony Bridgeman

Sponsors

EPAD (France): Bernard Audiberd
Norwich Union: Richard Perrin and Roger Richard
Plan Construction et Architecture (France): Ruth Marquès
The Rutland Group: James McAllister
Unifor (Italy): Sergio Serra

Invaluable support to the research was provided by a group of organisations who agreed to be the subjects of interviews and visits to their offices. They often also provided drawings and architectural plans to illustrate their workplaces. Many individuals in case study companies helped the progress of research, but particular thanks are due to:

Case study participants

AWK, Germany: Dr Marter and Herr Schmidt
Bertelsmann AG, Germany: Herr Bieker and Herr Nagel
Dent Lee Witte plc, UK: Richard Lee
Digital Equipment Corporation, Finland: Erkki Wirta
Edding, Germany: Rüdiger Kallenberg
Enfield Borough Council, UK: Colin Bullworthy
Glaxo Pharmaceuticals, UK: Dr William Proudlock
Greenpeace, UK: Colin Hines and Jonathan Smales
Health Education Authority, UK: Dr Spencer Hagard
IBM, UK: Andrew Bailey and John Jack
Independent Television News, UK: Michael Batchelor and Peter Ward
Instituut voor Milieu en Systeemanalyse Netherlands: Marcel Bovi and Wouter van Dieren
MEPC, UK: Roger Squire, David Parkinson and Nick Pakes
Olivetti Information Services Group, Italy: Luigi Rispoli
PA Consulting Group, UK: Paul Wakeham
Policy Studies Institute, UK: Bill Daniel and Eileen Reid
Spie Batignolles, France: Claude Caillard
Volvo Car Corporation, Sweden: Nils Blonde and Hasse Spetz

Thanks are also due to all members of the Responsible Workplace team, including our advisory group and the authors of the trend papers. Particular acknowledgement should be paid to both Simon Hodgkinson and Alexi Marmot who originated the idea for the research project when at DEGW, to Joanna Eley for her efforts with the case study research and to Natasha Owen for editorial work.

DEGW Research Team

Dr Francis Duffy
Tony Thomson
Dr Andrew Laing
Jay McMahan
Peter McLennan
Daniel C Mouawad
Alvise Simondetti
Janine Vasta
Sharon Chapler
Annette Gardiner

Joanna Eley and Paula Quirk, independent premises consultants.

Building Research Establishment

Neil Milbank
Dr Vic Crisp

Advisory Group

Dr Alexi Marmot, Alexi Marmot Associates
Adrian Leaman, Building Use Studies
Dr Vic Crisp, Building Research Establishment

Authors of papers

George Atkinson, Building Research Establishment
William Bordass, William Bordass Associates
Alan Flatman, ICL
Andrew Harrison, DEGW London Limited
Simon Hodgkinson, Touche Ross Management Consultants
Dr Andrew Laing, DEGW London Limited
Adrian Leaman and Iain Borden, Building Use Studies
Bruce Lloyd, South Bank University
Brian McDougall, EAL Property Research Consultants

Foreword

Roger Courtney, Chief Executive of the Building Research Establishment Executive Agency

Building research informs the future – and nowhere is that more evident than in the design of office buildings. A decade or two ago, when office work – based on what seemed then to be the ageless technology of the telephone and the typewriter – was stable, the architect's tasks were relatively easy. Today, office work is being transformed by information technology, new forms of organisation and global markets. In addition, office buildings have to meet ever higher environmental standards. The past is an unreliable guide in such a rapid period of change. Yet long life structures have still to be erected to accommodate increasingly volatile organisations.

In this situation, how does one attempt to foresee future requirements and identify future opportunities? This was the task that BRE and DEGW set themselves in The Responsible Workplace.

The investigatory techniques adopted – trend papers, brainstorming sessions with sponsors, international case studies of advanced organisational and design practice – provided the necessary insights. From them, we could form hypotheses about what the office environment at the end of this decade may be like. These hypotheses challenge existing stereotypes of office design, fundamental property management assumptions and many conventions in the planning of the urban environment. Lively debate is inevitable. What would be even better would be a radical new direction for the offices of the next century.

Introduction

The Responsible Workplace study emerged out of the recognition by DEGW and its research partners the Building Research Establishment that new responses to the history of office building experienced in the 1980s were required. In the UK the problems of rapidly taking up information technology and accommodating a booming financial services industry led to the invention and development of a new generation of office buildings, especially in the City. By the end of the 1980s, however, there was a sense of unease, both in the UK and in the rest of Europe. Had the immense scale of office development actually achieved all that it should have? Was a never-to-be-repeated opportunity to revolutionise the world of work, the systems of building patronage and procurement, the fundamentals of office workplace design seized with sufficient rigour and imagination? Was the quality of commercial architecture significantly improved over the decade? The answer seemed to be that the revolution, if that indeed it truly was, had been patchy. Much more remains to be done.

A mixed sense of achievement and dismay was the stimulus for the study. At first glance the British office boom seemed distorted by the unquestioning adoption of North American standards, both bad and good, to the exclusion of North European values. A second glance revealed a new generation of buildings that reflected a new global corporatism of organisations utterly dependent on information technology.

Yet all this investment and invention seemed all too often to have failed to solve a fundamental problem: that of the divergence between what people, individually and collectively, wish offices to be and what many offices have become: highly conventionalised stereotypes, the logic of which has hardly been challenged for decades.

The Responsible Workplace study is a response to this problem, an attempt to explore fundamental changes underway in the way we work and in the way that work should be accommodated. The project proceeded through three phases.

The first was to commission a set of trend papers (chapters two through ten). The nine papers explore the factors likely to lead to change for the office workplace across a wide canvas, ranging through problems of location, the environment, information technology, and the new patterns of work of organisations.

The second phase was to examine case studies of innovative European organisations and how they have made and are making new kinds of decisions about the design, management and use of their workplaces (chapter 11). The case studies involved structured interviews and visits with personnel responsible both for strategic thinking for organisations and for decisions about the design and functioning of an individual workplace project. In this way the research targeted the critical links between the needs of organisations and their workplaces, rather than focusing on what might have been a conventional architectural concern with the interesting building, as such.

Finally the trend papers and case studies provided a fertile ground for proposing an overall strategic approach for conceptualising Responsible Workplaces (chapter 1) and a series of initiatives within an overall model of change and intervention through which Responsible Workplaces may be achieved (chapter 12).

The research participants are well aware that this period has been the right time to be taking stock. The lull in development activity caused by economic recession provides a welcome respite, of sorts, to reflect, research, evaluate and debate what an office architecture based on sounder attitudes to time, creativity, work, leisure, health and ecology should be like.

Note:

The study took place between October 1990 and October 1991. The data on case studies and in trend papers reflects the status of events at that time.

1 Findings in a context

The wrong buildings?

Something is very wrong with office buildings today. This judgement goes far beyond local and perhaps temporary British laments about empty offices and the ruinous consequences of oversupply. Our unease is about the essential nature of the office building itself – especially in the conventional forms with which we are familiar in both North America and Northern Europe. This conclusion is the result of rapid change in the worlds both of work and of real estate. It stems from the evidence gathered in this study.

The Responsible Workplace began as an examination of what office buildings would be like were they to be designed by architects with a profounder sense of responsibility for the aspirations of users and for the fragile and damaged ecology which supports these users. The time horizon we set for our investigations was the beginning of the next century. Predicting the future is a dangerous business: the limits of our evidence are obvious – nine trend papers, nineteen case studies drawn from the UK and Europe, and less than nine months of continuous study. Nevertheless the trends are so clear that we believe that the underlying message of *The Responsible Workplace* applies to the vast majority of office environments not only in Europe but to those in North America and Japan.

The fundamental lesson which we have identified is, quite simply, a divergence, which we believe is certain to increase, between what people, individually and collectively, wish office work and the office environment to be and what the majority of offices are actually like – highly conventionalised stereotypes, the meaning of which has hardly been challenged for decades. In the Anglo-Saxon world a limited kind of office environment – characterised by skylines from Chicago to Canary Wharf – has been dominant for over a century not because users want it (they are very rarely asked) but because such offices have been convenient to build, to manage and to exchange. This North American stereotype has, in effect, been reduced from its fine, highly particular and rational, late nineteenth century, origins to becoming simply the stock-in-trade of anyone anywhere who wishes to develop, design, and build for the property market. In Northern Europe, particularly in Scandinavia, Germany, and the Netherlands, another kind of office stereotype is the norm. This tends to be custom built and is, largely because of informed user pressure, far more user friendly. Attractive as such buildings undoubtedly are, we must question our collective ability, even in the wealthiest parts of Europe, to afford such high standards. Both the North American and Northern European stereotypes are in grave danger of becoming outmoded: one because fewer and fewer people really like working in deep space and controlled environments; the other because luxurious space and amenities simply cost too much. Alternative models of what the office of the first decade of the new millenium should be like are badly needed.

To suggest, to outline, to explore such models has been a key objective in *The Responsible Workplace*. We have presented trends and case studies not only for their own inherent interest but to use them as a platform to reach out for fresh, challenging and unconventional ideas about what forward looking office buildings and office interiors should be like. We have also sought to build a structure of ideas about the nature of the future workplace to bring together, to explain and to test what would otherwise be fragmentary glimpses of the future. Whatever ideas we have proposed have been identified for three reasons:

1 because they appear to have the capacity to respond to emerging user demands we have identified

2 because, simultaneously, these solutions appear to have the potential to bridge the gap between what is desired and what is economically feasible in organisations endowed with finite resources

3 because, cumulatively, they hold out the promise of sustaining rather than exhausting or polluting this planet's fragile eco-system upon which everyone's hope of survival for themselves and for future generations depends

To design – in the widest sense of that much underestimated word – what should be done to achieve better workplaces and eventually a better world has been an important objective. This explains the difference between those parts of *The Responsible Workplace* which are factual descriptions of research and analyses of case studies and those parts of our work which are much more subjective and value laden. Great care has been taken in the text to distinguish these two different but equally legitimate modes of thought.

Both observations and recommendations have been made in a period of particularly turbulent change. An attempt has been made in presenting the recommendations to establish a rough timetable for the likely adoption of new models for the office environment. Different users are likely to have diverse priorities. There is no such thing as the perfect office building. No one office prototype is likely to appeal equally to all. Diversity is both attractive and inevitable. Our recommendations are intended to offer an escape from the sterility of limited and limiting office stereotypes – both North American and Northern European – in the hope that increasingly demanding, ever more discriminating, and above all resource-conscious consumers will be able to exercise more rather than less choice in the design of their working environment.

Supply and demand

Trends in demand

A number of major trends have been isolated and elucidated in *The Responsible Workplace* which seem likely to influence the design and use of office buildings. What follows is a brief summary of the trend papers. The general theme which emerged can be summarised in a single phrase: an insistent demand for more.

All the Trend Papers tended in the same direction: more flexibility was wanted for business and more options were demanded for end users. More and more diverse technology was anticipated as well as the need to accommodate far more building intelligence. More natural environments were wanted but combined with more capacity in artificial building systems. More environmentally friendly buildings, more locational freedom, more discretion in the use of time were all in demand. Yet more choice was expected to be combined with more environmental responsibility. Driving rising expectations of more user choice and more stringent environmental standards are two closely interconnected realities: more powerful information technology (IT) and more powerful and discriminating users.

1 Changing businesses

Routine assumptions about the way office organisations should be structured are being overturned, often with paradoxical results: tighter control can be achieved within looser structures; organisations want to enjoy simultaneously the benefits of being both small and large; economies of scale are being replaced with economies of scope; the simple access to information resources characteristic of the early waves of the take up of IT are being converted into a demand for the creative use of knowledge; locational freedom in the conduct of work is the obvious result of ever more excellent tele-communications; freedom in the use of time is seen as being a higher freedom than control of place; traditional patterns of work, time, and location are being challenged and transformed. *Consequently, our prediction is that workplaces will have to be designed to accommodate much greater flexibility in the use of space and time, to provide more rapid responses to business and operational needs, and to allow employers to adjust to employees' rising expectations of workplace quality.*

2 Changing user expectations

Currently the freedom of office users is constrained by a hierarchical and usually sequential series of decisions about site location, the configuration of the building shell, the distribution of building services, and the layout of interior scenery. This sequence of discrete decisions is likely to be revised radically as a result of more effective, practical, and routine performance monitoring and user feedback, allowing a closer and more continuous relationship between the suppliers and users of the working environment. *Consequently, we predict that new workplaces and systems of managing the working environment will have to be designed which constrain users much less, and which enhance the quality of working life as well as productivity.*

3 Changing technologies

Networks of smaller and more powerful workstations linked to central databases are predicted. Cabling of considerably enhanced capacity will be more and more integrated with buildings in an increasingly structured and unobtrusive way. Many of the problems associated with the introduction into offices of the first wave of distributed intelligence will be overcome. *Consequently, we predict that workstations will be freed from the locational constraints of the traditional office; more kinds of work will be possible in more places; the free address environment will become viable for many – although not all – kinds of work.*

4 Changing IT and intelligent buildings

An increasing dependence of building managers as well as building users on a greater variety of increasingly powerful and attractive electronic devices is predicted, many of which will have the power to be used ubiquitously. Barriers between home and work – and leisure – will be eroded. Office uses of IT will converge with the use of electronics in managing building services. Office buildings will become increasingly difficult to distinguish from computer systems for which buildings exist increasingly simply to provide the infrastructure. *Consequently, we predict that the office environment will be much more closely related to business success. Performance measures will become critical. While there will be continual changes and improvements in the design of workstations, it is equally likely that there will also be substantial differences in shared spaces, in the amount and type of meeting rooms, in greater user control, in the provision and management of more intelligent working environments, and in greater mobility both at work and between work and home.*

5 Changes in building performance

User demands for a better, more responsive, more controllable working environment will have a big impact on the design of building services resulting in much greater integration of design, construction, and management. *Consequently, we predict that there will no longer be such sharp divergences between the design of long term shells and short term scenery; nor between natural external environments and artificial interiors. Building services will be more accessible to end users and will be used in a more sophisticated way, complementing and assisting natural systems. Building shells will need, however, to accommodate diverse and changing environments.*

6 Changing environmental issues

Priorities for the rest of the decade will be protection of heritage, avoiding hazardous building materials, dealing with the threat of global warming, ensuring greater energy efficiency, and devising transportation strategies that are less polluting and wasteful. *Consequently, we predict that responses to these priorities will include the development of environmentally friendly building products, the preparation of design and product guides for environmentally sensible design, the harmonisation of higher standards across Europe, more radical transportation policies, and the increasing use of information technology to manage buildings and their services for improved environmental performance.*

7 Changing locations

Offices and office work will become more footloose. Advances in telecommunications and in office automation, improvements in transport and business infrastructures, and increasing international migration opportunities will liberate office location from traditional constraints. *Consequently, we predict new patterns of location which take into account the conflicting demands of exploiting existing infrastructures and emerging user aspirations; that more office work will be undertaken from home or other remote locations; and that many staff will choose to work and live in non-urban locations to achieve improved quality of both working and living environments.*

8 Changing patterns of office work

The importance of office work for the economy will be more and more recognised as will the fact that office buildings already are, and will continue to be, the largest single item in any nation's asset base. *Consequently, we predict that changes in office location, in work and life styles, and in work patterns will be much more energetically seized by employers if they are shown to contribute to increased office productivity. Effective utilisation of the resources of space and time will become more critical.*

9 Changing regulatory perspectives

The UK regulatory process will change as a result of the influence of European rather than national technical specifications, the adoption of EC directives, greater emphasis on environmental issues, and the potential of IT in managing and integrating regulatory compliance and surveillance. *Consequently, we predict that there will be increased awareness of the legislative framework among both users and providers of the office environment. There will not only be a tendency to shift responsibility to constructors but a considerable reinforcement of the rights of end users to control the quality of their working environment.*

Changes in practice

If the direction of the trend papers was towards rising expectations, the response from the field in our case studies was tempered by greater caution and sharper pragmatism.

Nineteen case studies (eleven in the UK and eight elsewhere in Europe) were studied. They had been chosen as examples of advanced organisations noted frequently in the management literature and elsewhere for attempting innovation in matters relevant to this study: introducing advanced information technology, devising organisational structures which can cope with change, searching for new ways of increasing productivity and of using time more effectively, responding to burgeoning expectations of a safer working environment, taking environmental responsibilities seriously on an increasingly endangered planet. The case studies were not chosen primarily because they are prima facie interesting buildings but because in each case there is evidence that intelligent and practical attention had been given by the owners and users to negotiating between emerging demands in business and technology, the changing preoccupations of users and user organisations, and the procurement and management of architectural resources.

The constraints imposed by pressure on resources within these user organisations were real not theoretical. Not least among the many scarcities observed was a shortage of architectural imagination. The aspirations of the users were frequently greater than the space, environmental systems, buildings, furniture available to contain them. Many of the innovations observed were, of necessity, modifications of the existing, very limited range of office building stereotypes. The overall picture in the case studies was of organisations which were endeavouring to add to their effectiveness despite limited resources.

Priorities were much on the collective minds of the case study organisations. The form of questioning adopted was designed to elicit from each the order in which they would choose to use environmental resources to achieve their particular organisational objectives.

- The most important pressures of change reported are still to do with *information technology, telecommunications and organisational structure.*

- The workplace decisions that were reported as most important are to do with *location,* servicing the workplace, layout (enclosed or open offices), and security/access.

- For the future, organisations reported that the issue of adapting the workplace to changing organisational needs as well as making the workplace more responsive to users' needs will be their most important workplace decisions.

Some summary idea of how the case study organisations were using and manipulating architectural resources to achieve these objectives is given below.

1 Using space to facilitate changes in organisational structure

Organisations are restructuring to manage with less hierarchy and are working more with groups and teams. Physical consequences observed include playing down hierarchy, the deliberate allocation of space by need, the

Table 1.1 Pressures for change most often considered very important (in rank order where 1 = most often)

Pressure of change	UK cases (11)	non-UK (8)	Total (19)
Organisational structure/relationships	2	1	1
Information technology /telecommunications	1	2	1
Productivity pressures	3	2	2
Human resources	4	2	3
Time pressures	5	3	4
Comfort/welfare	6	3	5
Green/environmental	7	3	6

Source: DEGW and Building Research Establishment

acceptance of shared space, the acceptance of open plan and undifferentiated workstations.

2 Making the most of human resources

The wellbeing of valuable human resources is being strengthened as staff participation increases. Physical consequences include the working environment being redefined in traditional and even domestic terms, e.g. through more access to daylight, natural ventilation, opening windows. Desirable amenities include

Table 1.2 Workplace decisions most often considered very important (in rank order where 1 = most often)

Workplace decision	UK cases (11)	non-UK (8)	Total (19)
Location	1	2	1
Servicing	3	1	2
Open/enclosed offices	2	2	3
Security/access	2	2	3
Settings/furniture	4	2	4
Procurement	3	4	4
Forms of environmental control	4	3	5
Floor size	5	2	5
Site	4	4	6
Depth of space	4	4	6

Source: DEGW and Building Research Establishment

Table 1.3   Ranking of issues in degree of importance for future workplace decisions (in rank order where 1 = most important)

Issue	UK (11)	non-UK (8)	Total (19)
Adapting the workplace to changing organisational needs	1	1	1
Making the office workplace more responsive to user's needs	2	2	2
Making the office workplace more productive	3	2	3
Using information technology	4	3	4
Comfort and welfare of staff	5	4	5
Designing the workplace to respond to time pressures	6	5	6
Green issues at the workplace	7	5	7

Source: DEGW and Building Research Establishment

attractive sites, location near excellent transport and shopping facilities, as well as healthy working environments – absence of sick building syndrome, no-smoking policies and stress management. Amenities include features which transcend the workplace such as terminals to use at home, car phones, and childcare.

3 Increasing productivity

Organisations are examining the workplace as an asset, charging for the use of space and facilities, and seeking to understand better the relation between the use of space and productivity. Innovations include new ways of supporting group and team work, finding physical ways of bringing together groups and departments, and reinforcing communications both electronically and spatially. Cultural change is considered a prerequisite to improving pro-

ductivity. Physical consequences include the intensification of the use of space often aided by charges to user departments for the use of space.

4 Accommodating information technology and telecommunications

IT is a basic requirement and all organisations must find ways of accommodating IT satisfactorily. IT is enabling innovative companies to support working patterns that alter radically traditional notions of the design, use, and management of workplaces. In particular IT/ telecommunications allows organisations to use labour flexibly across several locations. Physical consequences include not only the universal taking for granted of a high level of provision for IT/ telecommunications but also, perhaps more significantly, experiments in sharing workstations (only possible with universal networks) and the elimination of individual desks – in one case using 45% less space.

5 Comfort and welfare of staff

The importance of attracting and retaining the kind of staff whose creativity as well as diligence are essential for organisational survival was stressed by many of the case study organisations. Physical consequences include high quality office environments, good levels of daylight, locally controllable services, policies to support health, provision of local amenities such as shopping.

6 Using time as well as space more effectively

Using time better was usually subsumed by respondents under the wider problems of productivity or organisational change. Physical consequences include more care in choosing location as well as flexibility in working hours.

7 Using environmental resources more responsibly

For many firms green issues were expressed through a discussion of energy efficiency. Avoiding the waste of resources and minimising occupancy costs are closely related. Physical consequences include the integration of the minimisation of waste into the design, management, and use of buildings. Other organisations related green issues to the provision of a healthy environment: naturally ventilated and highly daylit spaces being seen as both green and healthy. Conversely air-conditioning, deep plans, and the use of non-sustainable resources (such as tropical hardwoods) are seen by some respondents as irresponsible and the opposite of green.

Aspirations and reality

The attention of the managers in the case studies seems, very understandably, to be focused most sharply on the most easily realisable and practical options for organisational survival. Hence the importance the case study interviews placed upon the three top

priorities for decisions about the workplace in the future:

- adapting the workplace to changing organisational needs
- making the office more responsive to users' needs
- making the office workplace more productive

Decisions which appear to involve major reconceptualisation of time and space or which take up a philosophical position on humanity's relationship with the environment are, in this context, given lower priority. These priorities nevertheless are very much in evidence in many of the case study interviews. Three things became very apparent to the Responsible Workplace team:

First, the uncomfortable gap between what innovative organisations were attempting to achieve to ensure their future and the buildings available to them. Some of the best minds on the supply side of the world of office building had not been able to provide what is really wanted.

Second, the diversity of demand – all the trends predicted in the trend papers were encountered in the case studies – but as more or less isolated incidents and in an apparently fragmented way. At this stage of development of emerging ideas about work and the workplace such apparent lack of coordination is inevitable. However, it is also literally true that if all (or even many) of the features of change recorded in the case studies were to be collected in one place, the resulting physical environment would be so startlingly innovative that it would be unrecognisable as an office from the conventional viewpoint of today.

Third, while there was an enormous amount of innovation and optimism on the part of those interviewed in the case studies, it became gradually and cumulatively clearer to the Responsible Workplace team that in practically every case even more could have been done. The users' aspirations seemed higher than the physical resources and design imagination available to them.

One possible and very pessimistic conclusion is that, in the world beyond these relatively privileged case studies, aspirations and demand are generally so much weaker and user expectations generally so much more modest – the case studies, remember, are of some of the most advanced users to be found in Europe – that innovation on the part of developers and architects is simply not likely to be justified. We believe that exactly the opposite conclusion ought to be drawn.

The tyranny of supply

Let us now put the trend papers and the case study data into a wider perspective derived from the experience of working for many user organisations in several countries.

Office design is at a turning point. For many decades, especially in the developer dominated Anglo-Saxon world, office users have tended to be passive. Vendors of offices have concentrated on perfecting the delivery of office buildings – obviously at most profit, least risk, and maximum convenience for themselves. During most of this period, from 1920 to 1970, office organisations, office technology, and the expectations of office workers remained more or less constant. During this half century, in the most advanced white collar economy, the USA, the architecture of office buildings, the delivery of office services, and the design of office equipment were greatly improved and refined but within a framework that was hardly questioned. The office manuals of the early nineteen twenties and those of the nineteen sixties differ little in content and not at all in their underlying assumptions about the mission and conduct of office work.

The advent of the computer – first the mainframe in the fifties and sixties, then the mini in the seventies, and since the early eighties the increasingly networked personal computer (PC) – has been at least as great a destabilising influence on every aspect of office design – from location to the design of the workstation – as the introduction of the telephone and the typewriter in the last decades of the nineteenth century. The electronic office cannot be accommodated as easily as the old office technology. Information technology is too potent and destabilising an agent of change for that.

What has always been the principal excellence of the supply side, especially as practised by developers in North America, has been to provide office buildings which are as

simple and cheap to construct as possible. The kinds of buildings that result are, almost by definition and certainly as a result of historical experience, designed to satisfy the relatively simple demands of highly routinised and unchanging organisations. Whether such office buildings will be capable, without substantial modification, of accommodating the emerging requirements of organisations (which seem likely, from the trends papers and case studies of this report to be far less stable and much more demanding), is the key question which must be addressed by *The Responsible Workplace*.

This question has particular significance in the UK property market. British office buildings were until the early eighties a provincial variant of the North American developer system, financed in much the same way but in architectural terms much smaller, far less efficient in construction as well as plan form, less well serviced, and much more influenced by external considerations forced upon the developers by the importance of the British planning system. The globalisation of the financial services industry (in the City of London particularly), combined with the simultaneous explosion of information technology resulted in the construction of a novel class of office buildings. Their chief features are the direct consequences of the importation and imaginative adaptation of North American office design and construction practices. At their best these buildings, because their construction was timed to benefit from the opportunity to incorporate what had been learned about the direct impact of IT on office design, represent the most advanced developer-led offices in the world.

The contrast between the best new, North Americanised London offices such as Broadgate or Canary Wharf with the best North European offices such as SAS, Colonia, NMB Postbank buildings – the sorts of buildings produced when the developers' influence on office building design is relatively weak – is very striking.

User influence on office design in Scandinavia, Germany, and the Netherlands has been direct and considerable, resulting, for example, in narrow rather than deep plan forms, in very high degrees of cellularisation (the so-called 'Combi office'), and above all in extremely high standards of space, amenity and comfort for

Table 1.4 Planning and design criteria for various types of office

	Bürolandschaft offices	Traditional British speculative offices	New 'Broadgate' type of British speculative office	Traditional North American speculative office	The new North European office
No. of storeys	5	10	10	80	5
Typical floor size	2000 sqm	1000 sqm	3000 sqm	3000 sqm	Multiples of 200 sqm
Typical office depth	40m	13.5m	18m and 12m	18m	10m
Furthest distance from perimeter aspect	20m	7m	9-12m	18m	5m
Efficiency: net to gross		80%	85%	90%	70% (lots of public circulation)
Maximum cellularisation (% of usable)	20%	70%	40%	20%	80%
Type of core	Semi-dispersed	Semi-dispersed	Concentrated: extremely compact	Concentrated: extremely compact	Dispersed: stairs more prominent than lifts
Type of HVAC services	Centralised	Minimal	Floor by floor	Centralised	Decentralised: minimal use of HVAC

Source: DEGW

office workers. Buildings which have been shaped by direct user influence – through highly professional programming, through the competition system, and above all through Workers Council negotiation – are sufficiently different to the supply biased, developer oriented offices of the USA and the UK to demonstrate that an alternative kind of office is achievable, but obviously at a cost.

Why these Scandinavian, German, and Dutch offices are so important is not only the fact that they provide an alternative model to the supply side dominated offices we are so familiar with in the UK and USA but also that they are evidence of what happens when decisions about the form and shape of offices are influenced by another economic dimension – which relates office design much more directly to achieving organisational goals. These custom built office buildings are not the product of a self-contained and independent financial system; they are a direct corporate investment. The measure of their success is not that they are efficient in conventional real estate terms – which they certainly are not – but that they are intended to add value to the organisations which not only occupy them but use them.

That by the best developer standards these customised buildings should be so inefficient to construct, so profligate in the use of space, especially circulation, so untouched by conventional norms of efficiency, and thus so difficult to trade or exchange is a matter of considerable concern. Equally worrying is the view of developers' buildings from the user dominated side of this debate. What do these buildings add to the company's mission? How is it possible that people are allowed to work in such poor and unhealthy conditions, without direct aspect, in windowless offices, without natural ventilation, at such uncomfortable densities?

We have identified, in short, what we believe to be a severe and developing conflict between the developers' iron logic of rapid and minimalist construction, which expects to follow well established norms, and a comparably strong corporate and users' logic which we believe is increasingly likely to stress the necessity of finding new ways to accommodate organisational change.

That both sides in this interesting debate are, to some extent, right makes the resolution of the conflict particularly attractive. That such a resolution could be achieved at a time when there is increasing apprehension about the damage we are doing collectively to our fragile eco-system, through building and working in the way we have become accustomed to, gives an added urgency to the search for new models for the office.

Figure 1.1
The nature of work and change for office organisations. (Source: DEGW and Harbinger, 1985)

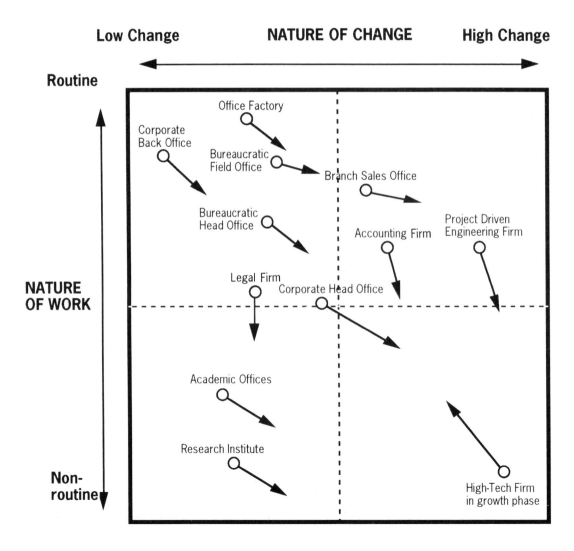

Types of user

How can the rate of change in the office be measured? One thing that is very clear, even from the limited evidence of this study, is that not all offices are the same. In the ORBIT 2 study on organisations, buildings, and information technology which we carried out (with Gerald Davis, Franklin Becker, and William Sims[1]) in North America in 1985, it was argued that one of the principal consequences of IT is that all organisations will tend to move, at varying rates and in different degrees, away from routinised work practices towards less predictable patterns of work. A second such consequence is that IT will, sooner or later, have the effect of accelerating organisational change in all organisations. What was also argued in

ORBIT 2 is particularly relevant to the Responsible Workplace: that, as organisations become less routinised and change more rapidly, they are likely to make greater demands on buildings and consume more environmental resources.

An attempt was made by the Responsible Workplace team to characterise the nineteen case study organisations within the framework of the ORBIT 2 model. This produces an interesting spread of organisational types with a marked bias, as might be expected, because all nineteen cases were selected as examples of advanced organisations, away from routine operations and stability and towards unpredictability and change.

The most interesting finding of this exercise – limited and informal as it is – is that, as expected, the most 'advanced' case study

Figure 1.2
Responsible Workplace case study organisations informally characterised in terms of nature of work and change. (Source: DEGW and the Building Research Establishment)

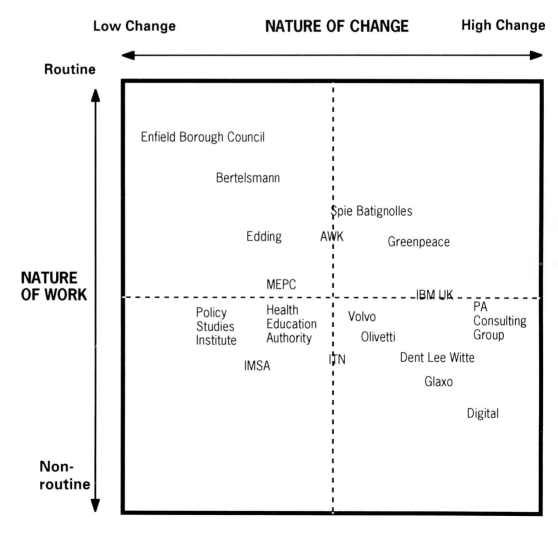

organisations – the ones experiencing the most unpredictable patterns of work and the most rapid organisational change – are attempting the most innovative arrangements in their workplaces. Design innovations, it seems, are most likely to happen when energetic organisations put pressure on scarce architectural resources.

More importantly, this observation is a clue to the sequence in which innovation in the design and the management of office space is likely to be achieved. Some organisations are more susceptible to arguments for adopting new ways of accommodating themselves than others. Under what conditions will new models be generated? Obviously not all innovations will happen at once nor will all such innovations be equally attractive to all organisations. The question is whether there is any reliable means of predicting the direction and the rate of innovation.

A perspective of inevitable change

The objective is to find new types of office which combine the advantages of:

- adding value to organisational performance;

- minimising occupancy costs;

- in such a way that sustains rather than diminishes the environment.

Adding value to organisational performance will become much more important during the next decade for all office organisations. This is because of the increasing importance of the office not just as the locus for information and control but, as routine operations are automated, as a place for stimulating intellect and creativity. Given this scenario, the importance should be obvious of finding clever and interesting ways – perhaps similar or even better than features found in offices in Scandinavia and Germany – of making the office environment more attractive to increasingly important, elusive, and demanding office workers.

Similarly, minimising occupancy costs will become an increasing preoccupation for all but the very richest user organisations. Increasing professionalism in the management of office facilities will make this goal more and more achievable. We predict that ever greater pressure to control and diminish the costs of space occupancy, coupled with the potential that building intelligence offers for managing of space more effectively, will influence the design and use of all buildings whether owner occupied or purpose built.

Organisations will pursue policies directed towards adding value and minimising costs in a popular climate which will be increasingly influenced by their employees, by government, by shareholders, by the press (and even, some would argue, by rioting in the streets), all of which constituencies will be exerting pressure on building owners, developers, and architects to achieve a more sustainable, healthier, more responsible environment. Few user organisations, we believe, will be able to escape this influence.

The most revealing way of explaining what we have learned from the case studies and from the trend papers is to show how different degrees of importance assigned to adding value and to minimising occupancy costs, in a climate of increasing concern not just for the quality of working life but for the sustaining of life itself, have led to certain characteristic behaviours and patterns of innovation.

The direction is obvious. Vectors which combine frugal use of environmental resources with the potential of unlocking human productivity and enhancing creativity are the ones to watch. The Responsible Workplace, in a time of constrained resources, within a threatened ecosystem, is defined, quite simply, as the most effective combination of use and exchange.

Strategies for achieving this benign alliance are, as can be glimpsed from the case studies, unlikely to be conventional. Consumers of office space will all be seeking, with varying degrees of urgency, to use built resources in more and more innovative ways to resolve their organisational problems. Invention is likely to be forced on these consumers, caught up as inevitably they will be by pressures for change.

Recommended initiatives

At what rate and in what order will innovation occur?

One powerful way to answer this question is from the point of view of the typical user of

Figure 1.3
*Responsible
Workplace case study
organisations
informally
characterised in
terms of adding value
and minimising costs.
(Source: DEGW and
the Building Research
Establishment 1991)*

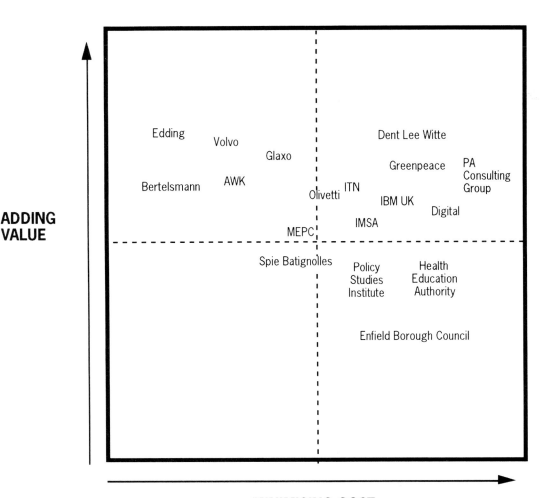

ADDING
VALUE

MINIMISING COST

office space. From this perspective some features of office design and space management (such as office layout and furniture) are relatively easy and quick to shift in order to achieve corporate objectives; other objectives are much more difficult to achieve in the short term because they involve interventions which involve totally different physical and temporal considerations (such as decisions about location).

Ten kinds of initiative have been identified. These are presented in order of how easy they would be, from the point of view of the corporate user or office user, to put into effect. This sequence, useful as it is for presentational purposes, is somewhat arbitrary. In reality different users with different priorities and opportunities are free to enter (and leave, and re-enter) the process at different points.

1 Facilities management

As facilities management moves from minimising costs to supporting organisational effectiveness, we expect more *managerial grip* – such as innovative leasing arrangements, more sophisticated contractual arrangements with vendors, and more *service*, such as more support to end users and less control, more use of data and feedback to relate space to organisational performance.

2 Furniture and settings

Furniture is a highly accessible way for user organisations to add value to organisational performance. We expect a *reconceptualisation of furniture priorities* – such as more emphasis

Figure 1.4
*Levels of initiatives to achieve Responsible Workplaces.
(Source: DEGW and the Building Research Establishment)*

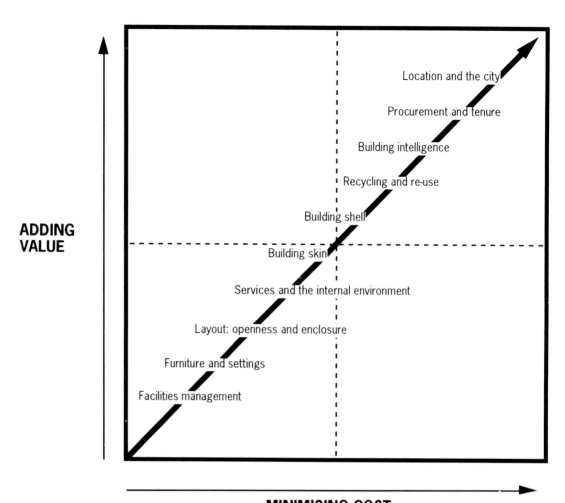

on furniture for group as well as individual activities; *greater capacity for problem solving,* for electronic storage, for the distribution of services, and more *tacit management* – such as the use of strong interior concepts in the management of the use of space for organisational purposes.

3 Layout

We anticipate a shift in the balance of both cellular offices and open plan as well as between individual and group spaces. *More diversity* can be expected to accommodate different work styles and more intense patterns of space use. *More mobility* will mean the use of a greater variety of locations.

4 Services and the internal environment

While the demands of IT on servicing the internal environment are expected to decline as machines become more energy efficient, the expectations of users will be towards mixed mode environments which will be naturally serviced while still being capable of supporting highly intensive IT work. *Built-in simplicity and structure* will be the chief characteristics of both cabling and environmental systems.

5 Building skin

Building skins and particularly windows, the interface of buildings with the natural environment, will take on more significance in maximising building performance while meeting changing needs. Building skins will become *more independent* of structure to facilitate change, and *more operable by users* at the same time as being capable of environmentally *higher performance*.

6 Building shells

The critical innovations will be in the direction of combining *cheapness* and *simplicity* with the capacity to accommodate *individual and highly tailored adaptation*. *Shallower* plans are to be expected but generous *volumes* will continue to be important for environmental and adaptability reasons. The difference between *lightweight* and *movable* elements (e.g. the skin, the interior) and the *long-term* and *environmentally* critical residual bulk of the building will become accentuated.

7 Recycling and reuse

Green pressures will not only exert pressure for avoiding *dangerous*, *deleterious*, and *wasteful materials* but building elements as well as entire buildings will be designed for *recycling and reuse*.

8 Building intelligence

Intelligence in buildings is valuable to enable users to manage, control, and use their workplaces in more effective, less resource hungry, and more user friendly ways. This will lead to the development of ways of using building intelligence to achieve organisational purposes such as *more distributed and more controllable building management systems*, a shift from *prescriptive* to *responsive* building management, and the development of such novel building products as *adaptive facades*.

9 Procurement and tenure

A closer match between user requirements and the supply of office buildings through a better managed procurement process will lead inevitably to more flexible *leases*; new, more rational and user-based methods of *valuation*; and *longer term and more service-based* relationships between developers and their tenants.

10 Location and the city

More attention will be focused on maximising locational advantages and in relating them more directly to organisational performance, avoiding the *social and environmental costs of wasted commuting*, exploiting existing infrastructures, providing more *intensive ways of using valuable central premises*, and ensuring that people have access to *amenities of the highest quality*.

What this programme of ten points means is quite simple: not only the remaking of the working environment but the invention of the cities of the Twenty First century. It is towards these goals that *The Responsible Workplace* is intended to lead.

References

1 Davis, G., Becker, F., Duffy, F. & Sims, W. *ORBIT 2: Organisation, Buildings, and Information Technology*, Harbinger, 1985, Norwalk, Conn.

2 The Responsible Workplace: user expectations

Adrian Leaman & Iain Borden, Building Use Studies

Summary

The Responsible Workplace derives from a design and planning strategy which gives building users the least possible amount of constraint at their workstations. This will increase social and economic productivity.

This paper proposes a model for understanding how the behaviour and degrees of freedom experienced by building users are currently constrained as a result of a hierarchical sequence of decisions about workplace location, site, building shell, services and settings of the office. What was previously considered as an efficient division of responsibility for the production of these various aspects of the workplace in fact contributes to the constraints experienced by the user at the end of the process. The creation of Responsible Workplaces will require attention to how the critical decisions about the workplace are taken through this sequence in both a space and time context. The Responsible Workplace will result from refining the performance monitoring and feedback responses into the decision making process, allowing a more integrated process of relationships between the decision steps in the creation of the workplace. Ultimately, the purpose of the Responsible Workplace is to change perspectives about workplace buildings in order to minimise the constraints experienced by users.

Introduction

The Responsible Workplace derives from a design and planning strategy which gives building users the minimum amount of constraint at their workstations. This is necessary because the more people are constrained, the less likely they are to work in a socially and economically productive manner. The more choice people have, the happier and more productive they are. The Responsible Workplace puts choice back into buildings. This must be achieved in a socially, economically and environmentally responsible way, by looking systematically at buildings and their inter-relationships with people, resources, organisations and the environment.

The process of giving people choice, however, must not be confined to individuals. The Responsible Workplace is not simply about giving people more control over their time and their immediate environment. The reason why many people under-perform is because their behaviour and degrees of freedom are systematically reduced by decisions over which they themselves have no control – decisions about building location, site, shell and so forth. Many problems in modern workplaces derive from poor decisions made higher up the hierarchy of control. Much more attention must be paid to how such decisions are taken and to their consequences in a context of both space and time. Strategic and tactical decision making about workplaces must be improved on the basis of performance monitoring and feedback.

At one level these arguments are truisms. At another, they are tantalisingly out of reach. Models of lateral, rather than vertical, integration in the design process do not create a logical inheritance between hierarchical levels. They do not examine how effects are transmitted downward, and they do not emphasise or define what is possible. The Responsible Workplace rectifies these deficiencies by changing peoples' attitudes to buildings.

This paper offers neither an exact identification of the specific characteristics of any workplace, nor a prescriptive list of responses. It is a speculation about future trends in office staff expectations of their workplaces – one of a series of scenarios which explore the idea of the Responsible Workplace.

The Responsible Workplace

A distinction is drawn here between individuals using their workstations; and organisations, and groups within organisations, occupying workplaces. The workplace is a setting on a larger scale than the workstation. The Responsible Workplace is a workplace within an office building which meets the following conditions:

- it provides a workstation environment for individuals which fulfils basic health, safety and comfort standards, and also contributes to individuals' human potential

- it offers a building environment for the organisation which responds economically and effectively to changing functional demands, and which offers opportunities for development and growth in the future

- it is situated in a geographical location which maximises opportunities for the building's occupants, their families and colleagues, the occupying organisation and the local community

- it is a workplace which minimises individual, social and environmental disbenefits such as

excessive energy costs, long commuting times, individual and organisational stress, and ill health.

Throughout this paper, the importance of hierarchical relationships between individuals, organisations, the workplace, buildings, and locational factors is repeatedly stressed. A Responsible Workplace is one in which needs at each of these levels will be met, but it is also one in which the relationships between the levels are properly managed and integrated. For example, geographical location raises questions further down the hierarchy about the energy costs of commuting; site; microclimate; aesthetic appropriateness and other aspects of environmental impact.

The cumulative effects of decisions taken at different levels in the hierarchy progressively affect, and act as invisible restraints upon, those levels beneath. Thus a new theme in the planning and design of the Responsible Workplace is how this pattern of inter-related decision making works, especially in the ability of organisations to perform their core functions in a socially responsible and cost effective way. The focus in future will be on the vertical integration of the decision making process across planning, design, management and use of buildings, a strategy which cuts across existing professional boundaries.

Different expectations and needs exist within the hierarchy. It is relatively easy to characterise need at each level because it normally falls into discrete areas of professional responsibility, but it is more difficult to understand how different needs interconnect and change over time.

In the Responsible Workplace, individual, social and organisational factors are understood within the context of accelerating social and technological change. In general, a hierarchy of constraints filters down from the building's location through site, shell, services, layout, settings and workstations, and finally reaching individuals. In the Responsible Workplace, the effects of constraints at one level are minimised for the next level down.

These conditions form the constraints under which needs can be met. Constraints can act usefully and positively, or negatively as inhibitors. The language of briefing and strategic design uses terms which reflect this: 'flexibility', 'adaptability', 'loose fit', 'contingency', 'redun-

Figure 2.1
Different spheres of influence within a hierarchy of relationships. (Source: Building Use Studies)

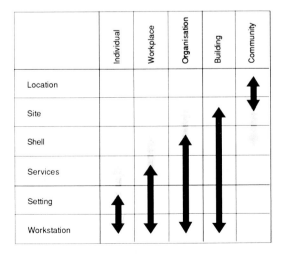

Table 2.1 Examples of discrete areas of professional responsibility

	Professional responsibility (examples)
Location	Planner, developer, organisation executives
Site	Architect, landscape architect, surveyor
Shell	Architect, structural engineer
Services	Architect, mechanical engineer
Setting	Facilities manager, interior designer, space planner
Workstation	Facilities manager, departmental manager, individuals

Source: Building Use Studies

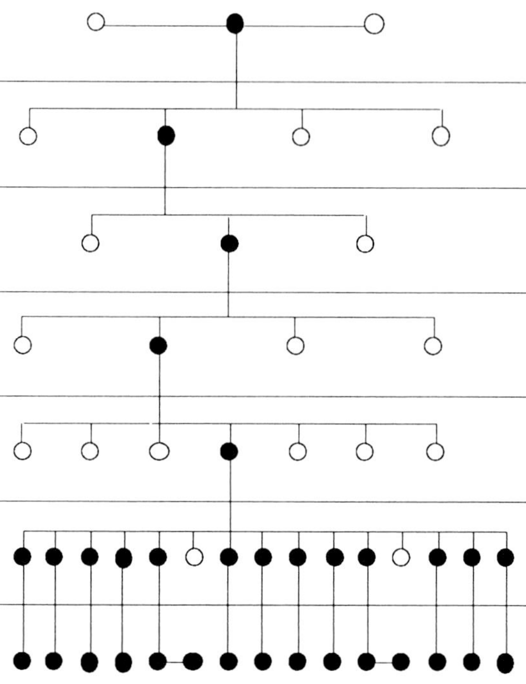

Figure 2.2
*A notional hierarchy of control showing the relationship between different levels in the building hierarchy, and the time and space scales associated with them[1].
(Source: Building Use Studies)*

Scale	Time period	
Location/Regional	Centuries or decades	
Site/Local	Decades	
Shell/Building	Decades	
Services/Building	Decades	
Setting/Floor	Year	
Workstation	Year	
Individual/Personal	Day	

Table 2.2 Possible types of constraint occurring at different levels of the office building

	Types of constraint (examples)
Location	Geography, climate, local economy, natural resources, labour, social facilities
Site	Micro-climate, transport, natural resources, landscaping
Shell	Structural load, floor plate, floor to ceiling height, entrances
Services	Service load, IT integration, health standards, safety standards, comfort
Setting	Space, support equipment, interaction, communication, work functions
Workstation	Privacy, control, task performance, comfort, IT and support equipment

Source: Building Use Studies

Figure 2.3
Speculative offices are controlled at the broader scale in order to impose a minimum of constraints on organisational function. Purpose designed offices have the advantage of including group tasks and workstation requirements within the brief.
(Source: Building Use Studies)

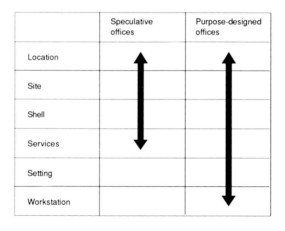

dancy'. Under certain conditions of technical and social change, constraints imposed at one period in design history make the building unusable at another, hence the language of functional failure: 'obsolescence', 'uncertainty', 'risk'.

The greater the unwanted constraints, the less likely that needs at all levels are fulfilled. But these constraints are often impossible to predict: thus, in general, the designer's task is to find building solutions which impose the least number of constraints, now and in the future, at each level in the hierarchy of control. For example, speculative developers may influence building location, site, shell and services to provide as constraint-free an environment as possible, but they will always be working with relatively little knowledge about tenants' real requirements.

In purpose designed buildings, there is potentially much greater knowledge about individual, group, departmental and organisational requirements, and, indeed, it is often the case that purpose designed offices perform better on user satisfaction criteria than speculative offices. This is probably because a purpose designed building delivers a wider 'bandwidth of control' to users at different levels in the hierarchy. In general, the building is more usable for more purposes for longer periods of time.

Problems in the workplace

One of the main themes of this paper is that offices of the future will deliver more types of responsive control to different types of users at different levels in the hierarchy. The problem of the Responsible Workplace, therefore, concerns the nature of the constraints within each level and how relationships between different levels are formed. In both areas, our knowledge is deficient. We do not understand enough about the overriding constraints which affect buildings and their use, and the way these constraints are changing over time. Nor do we understand fully how different levels in the hierarchy connect with each other to form lower level constraints.

At the bottom of the hierarchy are the sedentary clerical office workers sitting at their workstations. The problem of lack of user control amongst clerical staff is widely reported in studies of sick buildings[2]. In buildings with a large number of constraints, it is more likely that these people more than any others will be adversely affected by their working conditions, which may be cramped, hot, draughty, smoky, noisy, uncomfortable or lacking in privacy. They may respond by leaving for home early, working at lower levels of productivity, or leaving the organisation altogether.

In general, staff expect that the number of constraints affecting them at their workstations will be progressively reduced in the future, so that they will be given more choice and control over the quality of their immediate ambient environment. As a result, their ability to perform their work tasks will be improved, and their control over their personal space and time will increase.

Staff are also increasingly likely to compare working conditions with those of their peers and make job and career decisions based not simply on pay and conditions, but also on lifestyle criteria such as journey-to-work, housing and holiday periods. These are not simply value added features in the workplace, such as leisure facilities at work or perks and entitlements, but a more complex set of factors which are perceived to enhance the quality of their personal lives.

At present, in the early 1990s, quality is perceived as a bonus given by better employers; but later, when the personal and organisational benefits are clearly understood and demonstrably proven, it will be seen as a basic right for the individual and a basic need for the organisation.

Processes of qualitative improvement arise from observation, monitoring and the feedback of knowledge about performance. Knowledge becomes increasingly focused, and divides into smaller and smaller sub-specialisms. This has the effect of increasing the range and detail of knowledge, but it also increases the likelihood that it is not communicated laterally across sub-specialisms.

The process of modernisation constantly challenges and overthrows disciplinary boundaries and processes of decision making. It can induce a knowledge crisis, because existing theories break down, and it constantly introduces new knowledge formations to deal with the changes. In the modern office, the most obvious recent example is the growth of facility management.

The Responsible Workplace, then, is about the social consequences of increasing sophistication and complexity in the workplace, and finding appropriate responses to it.

Summary

Social responsibility arises from improved mechanisms of feedback, operating across disciplinary boundaries and in response to improved building monitoring. The progressive layering of constraints in a hierarchy of control ultimately adversely affects building users at their workstations. The conditions for staff in office buildings must be improved by a total approach to design and management, not a superficial treatment of insignificant parts of the whole.

Lifestyles

Time

In order to understand how individual need is affected at the workplace, it is necessary to characterise how lifestyles have changed during the life of the office building. Individual needs are both expressed and restrained by the lifestyle which the individual adopts. The balance struck between needs and lifestyle varies in the lifetime of the individual, and varies according to broad historical patterns. Understanding these processes is an important aspect of the Responsible Workplace.

The use of time is also related to lifestyle. As living standards rise, time becomes scarcer. Living standards are connected with rising productivity, so that as productivity rises, abstention from work (and absenteeism) costs more than in the past. The cost of leisure is then the cost of time that could be spent at work. As long as productivity continues to rise, time

Figure 2.4
Suburban life purports to allow people to maximise the potential of working life, social life and personal life. By contrast, typical working class life patterns merely satisfy working life and personal life while minimising the potential of location. (Source: Building Use Studies)

	Suburban life	Working class life
Working life	●	○
Location	●	○
Personal life	●	○
● Maximum ○ Satisficing ○ Minimum		

becomes more scarce. This has profound consequences, as Michael Young describes:

> One would expect this relationship between time and riches to have some effect on the hours of work. The effect should depend on which is stronger, the income effect which provides that as incomes rise people will be able to achieve any given standard of life with less work; or the substitution effect which operates so that the more they work, the higher the standard of living they will get and the more goods to substitute for leisure. According to economists, because working hours have fallen for the majority of people in industrial societies, the income effect must have swamped the substitution effect. In industrial societies people have at least had more leisure, even if it is more expensive in goods and services foregone, and even if they are more and more occupied with the unpaid work a higher standard of living generates. It takes so much work to maintain their property in houses, cars, hi-fis, TVs, videos, computers, microwaves, books, mixers, freezers that they may sink under the burden of civilised living. 'If I keep a cow,' Emerson wrote, 'that cow milks me'[3]

The cost of time should not only be measured in economic terms. The cost of doing anything can be measured in terms of other things that have been given up as alternatives. So these also add to the cost, and make people more conscious of the shortage of time. The shortage of time then becomes a commodity and items are sold in an attempt to supply more of it – timeshift video recorders, pre-prepared meals, answerphones, and so on. Of course, the effect is the opposite: time is not saved, more of it is consumed by people working more feverishly or carrying out more than one task at a time.

Time and resources spent on commuting to the workplace is the greatest social and environmental disbenefit of the modern workplace. Workplaces are still relatively fixed, which means that most people have to adjust the use of their time to suit the vagaries of location and their journey to work. As workplaces become less fixed (see below) the distribution and cost of both time and space will change.

Working life, location and personal life

The classic historical image of the office worker is the commuter, travelling to the office workplace in the city centre every weekday, and returning home to the suburban family in the evening. This lifestyle allows the nuclear family to live in a stable and secure environment with easy access to the countryside, while also allowing wage earners to maximise the potential of their working life, location and personal life. Given a substantial income (in the past usually that of the male, but now often a joint income), a partner tending to the needs of the family, and good quality education and community support, the suburban home purports to be the perfect realisation of archetypal middle and upper working class aspirations, enabling all three components of working life, location, and personal social life to be satisfied.

Despite this apparent coherence, suburban life is often divisive and alienating: the family frequently spends time apart, weekdays spent at home can be sterile and tedious, and the environmental advantage of location has been eroded by continuing housing and infrastructural development at the city periphery.

Location is also problematic for those who cannot afford the suburban lifestyle. People can be fixed to their place or region of birth, and are forced to find employment and build their family lives around such constraints. Those who do migrate are often forced to live in sub-standard accommodation. Conceptually, this produces two extremes.

These extremes, which characterised polarised lifestyles of the 1920s and 1930s, have been replaced by less prescriptive, more flexible lifestyles. This is primarily the result of increasing wealth and mobility, demands of women to have an active and independent role outside the home, a proliferation of consumer

Figure 2.5
Different lifestyles, such as the three examples above, allow different exploitation of work, location and personal opportunities. (Source: Building Use Studies)

	Young city professional	Hampstead professional	Rural teacher
Working life	●	●	○
Location	○	●	●
Personal life	○	●	●

● Maximum   ○ Satisficing   ○ Minimum

choice, and increases in the availability of and demands on leisure time.

Of the three essential components of sub-urban life – working life, location and personal life – people now tend to seek maximum benefit from only one or two. Which components they emphasise depends on the stage of life and personal choices of the individual, and therefore tends to change according to long term rather than short term patterns.

Within such scenarios, people alternatively change organisation and location or settle in one organisation and location as their priorities change. For example, if the main priority is working life, they will tend to live as close as possible to their place of work, such as young professionals working at Heathrow who live in bedsits or flats in West London. As people grow older they often choose between their profession (and move from job to job) and allegiance to a single organisation (and settle down in one or possibly two locations).

From an individual's point of view, working life, location and personal life are variables to be manipulated according to personal needs and desires. These variables have to be juggled in relation to a relatively fixed parameter – the workplace location. At the beginning of the 1990s, the location of work itself is still fixed, and therefore is still a parameter.

As the decade unfolds, the location of work will become a variable, a view which is now being voiced within IBM:

> We will see the end of the office as we know it today. Work will be moved to the people and the office will be a place to meet colleagues, the boss, customers and clients.[4]

Through information technology, work can be displaced to multiple locations, of which the home is just one. 'Homeworking' as such does not replace the office. Other possible locations include satellite offices, and temporary sites such as the train, hotel or car. In the future, the office itself will contain fewer workstations and a greater proportion of space devoted to meetings, conferences, eating, socialising and leisure. Some of the activities which take place at the workstation are likely to move out of the present day office: these include single person tasks requiring concentration and quiet, such as report writing; and repetitive tasks, such as data entry. Some of these activities will eventually seek out low cost labour markets or least cost locations or a combination of both and move out of the country completely.

The cultural ecology of the organisation, by which is meant the network of personal, political and cultural relationships which make up organisations, will remain and become more important. Greater emphasis will be placed on inter-personal and inter-client relationships, and these will be expressed through a more varied and rich cultural life in the office. This activity will increasingly be focused upon the workplace and office building, and perhaps also on rural retreats and conference centres. Greater emphasis will therefore be placed on the expression of cultural values through the design and management of office spaces such as reception areas, hospitality suites, restaurants and other social spaces in the building. Greater emphasis will also be placed on understanding the dynamics of organisations, and on expressing these in the workplace.

The working week

The effects of movable work are profound. The periodic cycle of the working week is altered, because people are able to choose how to use their time. For example, it may be possible for

Figure 2.6
People at different lifestages have different priorities for their working life, location and personal life. (Source: Building Use Studies)

	20-30	30-40	40-60	60+
Working life	●	○	○	○
Location	○	○	●	●
Personal life	○	●	●	●

● Maximum   ○ Satisficing   ○ Minimum

an individual to log into his or her work-files from a hotel, car, home, or plane so that any one of these locations could become a temporary workstation. Workstations are likely to become movable, but workplaces – the organisation in its office – will remain fixed. The implication is that 'workstation space' and 'workplace space' will increasingly be distinct.

People will be able to approach their work in the same way as they approach a television programme with a video recorder, adjusting times to suit personal needs and lifestyles. As a result, the pattern of daily working life is likely to become far less defined. People will attend the office for face-to-face meetings and related activities, but will not need to use it as a workstation base. They may be able, for example, to attend the office on three days of the week, working away from the office for the rest of the time, and travelling during off-peak times.

Recognising time as a factor in working life and introducing choice and flexibility in time management is an important component of the Responsible Workplace. Professional core staff (see below) such as partners and senior managers still need to attend their workplace regularly. Professional contract staff and other contract and part time staff have weaker ties with their workplace, but they are more likely to need a properly serviced workstation whenever they are present.

Individual expectations

Individual expectations of workplaces are related to increasing economic wealth. Beside health, safety and comfort requirements, all of which can be legally enforced, as standards of living rise people introduce new criteria based partly on domestic standards and partly on comparisons with other workplaces. As a minimum, they expect office conditions to be as good as those in their own homes. They are also increasingly demanding that workplaces enhance their personal image.

In other words, people want to be associated with environments which add to their self-esteem. This applies both to the working environments and to the organisation to which they belong. The more the total working environment gives people personal and professional creativity, the more they like it and the more

they ask for it. This process is similar to the development of consumer choice in wider marketplaces. Cars, for example, have to meet basic safety and comfort standards, but actual buying choices are based on 'value added' features presented as reflections of lifestyle images. These features are specified partly by marketing decisions and partly by the consumer, so that very few cars are exactly the same in specification.

The process of office differentiation and customisation will follow a similar path. Far greater attention will be paid to specifying and realising individual needs and preferences, with workstations and workstation arrangements tailored to these requirements. This applies primarily to those who have permanent 'ownership' of a workstation and to those who are sedentary, staying at one place throughout the working day.

Organisational change

Professional, core, contractual fringe and flexible labour

Changes in staff expectations are taking place within the broader pattern of organisational change. Three categories of staff and change may be identified[5]. Critical to the organisation is the professional core providing both the knowledge base and continuity. The received view is that this component is becoming smaller. The contractual fringe consists of self-employed professionals and technicians in the early stages of professional life who have not made an allegiance to one organisation. This short term professional labour force is reconfigured from project to project, and a greater proportion of professional work is now being contracted to it. The fastest growing sector is the flexible labour force of part-time and temporary workers, hired and fired to suit market forces.

Each staff category has different requirements. The professional core is most likely to have workstations customised to its requirements. These workstations are often empty, because their occupants are mobile, but they are dedicated to individuals as a sign of status and perceived need. High up in a staff hierarchy, needs are less to do with technology and servicing and more with quality: office size,

Figure 2.7
Graph showing the traditional workstation and shared space occupation patterns for the professional core, contracted fringe and flexible labour force in an organisation[6].
(Source: Building Use Studies)

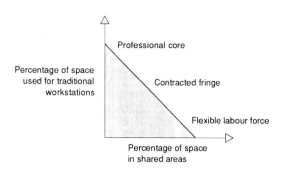

interior design and view take precedence over workstations and task equipment.

The contractual fringe is less likely to work in cellular offices and more likely to work in open plan offices with standard systems furniture, well configured but not exceptional in quality. These people tend to spend more time at their workstations and, in the future, will be more likely to use multiple workstations within the office. The flexible labour force almost always work at workstations dedicated for specific tasks located in less favourable open plan areas with relatively poor services. This will change as the relationship between poor working environments and lower productivity is better understood. In the future, people who spend most of the day at workstations will be more likely to have workstations with good natural light, views and high levels of user control.

Buildings and organisations

The relationship between buildings and organisations is becoming closer. Speculative developers are taking more care to define and provide for user needs. In purpose designed buildings, the briefing process is more detailed and wide ranging so that a greater 'fit' is achieved between buildings and the organisations which occupy them.

As we explained in the first section of this chapter, office buildings have a built-in hierarchy of control. The basic parameters of, for example, the shell (grid size, floor-to-ceiling heights, floor plate size) impose background constraints on the usefulness and performance of the building overall. Once set, these parameters are difficult and expensive to change.

The building shell sets constraints within which services can be provided. The interface between the shell and the services, and how they work in relation to each other, forms a crucial element in the performance and usefulness of office buildings. In surveys across different types of office buildings, temperature and ventilation are repeatedly the subject of the most vociferous complaints from users[7]. Office buildings are repeatedly reported as too hot, too cold, too draughty, too stuffy and as having poor air quality. Excessively fluctuating temperature and ventilation are primarily shell and services problems, exacerbated by changes in

Table 2.3 Each staff category – professional core, contractual fringe and flexible labour force – has different workplace and workstation requirements.

Professional core	Customised workstations Individual territoriality High specification of need High cost/high quality/high status Low change/reconfiguration
Contractual fringe	Systems furniture Group territoriality Functionality High quality support/high servicing High change/reconfiguration
Flexible labour force	Systems furniture Very high change/reconfiguration Less favoured location

Source: Building Use Studies

user requirements such as growing equipment usage and reconfiguration of accommodation[8].

Space planning is the architectural subspecialism which examines the relationships between services, settings and workstations so that functional configurations of workstations and support spaces are achieved. As space planning has developed, it has split into 'strategic' and 'tactical' branches. Strategic space planning examines the overall relationships between organisational accommodation requirements and the broad possibilities offered by a building's shell, services and settings. Greater attention is now being paid to the ability to accommodate change, and the nature of working group sizes. Increasingly, the size of working groups can become a generator of the overall space plan. This means that greater attention is being paid to the size, dynamics and functions of working groups in their space settings. The relationship between services and settings is proving crucial, especially in spaces where complex servicing technology is required. Such spaces include dealing floors, control rooms, laboratories and other uses which are not offices in the traditional sense. These spaces are becoming cleaner and more 'office like' and with other semi-industrial uses, such as graphic design and product design, are more likely to merge into office buildings in the future.

The relationship between services and the workstations at which activities take place is another crucial element in the hierarchy. Service provision constrains the possible workstation arrangements. These arrangements in turn constrain tasks, activities and behaviour patterns in the office space.

A great deal of attention has been paid in recent years to the problem of delivering all types of services (power, data, telecoms, heat, cooling, light) to the workstation; and, more recently, to giving adequate levels of service control to individuals at the workstation. There is no doubt that a higher level of user control at workstations is desirable, but there are dangers in providing it indiscriminately, especially if other types of control at different levels in the hierarchy of control are not taken into account.

The classic office design problem is that of windows. A recent unpublished study by Building Use Studies shows that user satisfaction with all types of office conditions (car parking conditions, restaurant quality, temperature and ventilation, for example) can all be 'explained' statistically by whether respondents sit next to a window. This result holds even after controlling for the effects of job type – managers are more likely to sit next to windows than clerks. Windows cross all levels of the hierarchy of control. They directly affect temperature, ventilation, lighting, noise and views out, and they indirectly influence many other variables. They are important for shell, services, settings and individuals at their workstations. Controlling windows, therefore, means that many aspects of the internal environment can be adjusted, and this adjustment affects different levels of building operation. Probably no single element of the office building is more important to the user than the window. Although technical knowledge about windows and performance is well developed[9], little is known about the behavioural aspects of how they are used.

Overall, modern office buildings appear to be failing in basic shell and services design. The inadvertent constraints which are imposed at these levels are often irreversible lower down the hierarchy of control. 'Failure' means, in this context, the inability of the physical infrastructure of a building to support the organisational activities carried out within it. As a broad principle, if the building fails at higher levels in the hierarchy, such as the shell, detrimental effects filter down to lower level activities where they are ultimately felt by occupants of workstations.

Building users

Different levels in the building hierarchy are normally treated as discrete subsystems, each with different levels of obsolescence, of contractual, legal and economic status, and of management approaches. Feedback loops therefore tend to operate within each discrete level rather than connecting between them. Several points of breakdown are possible, usually occurring between levels in the hierarchy (Figure 2.8).

Constraints tend to accumulate between levels, often culminating in problems with users. These users can rarely exercise control beyond immediate local conditions. In other words,

Figure 2.8
Diagram showing the filtering of constraints down through the hierarchy of a building, and the possible points of breakdown between levels.
(Source: Building Use Studies)

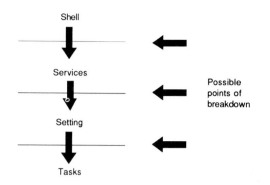

there is no vertical feedback mechanism which operates between levels. Recent evidence of user attitudes and responses in office buildings reiterates this view: there is a control problem between different levels of the building hierarchy which is related to an absence of feedback. In many buildings, users report most dissatisfaction with temperature and ventilation, while noise, lighting and smoking feature less strongly. The three graphs, Figures 2.9, 2.10 and 2.11, from recent research by Building Use

Figure 2.9
Levels of dissatisfaction with temperature for six British office buildings.
(Source: Building Use Studies)

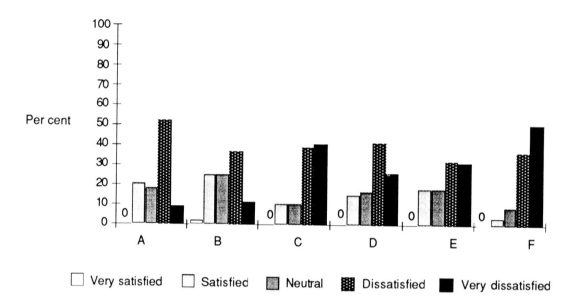

Figure 2.10
Levels of dissatisfaction with ventilation for six British office buildings.
(Source: Building Use Studies)

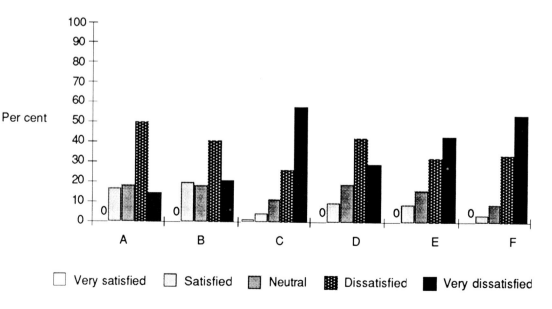

Studies, demonstrate this for six characteristic British office buildings. The cause lies in the way temperature and ventilation can be affected by changes at all levels in the building hierarchy, and, most fundamentally, by changes to the shell and services which are beyond the control of most users. In comparison, noise, lighting and smoking are affected mainly by changes to internal layout and workstation arrangements which can often be partly controlled by users.

Building users are demanding more control at their workstations of fresh air, natural light, noise and smoke. Lack of control can be significantly related to the prevalence of ill health symptoms in the office environment, and there is widespread agreement that providing more individual control is beneficial. Individual control must be balanced with other levels of control, as they are all equally important. Overall comfort conditions in the building are determined by the shell and services, acting as parameters, and by workstation positions, arrangements and activities, acting as variables.

For example, the facility manager of an air conditioned building adjusts building services for comfort conditions for staff which may not be suitable for individual tasks, creating user demands for more control. The question as to whether, in such circumstances, users should be able to open windows is about different levels of control: both levels are equally important, but at different levels in the hierarchy.

For the user, common problems in the office include stress, absenteeism and loss of productivity. Existing evidence suggests that poor quality office environments contribute to all three of these problems.

As Figure 2.13 demonstrates, there is a strong relationship between self-reports of productivity and ill health symptoms related to buildings: productivity decreases as ill health symptoms increase.

On the basis of such data it is possible to predict productivity losses: any building with an average of less than two symptoms per person is likely to demonstrate productivity gains among its occupants. The threshold level of two symptoms per person may then be treated as a performance standard.

All these considerations about buildings beg questions about buildings and the people and organisations who use them. It is possible, for example, that in a building with a reputation for being 'sick', occupants are more likely to report chronic ill health symptoms. In other words, occupants can change their attitudes and behaviour through changes in perceptions and so create feedback that is detrimental. In such circumstances it is often unnecessary to consider whether the situation was brought about by the environment or by the people themselves. Rather it should be treated as a causal circle that needs to be broken. Many environmental problems have the character of these

Figure 2.11
Levels of dissatisfaction with lighting for six British office buildings. (Source: Building Use Studies)

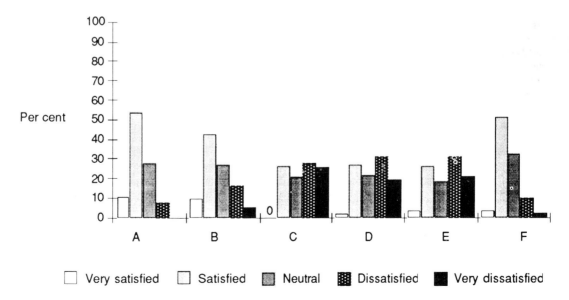

positive feedbacks; they are vicious circles of accelerating decline. Once the processes are underway, they become increasingly costly and difficult to manage.

The most appropriate management response is to stop them getting underway in the first place, through good design, rapid repair, and responsive management. All of these depend on the quality of information available about buildings and their processes of operation. The focus, therefore, moves from understanding the nature of constraints in the hierarchy of control – that is, how degrees of freedom are delivered in buildings at different levels in the hierarchy – to the nature of building related information and the quality of that information which is available for managerial decision making.

Figure 2.12
The relationship between self-reports of productivity and levels of control over temperature, ventilation, lighting and overall control. The graph shows that as control rises across all variables, so does productivity. (Source: Building Use Studies)

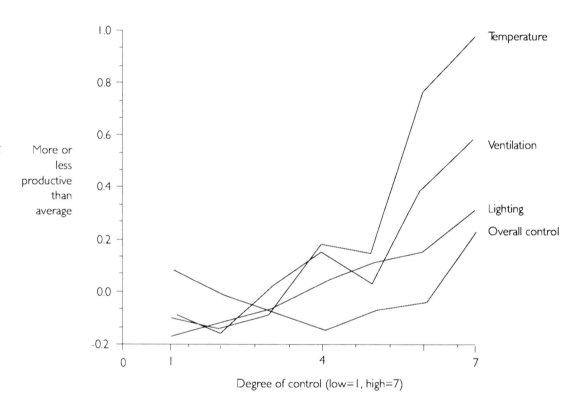

Figure 2.13
The relationships between staff self-reports of productivity and the mean number of sick building syndrome symptoms in a sample of 46 offices. This shows that offices with more than two symptoms per person are likely to show overall productivity losses[10]. (Source: Building Use Studies)

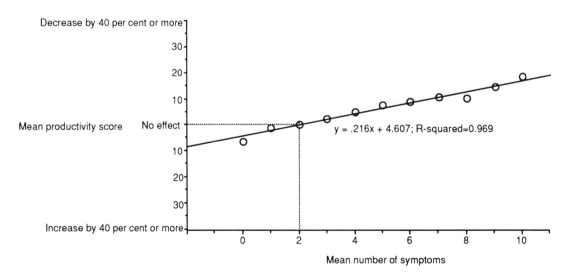

Figure 2.14
Levels of self-reports of stress (1 = low, 7 = high) against the number of hours per day spent in the office (n = 4600). People spending two hours a day report the same stress levels as those in the office for 10–11 hours a day[11]. (Source: Building Use Studies)

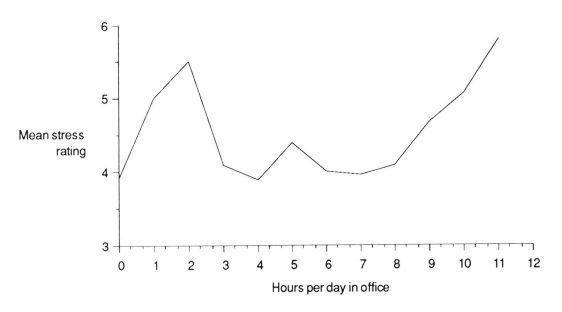

Figure 2.15
Staff who think that environmental conditions in their offices affect their productivity in six British office buildings. (Source: Building Use Studies)

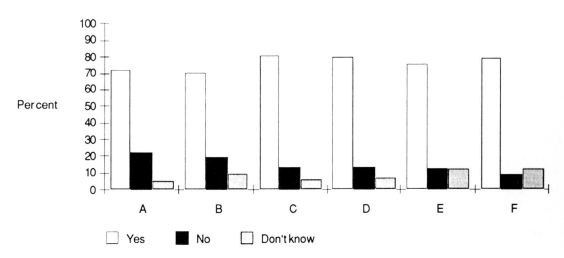

Table 2.4 Percentage of staff who left for home early in one calendar month as a result of conditions in an office building with sick building syndrome

Number of days	% of sample	Sample
Yes	41.8	202
No	58.4	284
Total	100.0	486

Source: Building Use Studies

Table 2.5   Number of days on which staff left for home early as a result of conditions in one office building with sick building syndrome. These data refer only to those who left home early

Number of days	% leaving early	Sample
0-5	87.7	128
6-10	9.6	14
More than 10	2.8	4
Total	100.0	148

Source: Building Use Studies

This leads to the final section of this paper. A crucial, but frequently absent, component of the Responsible Workplace is the capacity to make vertically-integrated decisions about building procurement, design, management and use; existing ways of developing and communicating knowledge and decisions about buildings are deficient because they are horizontally-integrated. Knowledge and decisions tend to stay at one level in the hierarchy. The problem is therefore the quality of decision making and the provision of management information which supports this process.

Making decisions

Managing constraints

In the foregoing sections it has been argued that a Responsible Workplace delivers minimum constraints at each level of a hierarchy of control. The effects of constraints are cumulative, so that people lower down in the hierarchy – the building users – are likely to be most affected if the constraints acting on them are too restricting.

Phenomena like sick building syndrome, which is a non-specific feeling of malaise experienced by people during the time that they are in a building, and overall dissatisfaction with the physical performance of buildings, are examples of the responses of building users to unmanageable constraints acting upon them. What is meant by 'unmanageable' is that the constraints are, on the one hand, known but too costly to undo ('The building overheats because there are too many people, too much equipment, and not enough volume of air to exhaust the heat, but we cannot afford to improve the air handling system or to move'), or, on the other hand, unknown and too costly to unravel ('Users feel ill, especially later in the week, and levels of absenteeism are high, but we cannot afford the expense of studying why this is happening, so we cannot cure it').

There are different management responses to each of these circumstances: deterministic, where a known cause or causes is diagnosed and treated; and, probabilistic, where risk factors are identified and changes made to the building, but where there is some likelihood that the problem will remain because the specific cause is not known. Many of the changes that are made to buildings are of the second type: they are guesses based on likelihood of success, although they may pretend to be of the first type.

The level of knowledge about building performance is rapidly increasing, but this in itself is causing a problem for occupiers and owners because new knowledge, often partial, speculative and untested, tends to increase uncertainty rather than decrease it[12]. Although there is now a wider literature available to designers and facility managers about building performance, much of this is presented in a form which is of little help to organisational decision making, because it does not present information in a way which aids decision making

Figure 2.16
Diagram showing isolated feedback loops within separate building levels. (Source: Building Use Studies)

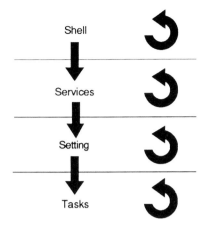

processes by describing the consequences of environmental change[13]. 'What-if?' questions about buildings are often unanswerable because the level of predictive knowledge about the consequences of change is still too poor.

Strategic planning and monitoring

Problems with the indoor environment are exactly analogous to those with the outdoor environment. They result from the lack of knowledge about the long term consequences of economic and technical intervention and change. The idea of a sustainable environment involves implanting negative feedback loops into decision taking about the economy and outdoor environment so that the consequences of change are understood, and the risk from environmental systems running out of control is reduced and, ultimately, minimised.

This can only be achieved by strategic planning and monitoring. Strategic planning views the overall operation of the entire environmental system guiding it in socially responsible

ways; monitoring provides the information and feedback by which the strategy can be guided. Thus strategy, monitoring and feedback are a vital part of a socially and environmentally responsible system.

Exactly the same applies to buildings: buildings must be strategically planned and monitored for similar reasons. Strategic planning and design covers the relations between geographical location, site, shell and services within the context of the overall needs of the occupying organisation; monitoring deals with ensuring that the performance of the building remains within acceptable criteria bands. For buildings, feedback loops have usually been horizontally-integrated; that is, they normally work only within levels of the hierarchy of control, or across adjacent levels.

In future the control and feedback mechanisms in buildings will be far more vertical, dynamic and responsive. This is not solely a question of the control systems of intelligent buildings responding to physical environment cues, but a much broader approach to a complete set of constraints and feedbacks across the broad range of building systems and subsystems.

In a Responsible Workplace, the total system includes geographical location and site (and therefore broad environmental responsibility) and the occupying organisation (and the performance of organisations as businesses or service organisations). The fate of environment, building and organisation are increasingly tied to each other as one system, although they continue to be treated separately.

The relationship between how systems work in terms of energy exchange and flow, including the capacity for efficient work, and potential for information processing and exchange has long been recognised as a proper basis for strategic decision making[14]. Buildings have a capacity as containers of organisations and are contained by and affect their ecological environment. As such, they have important systemic and interactive properties.

The science of making decisions

The process by which buildings are designed and used is one of variety reduction. Theoretically, at the initial stages of location, planning and design a building has an extremely large

Figure 2.17
Diagram showing vertical feedback from the workstation and task level in the building to shell, services and setting levels higher up in the building hierarchy. (Source: Building Use Studies)

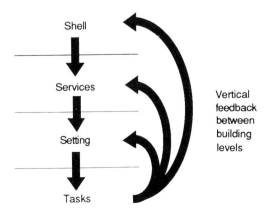

number of options: these are rapidly reduced as the process of design, construction and use unfolds. From a design point of view the variety of options, especially in a rapidly changing technical environment, can be intimidating. From a user point of view, the choice of options becomes critical. The user, at all levels of the building, wants to be left with as many options as possible; the designer needs to find ways of constraining those options without unduly taking freedom away from the user.

The implication for the future is that strategic and tactical decision making will become crucial for the Responsible Workplace, and that a science of decision making will develop around the total building system. This will have the effect of delivering usable information to managers in organisations in a form which they can act on, and it will create a new discipline of strategic thinking encompassing the physical environment, organisational ecology and managerial decision taking.

References

1 The term 'hierarchy of control' is taken from H H Pattee, 'The Problem of Biological Hierarchy' in C H Waddington (ed.) *Towards a Theoretical Biology*, Vol. 3, 1968–72. The terminology of 'shell' and 'setting' is taken from Francis Duffy: see, for example, F Duffy, C Cave and J Worthington (eds.), *Planning Office Space*, Architectural Press, 1976.

2 Health and Safety Executive, *Sick Building Syndrome: A Review*, Report No. 10, 1988.

3 Michael Young, *The Metronomic Society: Natural Rhythms and Human Timetables*, Thames and Hudson, London, 1988, p. 219.

4 John Jack, 'IT and the working environment,' *Environmental Quality '90*, 1990.

5 This process is described in Charles Handy *The Age of Unreason*, Business Books Ltd, 1989.

6 Adapted from John Jack, 'IT and the working environment,' *Environmental Quality '90*, 1990.

7 Satisfaction and attitude surveys of office users invariably show that temperature, ventilation, lighting, noise and smoking (in that order) are the objects of most user complaints.

8 Another example is the failure of certain shell designs to accommodate the requirements of information technology. See, for example, Butler Cox, *Information Technology: A Practical Guide For Designers*, Butler Cox plc, London, 1989.

9 For example, Pilkington Glass, *Fenestration 2000, An Investigation Into Long-Term Requirements For Fenestration*, 1989.

10 G Raw, A Leaman and M C Roys, *Further findings from the Office Environment Survey*, unpublished Building Research Establishment paper, 1989.

11 Ibid

12 For the rapid change in information levels see, for example, the difference between the first and second editions of S R Curwell and C G March, *Hazardous Building Materials*, 1986 and 1990.

13 Examples are J C Fischer, *Environmental Quality In Offices*, 1989, and F Steele, *Making And Managing High Quality Workplaces*, 1986.

14 P Checkland, *Systems Thinking, Systems Practice*, 1981.

3 Changing business: post-Fordism and the workplace

Andrew Laing, DEGW London Limited

Summary

The office workplace will have to be designed for increased organisational flexibility in the use of space and time, quicker response to market needs, and the higher expectations for quality held by employees. This will be the result of the pressures of change forced on organisations by the development of what has been termed the post-Fordist economy.

The theory of post-Fordism suggests there has been a major restructuring of market economies and business activities away from rigid traditional modes of operation to much more highly flexible and diverse systems. The nature of this new flexibility is reflected in ways of producing goods and services, organisational structures, employment and labour relations, patterns and locations of work, as well as through the impacts of information technology.

The routine assumptions of Fordist ways of doing things are overturned, often with paradoxical results. Previously contradictory or conflicting elements are combined by organisations, allowing them to maintain tighter control through looser structures; reap the benefits of small and large scale operations simultaneously; convert information into creative knowledge; locate in many places and have excellent communications; and transform patterns of work time and location.

Issues for the 1990s: interpreting changing business

Fordism and post-Fordism

The idea of Fordism and post-Fordism has emerged as a way of explaining the changes in economic structure and activity that have characterised market economies since the Second World War. Most authors who have developed the concept identify a further sharp turning point in the nature of economic activity from 1973 as a result of the oil price shocks and subsequent crises of competition, inflation and recession.

David Harvey[1], for example, provides a wide ranging review of the development of the concept of Fordism and its evolution into post-Fordism, the new type of economic regime which he describes as 'flexible accumulation'.

Fordism

The historical basis for the argument rests on the idea of the demise of Fordism with the end of the long post war economic boom. Fordism as a concept originated with the industrial practices and related social vision developed by Henry Ford at his automobile plants in Michigan around 1914. Harvey emphasises that while the industrial method of Fordism was based on innovative theories of 'scientific management' of the industrial labour process[2] it was at the same time a model for social consumption and lifestyles.

The Fordist industrial system broke the labour process down into detailed tasks according to highly specified time and motion analyses. Management, conception, control and execution were all separated into distinct hierarchies of function which resulted in the de-skilling of routine work at the point of production and the centralised codification of traditional practices into a core of managerial knowledge[3]. The increased productivity achieved by scientific management was intended to allow industrial workers to be paid enough to support a society of mass consumption and increased leisure. Fordism implied a new kind of worker and a new society.

Fordism became the dominant industrial model for the fast growing market economies in what are now considered to be the traditional industries: cars, ship building, transport equipment, steel, petrochemicals, consumer electrical goods. New industrial and urban regions emerged as core world centres of Fordist enterprise and society – the Mid-West of the USA, the Ruhr Rhinelands in Germany, the West Midlands of the UK, Tokyo and Yokohama in Japan[4].

Post-Fordism

If the central characteristic of Fordism was the mass production of standardised products, post-Fordism has been characterised by:

- increasingly flexible labour processes and markets

- programmable automated production

- heightened geographical mobility

- rapid shifts in patterns of consumption

- privatisation, deregulation, and reduction in state economic activity.

These developments are understood to be responses to the rigidity of the Fordist economy in which long term, large scale fixed capital investments for mass production have become out of step with market demands. Fordist enterprises were also associated with entrenched and antagonistic labour relations based on traditional unionised workforces typically in established urban centres.

The Fordist/Post-Fordist paradigm

In response to this rigidity new complexes of activities and enterprises have arisen that are flexible in their approach: new sectors of production, new kinds of labour process, new patterns of consumption. They include the new high technology sectors (in particular the electronics industry) as well as revived craft and design intensive industries (clothing, furniture, textiles) and the burgeoning business, financial, consulting and personal services sectors. Many of the new fields of post-Fordist activity have been key users of new kinds of information technology. The electronics sector has been particularly important in providing the technology for calculating, communicating, and processing that has enabled the restructuring typical of post-Fordist activity[5].

Kaye[6] has described how information technology has been used to create immense variety in product lines within tight cost con-

Table 3.1 Fordism and post-Fordism: keywords

FORDIST	POST-FORDIST
PRODUCTION	
industry	service
work on objects	work with people
manual	mental/manual
mass	niche/ customisation
rigid	flexible
economies of scale	economies of scope
hard growth	smart growth
ORGANISATION	
hierarchy	participation
command	initiative
control	learning
expansive	downsized, flattened
EMPLOYMENT	
core	core/periphery
full time	variable times
in-house	outworkers
blue/white collar	open collar
entrenched labour relations	flexible employment
job specialisation	no job demarcation
male	male/female
PATTERNS OF WORK	
layers of management	task teams
single task	multiple tasks
hierarchy	operating specialists
sequence of functions	synchrony
status	contribution
INFORMATION TECHNOLOGY	
automate	informate
data	knowledge
routine	creative
centralisation	integration and decentralisation
LOCATION	
places	networks
central	dispersed
transport	communication

Source: After David Harvey, 1989

straints, allowing increased production and distribution flexibility. Mass customisation has replaced the global products characteristic of the Fordist period.

A set of keywords compiled from several writings on post-Fordism is used in Table 3.1 to illustrate the dominant characteristics of the Fordist/post-Fordist paradigm, as it is expressed in terms of production, organisation, employment, patterns of work, and information technology. The keyword terms should be thought of as ideal types; simple polarisations of the attributes of the Fordist/post-Fordist dichotomy. In the discussion that follows, the relationship between the two poles is examined in more detail.

Breaking with the past?

To what extent do these post-Fordist developments mark a revolutionary break with the traditional Fordist model, or are they trends that coexist alongside pre-existing structures? To what extent will they become the normal way of doing business? Three approaches within the Fordist/post-Fordist debate are identified by Harvey. One school of thought sees the post-Fordist model as a complete break with the past, a revolutionary transformation of production socially, economically and geographically: 'a second industrial divide'[7]. Piore and Sabel identified entirely new forms of labour, organisations and locations of post-Fordist economy. A second school of thought sees the post-Fordist economy as a natural extension of an exploitative tendency inherent to the logic of capitalism: the casualisation of labour. In order for capitalism to maintain profitability and reassert control over workers, managers have instituted labour and employment policies that effectively marginalise labour and make it more easy to exploit. Authors in this school have focused particularly on the ways in which some sectors of post-Fordist enterprise have reused pre-capitalist and domestic organisations and marginal populations in their labour forces – for example: outworking, piece work, sweatshops, informal working arrangements exploiting Third World, minority and female labour forces[8].

Harvey argues for a third interpretation: new forms of flexible production and organisations are arising in conjunction with remaining efficient Fordist businesses, which are themselves being transformed by the post-Fordist innovations. The transition to post-Fordism involves combinations of new and older elements, some progressive, others exploitative. This interpretation allows the most flexible approach to understanding the complex interactions between the new and the old which characterise the new economic conditions.

Re-working old patterns

The historical transition from Fordism to post-Fordism and the future development of the post-Fordist economies is made up of a series of related developments which involve both entirely new kinds of activities and the re-working of older economic patterns in new ways. Examples of these include:

- growth of organised subcontracting and consultancy alongside major corporations

- revival of older forms of production: domestic, artisan, familial, outworking

- integration of informal economies with Fordist enterprises: underground, peripheral, marginal, (First and Third World).

Characteristic of the post-Fordist economy is the move away from high volume mass production to specialised flexible production systems:

> The economies of scale sought under Fordist mass production have, it seems, been countered by an increasing capacity to manufacture a variety of goods in small batches. Economies of scope have beaten out economies of scale[9].

In the same way that the new production methods of Fordism were accompanied by visions of a mass consumerist lifestyle, the post-Fordist economy presupposes a social vision: a rapid turnover of consumption catering to specialised tastes with diverse products.

Organisational structures and information technology

Flexibility and tighter control

Harvey describes the post-Fordist economy as undergoing an 'imploding centralisation'. Post-Fordist capitalism is developing in a paradoxical manner: increasing flexibility is achieved through tighter organisation. Geographical mobility, dispersal of activities, and flexibility in labour and consumer markets and in the organisation of work, are accomplished through tighter and flatter forms of organisation. The new flexibility is an expression of organisational effectiveness. Nowhere is this more clear than in the information industries and in the application of information technology to changing business practices.

Knowledge business

Knowledge itself has become big business. Knowledge depends on current information and very quick response times. Highly specialised consultancies in business and information services have emerged as a result. Competitive advantage is defined in terms of access to the right information. The production of knowledge can be thought of as a new productive sector located in such regions as Cambridge in the UK; the international Silicon valleys and glens from California to Scotland; Route 128 around Boston. These knowledge and information services have been developed furthest in the vastly expanded global financial services sector which has taken the most advantage of information technology[10].

Information technology and organisational change

Basic developments in science and technology have revolutionised computer and telecommunications hardware, a trend that is expected to continue to maintain a constant pressure of change for organisations and business activity. Computer hardware will continue to become smaller and more powerful. Alongside hardware developments are the immense increases in software power and much faster software production. The most powerful effects of this continuing change are thought to be on network systems. Organisations are being affected by the potential of:

- distributed processing networks to exchange data and information
- value added data services to link companies

- flexible accessible databases
- network management tools for distributed databases[11]

Businesses benefit from the reduced time required to record, reconcile, retrieve, analyse and present data. They also gain from the increased accessibility, consistency, and timeliness of data. Information can be adapted to changes in strategy and organisation more easily. Competitive pressures mean that organisations which fail to take on board these kinds of productivity improvements will be likely to fail.

What are the organisational impacts of information technology? The most obvious impact is the elimination of mediation between customer and supplier or the middleman in the organisation. Information technology enables the business to target market niches much more easily, to adapt products and services to consumer needs, and to forecast demand and control stock more efficiently. Kaye identifies a double process affecting business: the combination of what he calls 'disintermediation' and 'integration' which correspond to Harvey's idea of the coexistence of flexibility and tightness in the organisation. For example, the elimination of middlemen is combined with tighter control and response. Others have also identified the contradictory power of information technology to both stretch and shrink organisations, as it allows for greater centralised control through improved information but also enables the decentralisation of decision making. Information systems may become the heart and stable structure of new organisations, as they maintain corporate history, experience and expertise[12].

Changing organisational profiles

The organisational structures of post-Fordist enterprises are less hierarchical and more dependent on dispersed information. Unlike Fordist production systems which presupposed a clear hierarchy of skills divided among a privileged managerial elite and a de-skilled labour force at the point of production, the post-Fordist organisation makes use of a flatter organisational profile which encourages a more widespread distribution of knowledge and skills. Some organisations which have used information technology for routine processing of data or production automation are now developing into highly specialised knowledge based organisations. Organisational structures are changing to allow:

- realisation of benefits of small and large scale simultaneously

- flexibility in larger organisations

- blurring of distinctions between centralised and decentralised control

- focus on projects and processes rather than standard tasks and procedures[13]

Information technology transforms organisations

Information technology is the great transformer of organisational structures:

> 'as soon as a company takes the first tentative steps from data to information, its decision processes, management structure, and even the ways its work gets done begin to be transformed'[14].

Three major changes in business organisation in the last century have been identified[15]. First, between 1895 and 1905, management was effectively separated from ownership, a major breakthrough in organisational structure. Second, by 1925 the command and control model of organisation was established and taken up by leaders of industry (Sloan at General Motors, for example). Fordism required clear hierarchies to enable complex large scale operations to separate policy and management as well as the functional specialisation of departments. Drucker argues that there is now a third initiative that is reshaping organisations: the shift from the command and control model to organisations of knowledge experts, based on information.

Information technology is affecting how organisations do the work of thinking, communicating and acting[16]. Information technology has fundamentally changed methods of gathering, observing and analysing information; the creation and evaluation of ideas; and the resultant decisions for action. The typical organisation of the future will be knowledge based: 'composed of specialists who direct and discipline their own performance through organised feedback from colleagues, customers and headquarters'[17].

Information technology and management

It is generally assumed that the role of middle management is under threat by the powerful information technologies that are transforming work and organisations. Drucker expects that in 20 years time organisations will have half their current levels of management, and a third the number of managers. Some authors suggest that in the US organisations shed one million managers between 1979 and 1988:

> 'information technology which had once been a tool for organisational expansion, has become a tool for downsizing and restructuring'[18].

The traditional role of managers in relaying decisions from top down is being superseded by more direct forms of communication using information technology. Distributed processing and communications systems allow fast dissemination of information and instructions across organisations. Performance feedback can also be tightened up.

Kaye argues that the role of management in problem solving will become more important, with increased responsibility for the fewer remaining managers at lower levels. Shop floor workers, for example, may be made responsible for more tasks at larger volumes of production; salesmen may have more responsibility for delivery and customer commitment; middle management may take on responsibility for more complex problems[19].

Multifunctional groups and task forces become effective ways of optimising the new information resources across organisations. For top management, the impact of information technology changes departmental boundaries and identities, making them more fluid. Information systems and databases can support new kinds of decentralisation which can be used to promote flexibility and avoid the rigidity of large centralised staff. Firms can in fact maintain the advantages of integration and control typical of a centralised organisation with the flexibility and responsiveness of a decentralised organisation[20]. Large organisations can be run like small ones.

Information is no longer only used as a controlling mechanism, as in the Fordist enterprise, but becomes knowledge used for the special purposes of the organisation. The information organisation becomes an organisation of specialists. In the highly information technology intensive organisation, what Zuboff calls the 'informated organisation', the data base and the electronic text become the heart of the organisation:

'a vast symbolic surrogate for the vital detail of an organisation's daily life. They are a public symbolisation of organisational experience, much of which was previously private, fragmented, and implicit'[21].

Employment, labour relations, and patterns of work

Employment flexibility

Fordist labour relations assumed a hierarchy of division of labour within the plant which specified tasks according to function. Job demarcation clearly identified tasks to be performed by full time employees. Post-Fordist labour relations are characterised by flexibility of work and labour contracts. There has been a major move away from regular employment towards part time, temporary and other forms of contract labour. A distinction is often made between what are considered 'core' employees and a wider periphery of labour defined through a variety of contractual arrangements. Core employees are defined as those with permanent status central to the long term future of the organisation. Peripheral employees are expected to have a much higher turnover. They may also work full time, but they will have skills that are readily available in the market and they will be employed for specific tasks required at particular times on a more flexible time basis: for example, temporary, part time, contract, or trainees. The overall trend has been to reduce the core element of the workforce and expand the use of flexible peripheral employment.

New patterns of work

When information is no longer used for the purposes of control but for the creation of specialised knowledge, the organisation becomes less hierarchical and patterns of work change. Workers in information organisations have to be more highly skilled and better trained, they are specialist problem solvers working in teams or groups rather than de-skilled workers performing standardised tasks. Work may be done by task oriented teams from various departments supported by distributed information systems.

Work functions become synchronous rather than sequential. Research, development, manufacturing and marketing may be undertaken simultaneously by teams of specialists. The reality of work is transformed by information technology:

'information technology essentially alters the contours of reality, work becomes more abstract, intelligence may be programmed, organisational memory and visibility are increased by an order of magnitude beyond any historical capability'[22].

Work may be done by task oriented teams from various departments supported by distributed information systems. Groups may form and disband to solve particular problems. Workers may be dispersed. Software is emerging to serve group and team working processes, the so-called 'Groupware' for Computer Supported Collaborative Work (CSCW)[23]. CSCW allows work on a project to be undertaken in one or several places, at the same or different times, by a group of co-workers[24]. The work may take place in conference rooms, video areas, using electronic bulletin boards or mail systems. Ideas and drafts of documents can be captured and displayed in many different ways[25].

Whereas the Fordist organisation had clear demarcations of standardised tasks, the post-Fordist organisation involves projects and processes that are unique and tailored to special purposes in the market. Rigid hierarchies to organise the mass production of standard products or services are replaced by networked organisations that allow for fluid patterns of work.

Work time and space

As the typical corporate profile becomes flatter and employment patterns more flexible, a new pattern of relationships between work time and space within the workplace is established.

Groups form and disband around projects; consultants and outworkers come in and out of the organisation: there is a new fluidity in the use of space over time. Many core workers may be out of the office or away from their desks much of the time – with clients, working at home or working with project teams inside or outside the office. Other kinds of workers are coming in and out of the office. Why should the organisation provide every member of its staff with permanent offices and desk positions when they are often absent and when their productivity is enhanced by more intensive group work or time spent with clients? Desk sharing, the free address workstation, and the provision of a range of group shared spaces is one solution to this problem being explored by many organisations[26,27]. This push to realise office assets more efficiently and promote productivity is very much more feasible with advanced information technology and networking.

The impact of information technology on organisational change is raising questions about the notion of the place of work. The informated workplace, 'which may no longer be a "place" at all, is an arena through which information circulates, information to which intellective effort is applied. The quality, rather than the quantity, of effort will be the source from which added value is derived'[28].

Information technology has changed the management of work, separating control from reporting relationships[29]. Individuals are more likely to be specialists who can operate around goals which clearly state performance expectations. The rewards of work are defined individually within a unified vision of the organisation of specialists. Drucker notes that currently individual business advancement is organised through management positions and titles, rather than through rewarding specialists.

The creative workplace

Innovative organisations in the 1990s will be using information technology to support creative work. Workers will expect to be rewarded on the basis of the contributions they make rather than according to established hierarchies of rank and status. They will also expect the work environment to support their creative work:

'Because workers will be highly skilled and the organisation will offer fewer opportunities for advancement, employees will expect the work environment to be rewarding. If they are not stimulated or if their independence is threatened, they will go elsewhere'[30].

Locations of changing business

Post-Fordist locations

The Fordist/post-Fordist debate is related to arguments about the spatial distribution of economic activity. Is there a geography of location that corresponds to the post-Fordist model? New regions of high employment growth and new manufacturing have emerged since the 1950s, expanding rapidly in the 1970s and 1980s. They tend to be in what were once marginal areas without established industry and in revitalised zones of older industrial and urban centres. Many such areas have been associated with new high technology industries, but others are also associated with craft, design, and artisan industries. Scott argues they are a series of new industrial spaces for new kinds of capitalist economic activity. There has been widespread debate over spatial changes associated with new forms of economic activity[31].

These new locations of the post-Fordist enterprise are further supported by the impact that advanced information technology has on the way they do business. The capacity for information technology to shrink distance favours global operations. Global networks convey sound, vision, text, and data to enable salesmen to reach global markets, to support global manufacturing, and to provide global services[32]. Information technology helps firms to deal with the complexity of operating in many different markets and enables new economies of scale to be developed. Information technology allows a new flexibility in the location of work, at the same time empowering global communications and enabling work to be done from home. Information technology can allow networks of small dispersed offices to remain in effective communication with each other.

The post-Fordist industries and business activities have indeed developed their own particular patterns of location. Scott has analysed a series of case studies of geographical regions in the Western economies that represent new centres of post-Fordist economy. They include the 'Third Italy' – the fashion, design and craft artisan industry of the many towns around Bologna – the so-called 'Scientific City' to the south of Paris, and the Silicon Valley of northern California[33]. Scott argues that post-Fordist industries and activities tend to locate together in areas where their requirements of flexible production systems using specialised local labour can be met. Many post-Fordist centres of economic activity have been established in new or marginal regions, sometimes to evade the unionisation and political activism typical of the established culture of older industrial regions. For example, high technology post-Fordist activities have tended to locate in suburban sites outside established industrial areas or in entirely new industrial areas – Route 128, Boston; Orange County and Silicon Valley, California; 'Medical Alley' around Minneapolis and St. Paul; the M4 corridor in the UK.

However, not all post-Fordist activity is established in new, suburban, or marginal areas. Some older industrial locations have also been recolonised by new industrial and business enterprises. Scott gives examples of post-Fordist enterprises outside the high technology and financial sectors which have 'recolonised' older urban industrial areas, some of which use cheap immigrant labour. These include the clothing, furniture and jewellery sectors in New York, Los Angeles and Paris; and craft centres in Denmark, southern Germany, Jura, Switzerland, and parts of France and Portugal.

Scott also argues that post-Fordist enterprises have colonised small and medium sized towns in what were formerly peripheral areas of the Fordist economy. Typical locations are: Austin, Texas; Boulder and Colorado Springs, Colorado; Cambridge, UK; Grenoble and Sophia Antipolis, France. These towns are characterised by having both highly skilled managerial and technical labour forces, often associated with universities and research establishments, as well as pools of low paid immigrant or marginal workforces[34].

Post-Fordist locations thus contrast with areas of traditional basic industry, which themselves are undergoing transformation as a result of a new international division of labour. This has resulted in much basic Fordist manufacturing plant activity being exported to peripheral developing countries.

Globalisation

Globalisation has become an economic imperative. On a competitive map of the world there are no national boundaries to the flow of business activity[35]. Information has made everyone a global citizen, but a citizen in a postmodern world in which individual difference and choice rather than a standardised global product are demanded. In Europe, the imperative of globalisation is the immediate target of the single European market, which at over 320 million people will be the biggest continental market in the world.

Changing business and the Responsible Workplace

To what extent will post-Fordist ways of doing business be implemented generally through the economy, and what effect will this have on the design, management and use of the workplace? Is the post-Fordist workplace also a Responsible Workplace?

The market for Responsible Workplaces

Before considering the impact of post-Fordist business on the workplace, it is worth recognising the limited extent to which newly designed workplaces will be created during the 1990s. The annual demand for all new built development in the UK is only about 2% of the total built stock. Occupiers concerned with the built environment both as a factor of production and as a shelter and appropriate environment for the production of goods and services will primarily be adapting existing buildings and facilities[36]. Yet it will be the growing and innovative firms that will be most likely to require new or additional premises, so the market for correspondingly innovative workplaces grows with these firms.

What do the post-Fordist trends suggest for the nature of these workplaces? Each of the characteristics of post-Fordism identified in this paper has implications for the design, use, and management of the workplace.

The productive workplace

If the productive potential of the post-Fordist enterprise is to be fully realised, the workplace should be designed to allow the flexibility of response to the market that is demanded by competition. An increasing emphasis on service orientation, on working with people as opposed to working on objects, on the customisation of goods and services, and on the definition of economies of scope rather than scale, all point to the workplace as being geared towards change and flexibility. The workplace must be capable of being 're-tooled' easily and quickly. Re-tooling will be facilitated by an intensified use of information technology to enable customised reactions to market-led change and to cope with highly flexible patterns of employment.

Accommodating the flexible workforce

The post-Fordist office workplace will be designed to accommodate a flexible workforce, ranging from the core employee to an array of consultants, part-time staff, temporary help and outworkers and subcontractors of many kinds. The organisation may itself be linked to other organisations in temporary and permanent relationships. How should the workplace respond to the different employment characteristics of the flexible workforce?

Post-Fordist workspace

The organisation is less likely to be a unit of equivalent employees differentiated only by rank, the latter expressed by different space standards allocated to grades of staff: traditionally enclosed offices for managers and open plan areas for secretarial and clerical staff. This traditional layout, favoured in the UK and the US, represents a Fordist approach to the definition of the social space of the office. The open plan layout represents the space for de-skilled routine work at the 'point of production'; the enclosed office signifies elite managerial status holding power and knowledge. The post-Fordist organisation will increasingly challenge this rigid pattern of space use.

Generic flexible space

The major implication of flexible organisational structure and employment for the design of the office workplace is the absence of a simple spatial representation of an organisation's pyramidal hierarchy. The definition of space standards from clerical open plan to enclosed executive office will break down. But, more than replacing the Fordist dichotomy of enclosed and open plan space, the post-Fordist workplace will introduce a range of working spaces that are generically more flexible and more supportive of particular kinds of work activity. The trend is likely to be an increasing provision of generic kinds of working spaces that can be used by different kinds of staff in varying numbers to perform a range of tasks. These generic workspaces will be supplemented by highly serviced support spaces that can be shared by fluctuating numbers of people. This kind of spatial solution to new working patterns has been defined by Stone and Luchetti as 'the multiple activity setting'[37]. In some European countries the crude Fordist dichotomy of open and enclosed space is being replaced by workplaces in which high proportions of cellular offices are being combined with a large degree of shared amenities and new types of workspaces, such as the German gruppenraum in which groups of people share offices[38]. The requirements of private work and public amenity are being provided in new ways.

Balancing efficiency and creativity

Designers of the Responsible Workplace in the 1990s are faced with a dilemma. The flexibility of employment and market response demanded by the post-Fordist organisation suggests breaking away from a traditional allocation of space[39]. Organisations are under pressure to rationalise standards, reduce occupancy costs and maximise flexibility[40], all of which prompt the use of more open plan space, or, in some cases, desk sharing. Yet the nature of office work has become more intellectual, less routine and requires greater privacy as well as provision for communication, group, team, and project work. The solution, then, is likely to be a variety of work settings that have less to do with rank and status and much more to do with the quality of conditions for creative work. The intensification of use of the office as an asset must be achieved through the design of environments that support high quality creative work.

Accommodating new patterns of work time and location

The most significant characteristics of the post-Fordist organisation in terms of the design and use of the office workplace will be an increased flexibility in both the location of work and the timing of work activities. This flexibility will provide the main challenge for firms to capture the potential increases in productivity to be gained from designing new kinds of workplaces.

Given the increased flexibility of employment there will be a constantly shifting population working in the office; these people will be interrelated with other kinds of personnel working outside the office in different types of locations. The office will be used most intensively by the full-time core workforce, but it will be used by them in more flexible ways. Core staff may prefer to work at home some of the time. Others may be working much of the time at their clients' locations. For some core staff the office may be used principally for meetings and other social activities or for accessing specialised technical resources and information. For all core workers, the office will be used at many different hours of the day and at weekends. For non-core workers the office workplace will be used more or less intensively depending on particular work requirements. Some routine non-core work can be done remotely or at home. Consultants and subcontractors and other kinds of outworkers will use the office on as required.

Matching new organisational structures and patterns of work to the workplace

While the key spatial characteristic of the post-Fordist office is likely to be a range of generic workspaces that can be used by varying numbers of staff at different times, supplemented by highly serviced support space offering specialised technical resources and meeting spaces, the quality of the office workplace will be transformed as well. As soon as the office is no longer primarily a space for routine, full-time processing activities, but instead a centre for creating ideas and taking decisions supported by intensive use of information technology, the workplace becomes quite a different entity. The workplace is more likely to be designed to facilitate interpersonal communication between groups that are set up to work on particular projects. Groups need to be supported by accessible and powerful technology in settings that are conducive to irregular and sometimes long working hours of intensive creativity. The 'back office' of routine processing will be shrunk or relocated away from central workplaces where the core business activity will take place.

Imagery and security

These fluid boundaries of the organisation suggest that the imagery of the office will need to be reconsidered. The workplace is where a variety of consultants, outworkers and colleagues meet to work together; as such it is highly exposed. Design constraints will be posed by the need to maintain in-house security in organisations that are much more open to outsiders in their daily operations.

Users' demands

Moreover, the employees in post-Fordist organisations will be much more demanding of their workplaces. They will expect suitable amenities to support their creative work and lifestyles – for example, provision for childcare, relaxation and refreshment, or advanced telecommunications and computing capacity[41]. They will expect an environment that is psychologically supportive and visually pleasing, one that enables them to feel comfortable and stimulated when working for very long hours with people they may not be familiar with. Without the security of their 'own' desk in their 'own' office, employees will expect other kinds of compensation: for example, the use of remote or portable technology to allow them to work easily from home or communicate by telephone and laptop when travelling. Instead of their 'own' space, office users may identify with an area of shared facilities belonging to the group of people they usually work with. They will expect a workplace that reflects their concerns for the environment: one that does not squander resources, waste energy or use ecologically harmful resources. They may expect to work in an environment that they can regulate more easily.

For the developers, designers, and managers of workplaces the decisions will have more to do with creating workplaces that are both able to respond to changing organisational needs and more finely tuned to the particular organisation's requirements. In this way, the design of the workplace parallels the paradoxical character of the post-Fordist organisation: it provides the flexibility to achieve tighter control, and focuses on economies of scope rather than economies of scale.

References

1 Harvey, D, *The Condition of Post-Modernity*, Oxford, 1989
2 Taylor, F W, 'Scientific management', in *Organisation Theory* (1912), D. S. Pugh (ed), London.
3 Braverman, H, *Labor and monopoly capital*, New York, 1974
4 Harvey, D, *The Condition of Post-Modernity*, Oxford, 1989
5 Scott, A J, *New industrial spaces: Flexible production organisation and regional development in North America and Western Europe*, London, 1988
6 Kaye, D, *Gamechange, the impact of information technology on corporate strategies and structures*, London, 1989.
  7Piore M, and Sabel, C, *The second industrial divide*, New York, 1984
8 Scott, A J, *New industrial spaces: Flexible production organisation and regional development in North America and Western Europe*, London, 1988
9 Harvey, D, *The Condition of Post-Modernity*, Oxford, 1989
10 Ibid
11 Kaye, D, *Gamechange, the impact of information technology on corporate strategies and structures*, London, 1989.
12 Applegate, L, Cash, J and Mills, D, 'Information technology and tomorrow's manager', *Harvard Business Review*, Nov/Dec 1988.
13 Ibid
14 Drucker, P, 'The Coming of the new organisation', *Harvard Business Review*, Jan/Feb 1988,
15 Ibid
16 Kaye, D, *Gamechange, the impact of information technology on corporate strategies and structures*, London, 1989.
17 Drucker, P, 'The Coming of the new organisation', *Harvard Business Review*, Jan/Feb 1988
18 Applegate, L, Cash, J and Mills, D, Information technology and tomorrow's manager, Harvard Business Review, Nov/Dec 1988
19 Kaye, D, *Gamechange, the impact of information technology on corporate strategies and structures*, London, 1989.
20 Applegate, L, Cash, J and Mills, D, 'Information technology and tomorrow's manager', *Harvard Business Review*, Nov/Dec 1988
21 Zuboff, S, *In the age of the smart machine, the future of work and power*. London, 1990
22 Ibid
23 Tesler, L. 'Networked computing in the 1990s'. In *Scientific American*, September 1991.
24 Johansen, R. et al, *Leading business teams, how teams can use technology and group process tools to enhance performance*. Addison Wesley Publishing Company, 1991.
25 Grenier, R & Metes, G. *Enterprise networking, working together and apart*. Digital Press, 1992.
26 Laing, A, 'Desk sharing: the politics of space', *Facilities*, July 1990.
27 Stone, P and Luchetti R, 'Your Office is Where You Are', *Harvard Business Review*, Mar/April 1985
28 Zuboff, S, *In the age of the smart machine, the future of work and power*. London, 1990
29 Applegate, L, Cash, J and Mills, D, 'Information technology and tomorrow's manager', *Harvard Business Review*, Nov/Dec 1988
30 Ibid
31 See, for example: Massey, D, *Spatial divisions of labour*, London, 1988
32 Kaye, D, *Gamechange, the impact of information technology on corporate strategies and structures*, London, 1989
33 Scott, A J, *New industrial spaces: Flexible production organisation and regional development in North America and Western Europe*, London, 1988
34 Ibid
35 Ohmae, K, 'Managing in a borderless world', *Harvard Business Review*, May/June 1989
36 Stone, PA, *Development and Planning Economy*, London, 1988
37 Stone, P and Luchetti R, 'Your Office is Where You Are', *Harvard Business Review*, Mar/April 1985
38 Duffy, F, 'The European Challenge', *Architect's Journal*, August 1988
39 Laing, A, 'Desk sharing: the politics of space', *Facilities*, July 1990.
40 Lloyd, B, *Offices and office work: the coming revolution*, Slough, 1990
41 See, for example, Becker, F and Steele, F, 'The Total Workplace', *Facilities*, March 1990

4 The future of offices and office work

Bruce Lloyd, South Bank University

Summary

Office work now involves about half the population in western economies. Office property is the largest single item in the value of a nation's asset base. Yet, it is notorious for its low productivity in terms of both people and buildings.

This paper analyses the poor performance of the office as a resource in terms of utilisation of time and space. Key factors of change are identified: the shortage of young skilled people as a result of European demographic change, the social and environmental costs experienced by office workers in urban areas which may prompt changing locations and work lifestyles, and changes in work patterns which can contribute to increased productivity of offices.

The nature of office work

Office work, like factory work, is not a clear cut category of activity: it covers a range of activities with different characteristics. What unites most office workers is that they work in a similar physical setting: the office building. The office is a building where the end product is essentially a piece of paper (in its physical or electronic form) rather than a piece of machinery, equipment or hardware.

Almost all the functions of an office are fundamentally to do with information processing activities and they are an integral part of all manufacturing and service functions. It is, however, important to recognise that by no means all service industries operate from offices, nor are all office activities related to the service sector. Although there is some overlap, it is essential to separate the office revolution from the service revolution; both will become increasingly important in the coming decade, but they should not be confused as they have significantly different causes, characteristics and implications.

One estimate[1] suggested that, in the UK, each office worker used 10% of the equipment of a production worker (this figure ignores building costs). Over the next decade this picture is expected to change as the amount of equipment employed in an office rapidly increases, due to the impact of information technology, and as it becomes increasingly imperative to include building costs in any evaluation.

The office building and its utilisation

Conservative estimates suggest that between 25% and 50% of the workforce in the UK and the rest of the industrialised world currently work in offices[2]. In terms of resources the figures are enormous: possibly one third of the nation's GDP is involved in this activity. Yet the whole sector, while providing a vital basic function, is endemically inefficient and wasteful.

Office buildings and white collar jobs are likely to come under increasing pressure over the next decade. It is perhaps paradoxical – but for historical reasons not all that surprising – that there is increasing pressure to utilise major capital assets such as coal mines, power stations and car assembly lines for 24 hours a day, seven days a week, whilst office buildings and the work that goes on in them are virtually ignored. Overall, the trend appears to be in the opposite direction. Office buildings are unoccupied for longer periods as the white collar working week shortens and holiday periods lengthen. However, as offices and office workers become increasingly subjected to the rigours of the evaluation of management and performance that are commonplace on the factory floor, it is likely that radically different priorities will result.

In order to highlight this contradiction, it is useful to start with some rough calculations on the utilisation of the office building itself. The building is a capital asset of perhaps £1m, £10m, £100m, or even more. It functions for 365 days a year and has to be paid for as a capital asset over that period. But for how much of that time is this precious asset actually being used effectively? If 365 days a year are taken as 100%, the utilisation of an office property is immediately reduced to 260 days (71%) by allowing for a five day working week. Annual and bank holidays (25 and seven days respectively) bring the figure down further to 228 days (63%). Office buildings usually function for only eight hours a day during the days they are in use. This factor reduces utilisation by two-thirds, and hence the overall use figure is reduced to 76 days (21%). The theoretical attendance time is only 21%; even then no allowance has been made for lunch, illness, lateness and early departure. It is probably reasonable to deduct one hour for lunch and another hour to cover all the other items. Hence, the office operating time is down by another 20% to 57 days (16%). That is the theoretical operating time. Yet, anyone who has spent any time working in an office will know that work attendance is one thing; effective work another. In practice, time spent in an office is invariably split between three activities:

- Purely social activity. Time spent organising private matters during office hours; office social events and other activity peripheral to the stated objectives of the organisation.

- Running the building and organisation. Time spent in meetings, preparing reports and other administrative rituals. Of course, some organisations avoid this but they tend to be exceptions rather than the rule.

- Real relevant work.

It is difficult to get precise figures for the overall proportions of the above three activities, but it is probably not unreasonable to estimate an even three-way split. This reduces the use of that precious capital asset down to 19 continuous days in a year, marginally more than 5% of the total time available.

Additionally, many office workers are out of their offices 'on the road' some of the time, which would reduce the utilisation figure even further. Furthermore, when people are actually working it is likely that many will be operating at little more than 50% efficiency, which could reduce the real figure closer to 2–3%. Not many factories or power stations are allowed to waste assets on such a prolific scale.

Why has this happened? Why is it important? How is it going to change? And what needs to be done about it? This widespread misallocation and waste of resources has arisen because of a combination of factors. However, it should be recognised that it has tended to be companies in the manufacturing sector, such as GEC and ICI, that have led the way in reducing their expensive office space to a minimum. These companies have been subjected to the greatest competitive pressures over the post war period, and hence they have had to be especially concerned about using all their assets as effectively as possible. Manufacturing companies with substantially under utilised office

Figure 4.1
Office utilisation.
(Source: Bruce Lloyd)

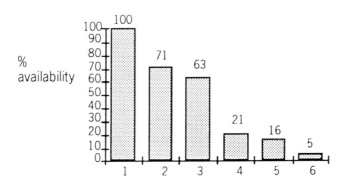

1. Office availability

After allowing for:

2. Five day working week
3. Annual/ bank holidays
4. Eight hour a day operations
5. Lunch/ illness etc
6. Social/ organisational activities.

Leaving real relevant work at 5% .

assets have also been particularly vulnerable as takeover targets.

Despite competitive pressures over the past 20 years, much office development has been a classic example of vested interest, combined with inadequate accountability and lack of market pressure to produce potentially severe distortions in the efficient allocation and use of resources over the longer term. Fortunately for most organisations, virtually ignoring the productivity of their office asset has not in general been too harmful to their 'bottom line' – so far. The bandwagon effect has caused the value of office space to continue to appreciate – in marked contrast to a factory where depreciation is an ever present reality. Gradually, perhaps even suddenly, the ultimate pressures of the marketplace will begin to show themselves in a significant change in attitude towards offices.

Radical changes are long overdue. They have been talked about for years[3] but, so far, relatively little seems to have happened. In the 1980s the position of London in general and the City in particular was supported by the influx of new institutions from outside the UK; particularly from the US, the Middle East and Japan, with some support from Europe and Hong Kong. The most difficult element to predict in the decade ahead is the level of overseas investment in the UK commercial property market. Without a significant inflow from somewhere, the changes predicted in this paper could be even more far reaching.

Changes are beginning to occur which will soon start to have a significant effect on the underlying position of the office property market. In the short term the change is probably more a reflection of high interest rates on the overall domestic and international supply and demand position than anything else, but the advent of new technology such as computers, fax machines and cellular phones is reinforcing the underlying trends, even before the greater economic, environmental and social pressures are considered.

Key factors of change

What changes are likely to occur over the next decade? How do they differ from the classical property cycle?[4] And what are the possible implications of these differences? Among the differences, discussed in more detail below, are:

- demographic change
- increasing awareness of social costs
- relocation trends
- changes in individual priorities and aspirations
- possible new international migration
- effects of greater competition
- growing impact of new technology

Today change is so pervasive that any straight line extrapolation of past trends to forecast the future is likely to result in very expensive mistakes.

Demographic factors

The 1990s will see a shortage of young skilled people across Eastern and Western Europe as well as in most of the rest of the industrialised world. Consequently the growing pressure to bring older people back into the workforce replaces the pressures for early retirement seen in the past decade. Fortunately, some organisations have found that their older staff are just as capable of learning new skills and adapting to change – if the right training is provided. Other factors which will add to the need for more flexibility are:

- The growing number of women in the workforce in professional and managerial positions. About 75% of office work is undertaken by women, but at present they are still very unevenly distributed in the hierarchy of nearly all organisations.
- A more mature, more educated workforce, with a greater desire to work independently.
- The demand for more flexible working arrangements, as more parents combine career oriented work with family responsibilities.

Social costs

A whole range of social costs, either paid for by the individual directly or by society as a whole, have tended to be ignored in the past and are likely to be given greater attention in the future. These include commuting, which is a major waste of time and creator of stress, and is unlikely to be tolerated by a more discriminating workforce; and the waste of resources resulting from the unnecessary infrastructure investment that is geared simply to cope with peak demands.

One example of the newly recognised importance of the social and environmental costs of commuting was highlighted in an article[5] which discussed the attempt by the city of Los Angeles to relate local smog to the commuter effects of office development. The average 100,000 sqft office building was estimated to attract about 500 rush hour commuters each day, pumping almost 1lb of carbon monoxide into the air daily. Yet the solution to the problem was still seen in traditional terms – more ride-sharing programmes for employees and 'build more roads' campaigns (although Los Angeles is now encouraging the development of electric vehicles). In many ways, London's commuting problems pale into relative insignificance when compared with Los Angeles, partly because London benefits from relatively static overall population growth. Yet, even in the US, scant attention is paid to re-evaluating what is going on in office buildings in the first place.

In discussing social costs it should not be forgotten that a growing number of new illnesses, for example 'Yuppie Flu', appear to be associated with new office buildings and their working environment. These too need closer study, particularly as studies of sick building syndrome have shown that the condition can be attributed to individual workers having little or no control over their working environment.

Relocation

Some organisations recognised a long time ago that it was both illogical and expensive to have major office buildings full of equipment situated on expensive city centre sites. The advent of computers and modern telecommunications has accelerated this trend. Despite these pressures, many organisations still have fully occupied office blocks operating in expensive congested areas, undertaking activities that are not 'place dependent'.

In the post-war period, manufacturing industry became much more flexible in its use of location and has tended to move to cheaper areas of production. Information processing

and much routine office work which does not have security implications could move in the same direction. Cost and efficiency pressures are likely to make Third World locations and homeworking much more attractive options in the coming decade, particularly since satellite links will free organisations from cable and other physical restrictions and so enable a much greater degree of operational decentralisation. There is already today no technical or managerial reason why a company's information processing needs cannot be provided for anywhere in the world, assuming political stability.

The decline of Central London as a headquarters location is illustrated in a recent report[6]. From 710 corporate headquarters in 1980, only 411 remained in Central London at the beginning of 1988. This was attributed to two major factors: relocation and the impact of takeovers and mergers. In the late 1980s, as in the early 1970s, organisations had to utilise their Central London office space more effectively or they would become takeover targets for their property valuation alone. For many organisations the question is not so much whether they should have a London headquarters, but rather what the function of the headquarters should be. A fundamental evaluation of this question should be a formal exercise for all organisations at least every five years. For some organisations, taking a radical look at homeworking could result in some offices and workers staying put, rather than relocating.

An increasingly important factor in a consideration of the relocation issue is the growing reluctance of managers to move, partly because of the higher priority now being given to 'quality of life' issues and partly because of the growing importance of dual career implications for couples. In the latter case a more flexible approach to work, including the introduction of homeworking, could make an invaluable contribution, but that option appears to be only rarely considered.

Relocation should be an opportunity to rethink the whole concept of what the office, and the work that goes on in it, mean to the organisation as a whole – and how it can be improved. Few organisations get more than one opportunity every 20 years to radically rethink the way they operate. Yet, even when this opportunity occurs, many managers become more concerned with how to invest their windfall capital gains obtained by moving to a lower cost area, and with the day to day problems of laying off and recruiting staff.

It should be emphasised that in almost all cases, even where relocation is not being considered, there is still usually significant scope, and urgent need, to improve the efficiency of office operations. Organisational constraints are all too often found to be the main reason why little radical progress is made. Companies are just not organised in a way that enables them to analyse and take the necessary decisions. Apart from the managing director or chief executive, it is unusual for someone to be able to cut across the traditional organisational divisions, and those at the top are usually too busy to look at these difficult long term issues. The overall organisation and efficiency of office work and office building utilisation ought to be an integral part of an organisation's strategic plan but this is rarely the case.

The implications of all these trends for the future of London cannot be over-emphasised. Approximately half of London's manufacturing jobs have disappeared since 1970 and the City's population has been falling over the past 20 years. Today, about half of London's working population can be described as office workers and about one third of the UK's office employment is still found in London.

Building flexibility

What can be done about this apparently inefficient and chaotic situation? Much wider consideration needs to be given to understanding changes in office work, and appreciating the implications of current trends. When considerable change takes place the key to survival and success is flexibility. A custom designed corporate headquarters may help to develop a sense of corporate identity, but at what cost? And how often are these costs explicitly identified?

Why is the whole question of office organisation efficiency going to become increasingly important? The answer is obvious: it has been ignored for too long and increasingly competitive pressures on the use of resources – both capital assets and people – will leave organisations no alternative if they wish to survive the decades ahead.

Much of the historic discussion, apart from the recent homework debate, has focused on such topics as the extension of flexi-time, rather than on the need for radical change in the whole area of office management. In the 1990s there will be an urgent need to redefine the role and method of operation of middle management because of the information technology revolution, which has had the effect of stripping down traditional layers of corporate management.

Sheena Wilson argues that: 'buildings are most crucial to contemporary performance, first, in enabling the organisation to adapt to change, and second, in sustaining staff motivation sufficiently to cope with the stresses of change'. But she concludes somewhat pessimistically: 'several trends in office design point the way to offices becoming more oppressive, more bland, certainly not stimulating or creative. For example, daylight is becoming a rare commodity as buildings become deeper and windows become thicker and more heavily tinted; ceilings are getting lower as channels for ducts and wire compete with habitable space; densities are getting higher as more machines are pushed into the space once occupied by people alone. Rather than enhancing productivity, many offices are simply increasing stress'[7]

A valuable recent BIM/CRESAP study[8] considered four different operating models for offices: Targeting, Guiding, Directing and Running. But apart from a functional breakdown, this study contained no discussion of what people actually did when they were in the office, or how much of it was place dependent, or how effectively the individual head offices were managed within an overall cost-benefit analysis. The report did not attempt to establish a basic framework within which such an analysis might be done. Nor were these issues discussed by Goold and Campbell in their major study of the role of the centre in managing diversified corporations[9].

The massive London Docklands development[10], which is expected to add 30 million sqft of new office space over the next five years, is increasingly dependent on extensive migration from other areas, rather than net new growth. In this and other major office developments little appears to have been done to take a more flexible approach to the dividing line between home and office working. This omission could prove to be a very expensive mistake. With office vacancy rates currently at record levels, the key question is how much more office space does London really need? How far have developers taken note of the changes that will take place in the 1990s and beyond?

The importance of building flexibility is emphasised by Bev Nutt: 'Buildings should be designed with much more long-term flexibility in mind, so that they cease to inhibit the changing characters, activities and procedures of the organisations which occupy them'[11]

Lifestyles

Many managerial and professional staff are looking for more congenial career structures and patterns of work that are not satisfied by traditionally organised businesses. This was underlined by a Henley Centre study[12]. Psychologically and socially, the study claimed, as much as three quarters of the population is well disposed towards homework. From the corporate angle, Henley identified the benefits of homeworking as lower overheads and the more productive use of knowledge workers. The study provided much useful background on tomorrow's workplace, within a discussion of the social costs and benefits of teleworking, but even this exercise had at least three significant omissions.

First, it paid little attention to the demographic changes over the next decade which could influence the underlying trends. For example, over half the adult working population today does not exist within the traditional category of a 'family with children' and this proportion is rising. Also, some account needs to be taken of the wealth factors identified in *The Inheritance Generation*[13] which could affect work attitudes for a significant and growing proportion of the population.

Second, there is an acute need for more analysis of what actually goes on in offices. How much of it is routine and how much is creative work? How much of it is 'place dependent'? The Henley analysis covered mainly relatively low-skill job areas such as mini-cab drivers, plumbers and travelling salesmen. But how far is this new opportunity for greater flexibility going to change the way in which middle class professionals live and work? Why should not solicitors and accountants increasingly work from home? What about car salesmen following

the pattern set by the life insurance industry? Then there are jobs that are dependent on computer processing, such as stockbroking and mail order selling; travel agents and bank managers. There are creative thinkers who are required to write reports and develop new ideas. Here the traditional office environment, particularly the open plan variety, and the effects of commuting are particularly wasteful.

A third weakness of the Henley study was that there was little discussion of the impact of the prospective changes in work patterns on office building supply and demand, although the report did include an extensive analysis of the impact on house prices.

The importance of an organisation having a strategy for the effective management of the growth of electronic office information systems cannot be over emphasised[14]. Yet another survey[15] found that few British companies incorporate long range planning into the organisation of their work space. In addition, management responsibility for office organisation is spread over a broad range of individuals making it very difficult to locate the right person. This is not the place to discuss the detailed organisational problems associated with introducing radical change, except to emphasise the importance of understanding all the factors involved, together with their implications, and the need for commitment at the top if radical change is to be implemented successfully.

A large number of traditional professions – surveyors, estate agents and developers – have vested interests which have prevented them from taking a proactive role in this area. Also, rarely are personnel issues discussed at a high enough level in an organisation for them to be the vehicle for radical change. Few recent books on personnel management appear to get further than scratching the surface of the changes expected in the operation and role of offices in the years ahead.

Emerging trends

Office efficiency and productivity

Robb Wilmot views these issues from a different, but complementary, perspective when he maintains that 'it is organisations that win competitive battles, not products, which are a symptom of competitive management; nor information technology, which is a tool.' He believes that many organisations could improve their competitive capability by 70–80% or more. The key question he asks senior managers is: 'how much of your time, in your own judgment is truly high value added, and how much relatively low value added?' He believes the answer follows the usual 80/20 rule and argues that 'despite information technology investment having tripled over the past decade, output per hour outside the factory has been virtually stagnant. Yet this now represents 80% of the total workforce'[16].

Wilmot concluded that most larger international organisations find it difficult to operate with less than five levels of management, and that in this hierarchical structure a manager is typically an information processor, probably spending 50% of his time in information exchange with his subordinates, 10% with his boss, 10% with peers in the matrix, and, if he is lucky, 10% with customers and a tiny fraction sponsoring innovation and orchestrating change. Large organisations suffer from inherent disadvantages in managing change, and the more change that is going on the greater their disadvantage.

Wilmot's view is supported by Paul Strassmann, former vice-president of information products at Xerox, and also former head of information technology at Kraft Foods. 'After studying a large number of US and European organisations my view is that, without exception, their overhead costs – that is to say their information costs – are excessive. An increasing proportion of the information technology budget is spent to support the demands of unnecessary people. Information technology managers and boards must not fall into the trap of automatically responding to users' priorities, which in fact may not reflect the strategic reality of the firm – which should be changing its overhead structure . . . The most profitable opportunities in the next decade will be internal streamlining'[17]. There is a big difference between using information technology and using it effectively, as two recent reports have shown[18].

In order to begin to make quantum improvements in office productivity it is useful for organisations to start by finding out about what exactly their employees do with their time in the office. One approach, which can be revealing and provide useful leads for future action, is to cross evaluate each worker's time with the four human functions and four organisational elements listed below:

Human

- thinking
- reading
- writing/word processing/computer operation
- talking/listening (communicating with other people, either directly or indirectly)

Organisational

- dealing directly with customers
- dealing with organisational issues that are directly customer-related
- dealing with non-customer-related organisational issues
- social activities

With this approach the organisational links can be further separated into 'up/down/peer' links and according to whether the links are within or outside the department or unit.

Most people will argue that some social activities have important organisational benefits. They may be a vehicle for establishing and building trust between people within an organisation, which is an essential element in the operation of any successful organisation. Nevertheless, it can be said that many existing offices appear to operate more as social organisations rather than as vehicles for doing real work.

Business centres

For the new small business there should be more flexibility in mixing office and residential needs, as well as encouraging further growth of specialist business centres where serviced rooms can be rented by the hour or day. These business centres have become increasingly popular with many large organisations. There are currently reported to be 6500 business centres worldwide[19].

Facilities management

The relatively new profession of facilities management could be seen as a step in the right direction, but this role must be integrated with progressive and flexible personnel policies to have a significant effect on the way the organisation will be organised in the future. Serious attention to facilities management has arisen predominantly because of the increasing drive by senior management for more operational efficiency at all levels of business. The tremendous growth in sophistication of office technology has further increased demand for effective facilities management. The profession now requires administrative and technical management skills which previously had never been demanded of the traditional 'retired colonel' type of office manager. This is essentially the difference between the traditional administrative approach and the need today to be at the front end of proactive innovation.

Jones Lang Wootton believes that UK companies spend £40,000 million a year on facilities to help them run their businesses[20]. Engineers, building managers, management consultants and architects are now all muscling into the facilities management field. This is a major step forward – and it is an essential element in any strategy to improve office efficiency – but it is unlikely to have a significant impact on asset and people productivity unless the whole question of new work patterns and relationships are also fully considered.

Shift working and flexi-time

One option for some offices will be more extensive use of shift working, as in factories and power stations. 25% of all manual workers are involved in some kind of shift work, although in some industries this is falling as production processes become more automated; yet the figure for office workers is probably less than 1%. Office efficiency could benefit from the lessons of traditional manufacturing sectors. Two areas where shift work will affect office workers in the future are operations for which extensive computer processing is involved, and financial markets, where globalisation will increasingly require 24-hour trading.[21]

These trends are likely to result in a greater separation between buildings for creative work, which can essentially be done anywhere, and buildings for high tech or production activity, where there will be increased pressure for greater utilisation. Over the longer term the value of many of today's – let alone tomorrow's – office building assets will depend on the ease with which they can be subdivided or converted to alternative uses. One development might, with a little ingenious design, be to see buildings used as hotels during the night and as offices during the day. Many hotels are already extending their office support services.

Part time work and homeworking

All the evidence suggests that, with a little thought and investment, a massive amount of unnecessary expenditure could be avoided by encouraging a more sympathetic approach to part time work and homeworking. There is some sign of movement in this direction – over two million people in the UK now work from home and the CBI forecast that figure to double by 1995. In the UK, between 1981 and 1985, self employment increased by 12%, part time employment by 22% and the number of temporary employees doubled to 1.3 million. In the US it is estimated that nine million people already work from home and the number is increasing by 15% each year.

One forecaster believes that by the year 2000, one third of British office work will be done at home[22]. This trend is confirmed by other estimates. A NEDO study estimated that 20% of the workforce would be working from home by the year 2010, with between 10% and 15% of the skilled labour force in telework by 1995[23]. The key questions today are how much work could be done at home, and what are the organisational (and other) constraints that prevent these figures from being reached.

Telecommuting or homeworking has a number of advantages, it can:

- reduce overhead costs

- boost productivity

- help attract and retain scarce staff

- enhance flexibility

- cut commuting costs and stress

- provide new work opportunities for groups such as working mothers, the disabled and semi-retired

- strengthen family and neighbourhood ties

- help relieve road and rail congestion

- help ease the prospective manpower shortage of the 1990s

Homeworking does, however, have wider implications in the areas of health, local legislation, housing design, zoning regulations and transport services, as well as retail and leisure facilities. Homeworking also raises a number of key management issues including the need for top management commitment and new management techniques; the need for greater emphasis on training, and the need for clearer objectives and a move away from paying workers to 'do time' in an office – instead they will be paid to 'do work' whenever and wherever they consider appropriate.

In addition, new contractual and security arrangements as well as new communication and control techniques and new organisational structures will be needed. A 'distributed' organisation has to be both flexible and highly formalised; combining extremely precise assessment and monitoring procedures with the flexibility that allows individuals to carry out their tasks in whatever way suits them. Only suitable jobs (or parts of jobs) can be non-location-dependent. Particularly suitable are those jobs that are oriented to defined outputs or projects, and those with a high creative input that cannot be fostered by the normal office environment.

The practical issues of teleworking vary depending on the nature of the organisation and the work involved, although some general principles apply widely, such as the importance of training, communication and top management commitment. The more any job can be defined, the greater the scope for flexibility in where it is done, unless there are specific organisational constraints that prevent it. How many organisations have ever undertaken an exercise that assumes work is not location dependent unless otherwise justified, instead of assuming that there is no alternative to organising everything the other way round?

Homeworking trends operate in two overlapping directions. On the one hand there are some jobs that could be almost entirely home-based, which would create a need for a new core or peripheral organisational structure. Other organisations could increase their effectiveness by realising that a significant proportion (10–50%) of almost all jobs could be home based. But it must be emphasised that not all jobs are suitable for a homework element and that, at least in the foreseeable future, homeworking is unlikely to suit everyone.

By the end of this century having an 'office' (including voice activated computer terminals; picture phones using a small video camera on top of the computer; networking and database accessing facilities; computer fax machines) at home could be as vital and as common as a kitchen. By that time much, if not the majority, of office work could be done more efficiently at home rather than within traditional office structures.

In the next decade the main employment growth areas in the UK have been identified as education, health, welfare, scientific work and management; all these are at least partly suited to homework. But it is not easy for an organisation to consider the radical changes suggested here; often there are organisational barriers which prevent radical options from being fully evaluated. If expensive mistakes are to be avoided, it is essential that anyone considering new initiatives in office organisation learn from the experiences of others. In many ways it is much easier to organise and manage an organisation that integrates these new principles from the start, then grow them as an integral part of the corporate culture. It is always much harder to introduce radical change successfully into mature, traditional organisations. A significant expansion of homeworking is just one element in a portfolio of policies required to produce a quantum improvement in the productivity of office buildings and the people who work in them.

What are the arguments against homeworking? Critics often point to individuals' need for the social element of work. But at what cost? And who is paying for it? And are there not more effective ways of providing that social network? Can the social element not be switched back from the office to the neighbourhood or home environment? Is the commuting nightmare really justified on social grounds? Surely there must be better answers?

Long term outlook

It is important to emphasise again that the office revolution is not synonymous with the equally relevant and challenging service revolution. There is obviously some overlap but, essentially, office employment is concerned with information processing, partly as a product in its own right, partly as a service function, and partly as an integral (in theory, at least) element of managing change within the organisation. The service revolution is, in essence, a recognition of the importance of the customer and the need to improve the customer/organisation interface.

Unfortunately many of today's office buildings are little more than indulgent management ego trips, and the capital tied up in them is not being effectively used at much more than the 5% utilisation level. With the gradual reduction in working hours and longer leisure periods, it is even more important that attention is paid to new initiatives for using buildings and equipment more efficiently. From this analysis and the figures quoted, it should be possible to achieve a 50% increase in the productivity of both office workers and office building utilisation – producing a net increase of up to 25% in GNP.

The present ineffective utilisation of office space can only be temporary. In the end offices will have to earn their keep, one way or another, just as factories have to. When that happens, life will be very different for a lot of people whether they like it or not. In the meantime there is an overwhelming case for investment in office space to be much more effectively evaluated across a wider range of options.

Many organisations have found to their cost that the inefficient use of their office assets has made them vulnerable takeover targets. The effective use of the physical and people assets of an organisation is the only basis for future success and only this will prevent the organisation from becoming a target for unwelcomed acquisition. In order to achieve this objective organisations will increasingly separate facilities use from facilities ownership and management. This should allow them to concentrate on the real strengths of the organisation.

The office sector is a key area for change and productivity improvement over the next decade. In many ways the office revolution is already with us[24] and the benefits are enormous for those employers and employees who can see the opportunities and manage them effectively. Those organisations who are one step ahead will, as always, survive and flourish.

As James Robertson put it: 'when future historians look back from the mid-21st century in 60 or 70 years' time, they will see that there had already taken place by the mid-1980s the first, hesitant, largely unconscious phase of the shift to a new post-industrial work order in which personal and local ownwork eventually became no longer marginal alternatives to conventional employment, but themselves came to occupy centre stage.' Robertson went on to conclude: 'the new work order will not be brought in by mass action responding to the requirements of a bureaucratic programme and reflecting the factory mentality of the employment age. It will come in as growing numbers of people, conscious of sharing the same vision of the future of work and of travelling the same journey towards it, find new ways of organising work for themselves and enabling one another to do the same.'[25]

The trends identified in this paper are beginning to happen and they will be liberating, if we understand them and are in control of them; but they will be enslaving and expensive if we allow them to control us. During the 1990s and beyond social trends and technological developments should give us more choice in how we live and where we work. For most people – at least those in the Western industrialised world – the options could be very different from those we have been used to. At the centre of these changes will be the revolution in office work and its organisation.

Britain led the way in the first industrial revolution. It cannot afford to be left behind in the equally important revolution that is now taking place in the operation and utilisation of offices. These changes could well determine how most of its population will be living and working in the 21st century, if not before.

References

1 *Office Work and Information Technologies*, G C Economic Policy Strategy Document No. 10, May 1983
2 According to David Clutterbuck and Roy Hill, *The Remaking of Work* (Grant McIntyre 1981), white collar employment accounted for about 57% of the UK labour force in 1980; the figure was growing and was expected to peak somewhere between 65–75%

3 Paul Cheeseright, 'Out of Step Means Out of Pocket', *The Financial Times*, 9 May 1990, p27

4 Ibid

5 'Whose Smog is it Anyway?' *California Business*, April 1988, p62.

6 *West End Offices: Corporate Headquarters*, Knight Frank & Rutley Research, 1988.

7 Sheena Wilson, 'Making Offices Work', *Management Today*, October 1987, p91

8 *The Effective Head Office*, BIM/CRESAP, 1988

9 Michael Goold and Andrew Campbell, *Strategies and Styles*, Basil Blackwell, 1988

10 The Independent 10 September 1988, p15; also Judi Bevan, 'Is City Lost in Space?' *Sunday Times*, 21 August 1988

11 Bev Nutt, 'The Strategic Design of Buildings', *Long Range Planning* Vol. 21/4, No. 110, p130

12 *The Development of Teleworking : An Economic and Social Cost-Benefit Analysis*, Henley Centre for Forecasting, presented at a Conference on Tomorrow's Workplace, CBI/British Telecom,14 September 1988

13 *The Inheritance Generation*, Elgie Stewart Smith plc, 1988

14 R.A. Hirscheim, 'Managing the Growth of Electronic Office Information Systems', *Long Range Planning* Vol. 16, no. 6, pp 59–67

15 Wilson S, Strelitz Z, O'Neill J, *Premises of Excellence*, Building Use Studies, 1986

16 Robb Wilmot, 'Computer Integration Management: The Next Competitive Breakthrough', *Long Range Planning* Vol.21/6 No.112 December 1988, pp65/70

17 Ian Meiklejohn, 'Making IT Work to Best Effect', *Management Today*, January 1989, p110

18 *Does Information Technology Slow You Down?* Kobler Unit at Imperial College, and 'The Puny Pay-off from Office Computers', *Fortune*, May 1986. See also, David Harvey, 'Dinosaurs in the Age', *The Director*, December 1988, p91

19 'Office Space A la Carte', *International Management*, December 1988 p67 and *Executive Travel*, December 1988, p16

20 Jones Lang Wootton, *Decentralisation Report*, 1988

21 B.B. Diamond, *Twenty four hour Trading: The Global Network of Financial and Currency Markets*, John Wiley, December 1988

22 Francis Kinsman, *The Telecommuters*, John Wiley, 1987

23 *IT Futures – It Can Work*, NEDO, 1987

24 See *Automation of America's Offices 1985–2000*, US Office of Technology Assessment, 1986; a 358 page assessment of home-based work and off-shore data-entry operations as alternatives to conventional offices

25 James Robertson, *Future Work*, Gower, 1985, p149

5 Trends in information technology and their impact on intelligent environments

Alan Flatman, ICL

Summary

Trends in information technology will have considerable impact on the design and use of office space through the 1990s; these trends will affect the evolution of information technology services for end users in the workplace (for example voice communication) as well as the development of related technologies themselves (for example, building control systems).

The implications for the design and use of future office space include reduced visual and environmental impact of terminal display screens; introduction of pocket phones and voice recognition phones in the office; document scanning, and the increased application of video technology. The personal processing power and range of applications will continue to grow dramatically. Significant developments in networking and interconnection technologies are also expected. The integration of information technology and building services will continue. Homeworking will be made more feasible by the introduction of Integrated Services Digital Network (ISDN) to the home by the end of the 1990s.

Energy use will eventually be affected by the decreasing consumption requirements of personal workstations, which also has implications for air conditioning demand. Structured cabling and flexible network infrastructures will facilitate greater mobility of people within the office. Information technology will converge with building services. Sharing of information technology resources by workgroups may allow for some reduction in personal workspace. Flat panel screens, video-phone and voice command/response technology may demand the redesign of desks and other office furniture. Demand for intelligent conference rooms will increase. Video conferencing may reduce the need for people transportation.

Implications for the design and use of office space

The 1990s will see dramatic change both in the nature and the application of information technology. Compared to a decade earlier, businesses and individuals are now far more ready to embrace new developments in information technology in order to generate real competitive edge (Table 5.1). At the same time, environmental awareness will demand a much more judicious use of information technology resources, and more environment-friendly equipment. This paper reviews those areas of information technology that are expected to have the greatest impact on the design and use of future office space.

Displays

Developments in flat panel display screens will be driven largely by the consumer market (Table 5.2). Widespread acceptance and use of flat panels will not occur until both price and performance approach that of the cathode ray tube (CRT). An A4-size high-definition monochrome flat panel with good viewing characteristics is not expected to become available at acceptable cost before 1994. An equivalent multicolour flat panel could emerge two years later. Given the increased use of multicolour displays, it is reasonable to assume that progression to flat screens will occur after 1995.

End user requirements

Table 5.1   The evolution of information technology oriented end user requirements

Service/Attribute	1990 1995 2000	Comments
Text – Alphanumerics	+ + * * * * * * * * *	Std keyboard design
Picture – Scanned docs	• • • + + + * * * * *	G3–G4 fax – OCR
– Graphics	• • + + * * * * * * *	Mouse/pointer
– Image	• • • + + + * * * * *	Hi-def 3D colour
Txt/Pic – Desktop publishing	• • + + * * * * * * *	2 x A4 hi–def display (landscape/spreadsheet)
Video – TV	• • • • • • • • • • •	Niche (eg dealer desks)
– HDTV	• • • • • •	Niche
– Surveillance	• • • • • • • • • • •	Special case
– Teleconferencing	• • • • + + + + + * *	Corp–departmental–personal
– Videophone	• • • • • + + + + *	Special–personal
Printing – Black & White	• • • + + + + + + • •	Personal – workgroup
– Multicolour	• • • • • • • + +	Departmental/niche
– Slides	• • • • • • • • • • •	Departmental/corporate
Voice – Static	* * * * * * + + + + +	Displaced by mobile
– Mobile	• • • • • • + + + + +	PCN service
– Hands free	• • • • • • • • • • •	Cellular office noise
– Recognition	• • • + + +	Cellular office noise
Control – Heating	• • • • • + + + * * *	Via keyboard in future
– Lighting	• • • • • + + + * * *	Via keyboard in future
– Ventilation	• • • • • + + + * * *	Via keyboard in future
– Air conditioning	• • • • • + + + * * *	Via keyboard in future
Storage – Paper filing	• • • • + + + + • • •	Reducing space
– Elect filing	+ + + + * * * * * * *	Magnetic–optical disks
– Secure/personal	* * * * * + + + + + +	Reducing space
Cabling – Power	* * * * * * * * * * *	(Ease of access, neat and integrated comms cabling)
– Comms	* * * * * * * * * * *	

Key: •   = Low level

        +   = Established

        *   = Ubiquitous

Source: Alan Flatman

Evolution of information technology technologies

Table 5.2 Developments in relevant technologies

Standard/Technology	1990 1995 2000	Comments
Displays		
– Colour CRT	* * * * * * * * * * * *	> 100 watts/bulky
– Mono flat panel	+ + + + * * * * * * *	Early size limited
– Colour flat panel	• • • • + + * * * * * *	Early size limited
Cameras		
– Colour CRT	* * * * * * * * * * * *	30 watts/bulky
– Colour CCD	+ + + * * * * * * * *	10 watts/compact
Printers		
– Monochrome	* * * * * * * * * * * *	(Mechanical noisy! laser printers
– Colour	• • • + + + * * * * * *	fast and quiet; colour later)
– Laser	+ + + + * * * * * * *	
Doc Scanners		
– Group 3 fax defin	+ + + • • • • • • • • •	Current fax definition
– Group 4 fax defin	• • + + + * * * * * *	Future standard
– Character recognition	• • + + + * * * * * *	OCR reducing in cost
Voice Recognition	• • • • + + + * * * *	Cellular office?
Storage Devices		
– Magnetic disc	* * * * * * * * * * * *	1 Mbyte/disk
– Optical disc	• • + + + * * * * * *	100 Mbytes/disk
Processor	* * * * * * * * * * * *	Increased performance for same cost & power
Systems Management		
– Multi media	• • • + + * * * * * *	(Early systems will be service-specific)
– Knowledge based	• • • • + + + * * *	
Building Control Systems		
– Integrated BEMS	• • • + + + * * * * *	OSI standards adoption enables integration
– Plus Access Control	• • • • + + * * * *	
Interconnect		
– Structured cabling	• • + + + * * * * * *	(2 metre x 2 metre grid to the desk)
– Optical fibre	• • • • • + + + + + +	
– Cordless	• • • + + + * * * * *	CT2 – CT3/DECT
Network Services		
– PCN	• + + + * * * * *	Becoming pan–European
– EDI	• • • + + * * * * * *	Becoming pan–European
– ISDN	• • + + + * * * * * *	Pan–European
– BISDN	• • • + + +	Pan–European

Key: • = Leading edge
      + = Established
      * = Mature/low cost

Source: Alan Flatman

There are several incentives for bringing forward the introduction of flat panel screens into the office. These include:

1 Reduced profile

The traditional 'sit-up-and-beg' CRT display is replaced by a slim (1 inch thick) package. Adjustable angles will be advisable to suit ambient lighting, reflections and personal preference. Different screen orientations will also be required for text, image and video application (0° – 90°).

2 Reduced heat dissipation

A liquid crystal display (LCD) A4-size screen would consume approximately 10 watts, compared with at least 100 watts for an equivalent CRT display.

3 Health and safety issues

In particular, X-ray emissions from CRTs.

4 Multiple screens

Certain applications (for example, dealer desks in banking operations) require multiple screens.

The development of larger flat panel displays suitable for wall-mounted dynamic display boards will also be driven by the consumer market. This technology could be available by 1996. Cost equivalence with CRT-based displays is clearly not a requirement for this type of application.

Keyboard

The keyboard is not expected to change in format or profile. The traditional keyboard will continue to command a central role within the desk, taking on additional functions such as personal control of heating, lighting, and air conditioning. The keyboard will continue to be mobile within the desk space. However, voice recognition may eventually become a competitor to the keyboard.

Pointers and markers

The 'mouse' is expected to remain as the standard electronic pointing device. This will probably continue to be wired, although cordless connection may be more appropriate, and would certainly be feasible. One obvious advantage of the alternative 'trackerball', or built-in, pointer is the improved elegance and man/machine interface (MMI) once the device is physically integrated into the desktop. However, there are overriding arguments against the integration of information technology equipment into office furniture, due to the different life cycles of products.

Cordless electronic markers may be used in conjunction with desk-based display units and wall-mounted 'intelligent' display boards. As technologies mature and costs fall, electronic markers will be appropriate at workgroup as well as corporate or departmental level. Electronic markers could also be used in conjunction with an electronic 'slate' as the basis of a personal telewriting service.

Voice applications

The traditional voice handset could be replaced by a combination of radio, cordless and hands-free operations, supported by speech recognition. It is estimated that 50% of professional workers will possess a 'pocket phone' by 1995. It is also expected that the Personal Communications Network (PCN) will evolve to support digital data services beyond 1995. The PCN could eventually present a logical alternative to the traditional hard-wired telephone terminal.

Voice recognition could also evolve to provide some level of hands-free operation within the workspace. This would facilitate telephone dialling, commands for information technology and Building Energy Management Systems (BEMS), and voice signature for security purposes. Future voice recognition systems will be able to filter through background noise to provide a precise, hands-free command or response facility within an open plan office environment. Sophisticated voice recognition systems such as these will probably materialise in the late 1990s as a competitor to the keyboard.

Document scanners

With the 'paperless office' still many years away from reality, document scanning is expected to be a significant requirement in the workplace in the 1990s. Document scanning has become widely accepted as a departmental facility through the public Group 3 (100 lines per inch) fax service. However, the need to process, store and transmit documents of higher quality and resolution, at faster rates and at lower costs is driving the next generation of service very hard. A fax service with Group 4 resolution (400 lines per inch) operated over digital networks should become commonplace between 1995 and 1997.

Document scanning opens up a number of interesting scenarios. It will enable incoming paper mail to be scanned at a central point and transmitted electronically, and a high resolution service such as Group 4 will also enable signed documents (for example, cheques) to be processed electronically. It is tempting to forecast the use of document scanning at a personal level – at the desk – but it is more likely that it will be limited to corporate and workgroup levels.

Printers

There has been a recent trend in many organisations towards the use of personal printers, as these are relatively compact, slow and low cost, mechanical devices. In the longer term, the trend will be towards a workgroup level printing facility. Workgroup printing will inevitably be laser-based, and thus reliable, high quality, fast and quiet (the latter being a significant factor in open plan office environments). Lower cost, draft quality, compact laser printers are expected to be used at a personal level in the medium term, with the gradual move towards the 'paperless office'.

Colour printers will emerge later in the 1990s, but these are likely to remain 'niche' applications (for example, in public relations or publishing businesses) for some time to come.

Image

The use of high definition images for text, graphics and pictures is expected to grow out of the existing niche areas of manufacturing and publishing into many other industry sectors, and so into the general office environment. This area is anticipated to grow at approximately 30% per annum through the 1990s[1]. The increasing use

of image services will have consequences for the technology deployed in personal workstations and the supporting communications network. The workstation will therefore require a high performance display screen and processor, and the supporting network will be required to provide high bandwidth operation, based on optical fibre technology.

Video

The application of video services is expected to fall into a number of areas:

1 Broadcast TV

The delivery of a range of public services to niche industry sectors such as financial services. High Definition Television (HDTV) support will probably be required in the late 1990s.

2 Training

This will initially be provided at a corporate or departmental level via a local Video Cassette Recorder (VCR), moving down to the workgroup and, eventually, to the personal level from a central library (video 'juke box') via high bandwidth networking.

3 Teleconferencing

This is possible today on an international basis, but is expensive to provide and operate. Sophisticated bandwidth compression techniques, industry standards and the global digitisation of the telecommunications network should establish an ubiquitous service after 1995. At present teleconferencing is an exclusive corporate facility, but it could become a departmental or even personal facility as costs fall and the service becomes widespread.

4 Videophone

The technological enabler will be ISDN. This service is expected to become well established in niche areas from 1995 onwards, and will possibly become generally visible in most office environments at the end of the century.

5 Bulletins

Given the establishment of video facilities for a range of applications, a video bulletin service could easily be provided – initially at workgroup level, and ultimately via personal workstations. Examples of video bulletins might be 'Company Results' from the Chairman, 'Organisational Change' from divisional heads, 'Business Successes' from the sales director and company award ceremonies.

6 Surveillance

Security and safety considerations may require video surveillance. Compact and low cost charge coupled device (CCD) colour cameras will enable excellent cover in future office environments. Security staff may then access cameras via dedicated screens, or, later in the 1990s, via any office workstation capable of supporting video applications.

Many of these services will gradually replace the physical transportation of people with the electronic transportation of their voices and images. The general availability of the underlying technologies and supporting services will therefore have a major impact on the efficiency and effectiveness of many businesses, particularly given the rising cost of energy and the forecast congestion of public transportation in the 1990s.

Personal workstations

The key characteristics of future personal workstations are functional application and processing power, physical size, energy consumption and deployment ratio.

1 Processor power

This is expected to double approximately every two years based on constant cost and electrical power. In simple terms, for every pound and watt consumed, available processing power will increase at a rate of 40% per annum. This will considerably enhance the performance of professional workstations, and also broaden the market for general purpose workstations, due to reduced cost.

2 Applications

Word processing, spreadsheet modelling, electronic mail and access to database and diary services will become commonplace in most office environments in the early 1990s. The use of complex graphical processing will increase for many applications through the 1990s[2] and video services will become established beyond 1995. The implications of this growing functionality are essentially twofold: first, the demand for local processing power will increase, and second, the dependence upon effective networking will become significant. There is a further, related implication for the management of software – in order to control misuse, viruses, and other forms of abuse, there will be a strong requirement for high bandwidth networking and central management and control.

3 Physical size

The shape and volume of a desktop workstation are expected to remain unchanged in the early 1990s. Beyond 1995, a reduction in size, due partly to Very Large Scale Integration technology (VLSI), but largely to the take-off of flat screen technologies, is likely. This trend may actually be reinforced by the increased use of high performance 'laptop' personal workstations. The establishment of a public radio-based Personal Communications Network (PCN), capable of supporting data services (after 1995) will enable the emergence of 'palm-top' workstations, but these devices will have limited functionality and will not therefore be direct competitors to desktop or laptop devices.

4 Energy consumption

The only significant source of reduced energy consumption is the use of LCD display technology, which is not expected to occur before 1995. This could reduce the energy consumed by a single workstation from today's typical figure of 150 watts to approximately 50 watts. Workstation energy consumption is expected to remain roughly constant until this transition is accomplished. This is a significant factor when considering the current and forecast deployment of workstations in the office.

5 Audible noise

Developments in disk mechanisms and cooling technology, coupled with the longer term reduction in energy consumption of workstations will lead to a reduction in emitted audible noise.

6 Deployment

The deployment ratio of personal workstations to people in the office is estimated to be 40% in 1990, and forecast to reach an average of 70% in 1995, with 50% of organisations anticipating 100% deployment in 1995[3].

Networking and interconnection

Client or server architecture will result in file transfers of large blocks of data, up to millions of bytes in size. This will result in increased burstiness, response time requirements and volume which existing network infrastructures cannot handle[4].

High bandwidth networking will be required to support the wide range of information technology applications envisaged for most office environments in the 1990s. Optical fibre technology is now maturing; it has been subjected to the rigours of industry standardisation and will clearly be the order of the day in many situations.

The network infrastructure will evolve to exploit the application of industry standard optical fibre backbones, coupled with low cost twisted pair local access connections, to offer end users a wide range of services and choice of bandwidth up to 100 Mbit/s. There will be a convergence of information technology services (voice, data, image, video) into a single, integrated services network around 1995. This will be very compatible with network technologies, for example, ISDN, emerging in the telecommunications network.

Structured communications cabling will provide users with a long term – typically 15 years – infrastructure within which they can easily evolve and migrate their information technology requirements without having to make any disruptive modifications within the building. Traditional 'modifications' have included the removal of floor and ceiling tiles to allow insertion of new communications cables or re-routeing of existing ones. Moves and changes are easily accommodated with today's structured cabling – a typical move can be achieved in approximately 10 minutes at a cost of approximately £10 per move[5].

Structured cabling will present standard access points to a communications 'utility' at typically 2 metre by 2 metre intervals across the office space. In the shorter term, up to 1995, the cable between the desktop workstation and the wall-mounted access point will generally be a single, flexible link of 5 mm diameter. The voice service will be connected separately via a single 5 mm diameter flexible cable. In the longer term, up to the year 2000, the trend will be towards a single communications cable between desk and wall, either of copper or fibre, and measuring 5 mm diameter.

Workgroup and departmental information technology equipment, for example, printers, document scanners, servers, will be interconnected via structured cabling in much the same way as personal workstations. Finally, all cable types, connectors, topologies and installation practices will be dictated by open industry standards.

Integration of information technology and building services

Given the planned integration of information technology services within the local building or campus network by 1995, and the forecast penetration of the ISDN public network within the same timeframe, it is logical to integrate further BEMS, access control, fire and smoke detection and security surveillance systems within the same network infrastructure. This task is not technically complex, has no regulatory constraints and makes economic sense. Total functional integration will also enable greater flexibility and allow a higher level of management and control.

Management and control systems

A coordinated management system based on a secure, resilient processor would provide a maximum level of control of the network infrastructure. This 'fail-safe' system would have a disaster recovery capability and would enable the management of, for example, security of access to sensitive data and building areas, software distribution and control, diagnostics and fault recovery, statistics gathering, power consumption and accounting information. A billing facility could easily be provided for multi-tenanted sites.

The functional integration of all information technology and building services within a single network infrastructure will facilitate these developments with relative ease, providing a high level of flexibility across the local domain and across the wide area network to other locations.

Evolution of the wide area network

Plans to digitise the international telecommunications network will have a significant effect on the services provided to many commercial organisations during the 1990s. Wideband services are expected to become available to business premises by 1995. ISDN will begin to penetrate domestic premises by this time. These events will have several implications for life in the office:

1 Support of high bandwidth services

Organisations will be able to transfer video and high definition images between sites on a more effective, flexible and economical basis. This will be possible on a national, European and international scale, and will enable the logical integration of geographically fragmented organisations.

2 Homeworking

ISDN to the home will dramatically improve 'telecommuting', and could thus impact the population of 'office bound' personnel.

Electronic trading

Electronic Data Interchange (EDI) enables the movement of commercial documents, such as orders, invoices, import/export forms or drawings, directly between the computer systems of customers and suppliers. This is becoming popular, especially in retail and logistics-based operations, and is expected to spread to many other industries during the 1990s. Initially, the replacement of paper and the speeding up of transactions between customer and supplier will dramatically reduce inventory and reduce the error rate on commercial documents as transcription will be minimised.

The sophisticated use of EDI will give rise to new working practices between companies linked by computer networks that can be configured and reconfigured to enable groups of companies to enter new market niches. Just as today's large information users, such as banks and retailers, are highly dependent on their information technology for day to day business success, so will many other companies become similarly dependent.

Conclusions

Energy Consumption

The dominant sink of electrical energy within the information technology system will continue to be the collective set of personal workstations. Energy consumed by the network and departmental information technology equipment will be secondary and is expected to remain unchanged over this decade. Energy consumed by workstations will remain roughly constant until flat panel LCD technology is adopted around 1995. The overall environmental heat contributed by personal workstations could therefore double over the period 1990–1995, based on forecast deployment[6]. Given the application of flat panel display technology, this heat contribution could then be reduced to the 1990 level by, say, 1997 or 1998 and possibly halved by the end of the century. This fact should be taken into account when specifying air conditioning plant.

Mobility

The increased use of structured cabling and flexible network infrastructures will facilitate greater mobility of people. Moves and changes will be accommodated quickly, painlessly and cheaply, with a typical payback period of three years for average 'churn' rates. This will be reinforced by the emergence of cordless voice and data services and possibly hands-free command and response systems based on voice recognition later in the decade. Structured cabling must be embraced as part of the building services essential to provide a high level of freedom and flexibility in office layout and design.

Management and control

The convergence of information technology and building services into a single, high performance integrated network infrastructure will enable a high level of management and control of the day to day running of the business as well as longer term strategic management, and will facilitate the 'free siting' of people within a highly networked organisation. This will not occur before 1995.

Workspace area design

The trend towards shared information technology resources (for example, printers and document scanners), electronic information storage, improved MMI and smaller workstations seems to indicate that a smaller work area is likely in the future, perhaps with slightly reduced desk space. Future desk design could assume a more ergonomic 'wrap around' orientation in order to maximise the MMI associated with multiple flat panel display screens, including videophone and voice command/response.

Departmental and workgroup support facilities

Structured building cabling will make it possible to attach shared resources (for example, servers and printers) flexibly, anywhere in the office environment. The need for 'intelligent' conference rooms will increase for much of the 1990s, before the full spectrum of information technology services becomes commonplace at the personal workstation. Intelligent conference rooms will be supported by multiple high performance display screens and electronic markers, teleconferencing and computing facilities.

People transportation

The emergence of global high bandwidth communications and the establishment of videophone and teleconferencing services could dramatically reduce the level of people transportation required in the latter half of the decade. Effective homeworking will then become reality, and people who spend a high proportion of their working lives in 'the office' may require higher comfort levels.

Drivers for the use of information technology in the 1990s

Technology drivers in the 1990s

Many of the technology developments described here are extrapolated from the trends of the last 10 years. For instance, the reduction in the cost of information technology, which makes it potentially available to a wider audience, and the improvement in the ease with which applications can be used by non-information technology professionals, are ongoing.

While these technologies are developing in their own right, it is the convergence of not only information technology and telecommunications, but also TV, radio and entertainment which will begin to bring significant benefits: flat screen, high resolution TV pictures are on the verge of commercial reality, and the affordable personal mobile phone is set to be introduced shortly.

The result will be a significant leap forward in the area of communications, allowing the connection of PCs, workstations and other new devices to new global services. In addition, the advent of widespread broadband ISDN networks in the second half of the decade will make digitised moving video a reality. This means that ultimately visual desk-to-desk conferences can take place across the world, which will have a major effect on businesses.

Trends

To achieve this, significant infrastructure investment will clearly be required by public telecommunications providers and private network operators. Yet there are a number of trends which could lead to this becoming economically viable, encouraging the advanced use of information technology throughout the 1990s:

Green issues

Reduced emissions, pollution and energy usage must be high on the agenda, and organisations and governments are already beginning to pay more attention to these issues, which may ultimately lead to a change in tarrifing and an increase in the cost of energy relative to other business costs.

Quality of life

The 'baby boomers' of the late 1950s and 1960s are now beginning to place more importance on the quality of life: their environment, time spent with the family, sport, health, where they live etc.

Demographics

Demand for professional workers will continue to increase, and the supply of graduate level output will not be sufficient to cope with demand. Hence there will be greater pressure on the time of a shrinking number of professional workers. This increased demand will probably cause a continuing rise in salaries in these professions, making the people costs of the business a relatively higher priority.

Europe 1992

As the single European Market develops after 1992, European companies will find themselves doing business with partners over a greater distance – a company in France will have customers, suppliers and collaborators in areas that are some distance from its home base. This will increase the volume and distance of business travel.

Transport

The transport infrastructures of most countries in Europe are becoming severely congested. There is a continually tighter scheduling of air services, with airports struggling to keep up with growing demand. Roads in and around major cities are becoming crowded and travel times for most commuters and travellers are increasing.

The combined effect of these factors suggests that:

1 transportation of people will become less acceptable, socially, economically and environmentally, and hence information technology will be used to reduce travel, particularly across Europe. The costs of video conferencing are declining quickly, making this facility economically viable for many medium sized companies. For instance, Nationwide Anglia has already invested heavily in video conferencing. The liberalisation of telecommunications, particularly in the UK, will create competition and drive down service charges.

2 information technology will be used in the workplace to maximise the productivity and efficiency of professional employees. As salary costs increase, this will be the only way to remain competitive.

References

1 Forrester, 'The Network Strategy Report' *LAN Futures, AFTAAN*, January 1988 p5
2 Butler Cox, 'The Future of the Personal Workstation, 1988–1993.' *Butler Cox Report*, 1988, pp4–5
3 Ibid
4 Gartner, 'Enterprise Network Strategies' *Emerging Technologies Research*, 27 September 1990
5 Flatman, A, 'Universal Communications Cabling: a Building Utility', *ICL Technical Journal*, May 1988, pp 117–136
6 Gartner, 'Enterprise Network Strategies' *Emerging Technologies Research*, 27 September 1990

6 The workstation, the building and the world of communications

Andrew Harrison, DEGW London Limited

Summary

The impact of information technology on the workstation, the building, and the world of communications is examined. In the future, national restrictions on telecommunications markets will reduce. The European community, however, has yet to adopt compatible practices and global standards are not complete.

Smaller, more powerful workstations using central databases are predicted. LCD screens and colour laser plotters will become common by the end of the 1990s. The workstation will develop as part of a networked environment that can be easily accessed by the user.

Structured cabling in buildings has made cabling a manageable problem; copper wiring will be replaced by fibre at least in risers, if not to the workplace. Cabling systems will increasingly be integrated into buildings, moving towards a single channel for voice, data, fax and video as well as for the building management system.

Communication between the organisation and the outside world is advancing with the introduction of private fibre networks, satellite communications, and third party communications services. Workstations can be freed from many locational constraints. Personal smartcards may be used to access technologies and systems in many locations. Voice and data services will increasingly become person rather than workstation based. As work can take place in many kinds of locations, the free address work environment will become more viable.

Introduction

The impact of information technology on organisations and people has been enormous during the last 20 years and it seems likely that the exponential level of growth of the information technology industry will continue. The value of the global computer and communications market was estimated at $320 billion in 1990, rising to $952 billion by the year 2000. The UK's contribution to this total is approximately 6.4%, or $33 billion by 1994[1]. Given such a rate of change, is it possible to predict the development of information technology over the next 10 years?

We can predict future developments in so far as most of the technology that will affect our lives in the future already exists, either as commercial products or as laboratory prototypes. The lengthy research and development time that is needed before a new technology can be introduced to the marketplace makes it possible to look some way into the future. However, as any reader of science fiction knows, there is always more than one possible future and the difficulty with information technology is predicting which one will occur – in other words, which solution to a given problem will eventually achieve market dominance.

This is because there are a number of non-technical factors influencing the development of information technology. One that has had a major impact on European development is restrictive telecommunications practices within each country. The role that national PTTs have played in the development of information technology to date has been central, but they now seem to be lagging behind the requirements of their customers. Many of the restrictions these bodies currently place on telecommunications seem to protect their own parochial interests rather than provide direction for the future development of the global communications network. The UK leads Europe in the deregulation of telecommunications, but until all countries in the European Community adopt compatible telecommunications practices, it is difficult to see how a single market can hope to function effectively.

An associated factor that has plagued information technology since its earliest days and that still causes major problems is standards. Divergent commercial interests led to the development of proprietary standards in virtually all areas of information technology and it has only been after years of work by standards committees around the world that a common basis for development has been agreed in some areas. Open systems interconnection (OSI) standards, for example, have done much to make the interconnection of computers easier but there is far more work to be done. The fact that it still takes three to five years to get a national standard adopted in most areas probably explains why de facto standards often become more important or a single proprietary 'standard' dominates the market by brute strength.

It is no longer satisfactory to think of national standards. Technical standards must be global, comprehensive and coherent if the global network, serving both individuals and the large transglobal corporations, is to become a reality. The international telephone network is a good example of what can be achieved through global standardisation – it is difficult to imagine how we could function if national telephone networks could not communicate with each other – but there are still many areas of information technology which would benefit from the development of global standards.

So it is possible to make predictions about the future of information technology, but the accuracy of such predictions remains uncertain due to the unpredictable impact of geopolitical factors. Just because something is a good idea doesn't mean it is going to happen.

This paper will look at how information technology may develop in three principle areas which impact directly on the future of the workplace. These are:

- information technology and the workstation

- information technology and the building

- information technology and the outside world.

It will concentrate on the implications of technical developments likely to impact the workplace during the next decade, rather than on the nature of the technical developments themselves.

Information technology and the workstation

Hardware

Computers will continue to get smaller and more powerful. The price performance of the underlying computer technologies improved by 20% per annum in 1990[2] and there is little reason to expect this trend to change in the future. One can look to Japan to see how the physical size of workstations is likely to change: laptops are now being replaced by 'palm-tops.'

With more organisations considering the benefits of 'free address' workstations and different types of work environment, the truly portable – as opposed to 'luggable' – workstation allows flexibility of location: at the office, at the client's office, at local work centres or at home. Smaller, battery powered, portable computers also help organisations to avoid many of the heat, power and space problems currently associated with information technology in the open office environment.

The standard memory size (RAM) of most workstations will increase significantly during the next few years as more sophisticated memory resident applications are developed and as graphic interfaces become more comprehensive and user friendly. The cost of disk memory will continue to decrease, but vast hard disks will not be needed by most people; more people will be working with large central corporate databases that are downloaded from a central location to the workstation for processing and manipulation. This has major advantages over distributed storage of data from a management and a security point of view.

Large storage volumes will increasingly be used for image storage and for running multimedia information systems using a combination of CD-ROM and hard disks to store their data.

Up to the mid-1990s, the processing in most workstations will continue to be serial (the computer only processes one instruction at a time)[3]. After this, workstations using parallel processing will become increasingly common. Parallel computers can process a large number of instructions simultaneously which makes them much faster than their serial predecessors and ideal for intensive processing tasks such as database management involving text, images and graphics, and the image processing required for factory and warehouse automation systems and security systems[4].

There are already more than 30 parallel computing products commercially available but their wider use is inhibited by their incompatibility with existing systems, the need for specialised programming skills to take advantage of the parallel architecture and uncertainty about the long term future of vendors and suppliers in what is still a very new marketplace[5].

The interaction between user and computer will remain largely unchanged over the next decade. The keyboard will be the main method of data input but will be supplemented by more touch-based and mouse applications. Voice recognition systems are unlikely to be practical within this timeframe but developments in neural networks are accelerating advances in this area.

The computer screen will continue to be based around the cathode ray tube for at least the first half of the decade. LCD screens will largely be restricted to portable computers where lower power consumption is more important. In the latter part of the decade, bright active matrix colour LCDs will become widespread, making the flat office screen a possibility at last[6].

The laser printer will continue to be the main method of output in the office; both price and power requirements will reduce while quality and noise output improve. By 1995, 300 dpi colour laser printers will be common along with more expensive, higher resolution colour printers which will be shared over local area networks[7].

The overall impact of these changes on the workplace can be seen in Table 6.1, produced by the Communications Group at Ove Arup &

Table 6.1   Scenario for the effect of information technology of building services

Parameters	Era						
	Ancient	Old	Modern	Contemporary	Soon	Later	Distance
Computer at workplace	Terminal	PC	PC-AT	386	486	Multi media	Responsive
Units per workplace	1:50	1:5	1:3	1:1	1.2:1	1.1:1	1:1
MIPS per Unit	0	0.5	1	3	10	20	50
Input	Keyboard			Keyboard plus mouse			Keyboard plus mouse plus voice
Output		VDU		VDU plus LCD & voice & multiple displays			
Mbyte RAM	0	0.064	0.6	4	20	50	100
Mbyte Storage	0	0.4	20	40	200	500	1000
Area per workplace (sqm)	10	10	10	13	15	15	15
Power/Heat per Unit (W)	200	400	300	250	250	150	100
Power/Heat (W/sqm)	0.4	8	10	19	20	11	7

Notes:
1   The Era is a flexible time period of between three and seven years
2   MPS = 'Millions of Instructions Per Second'
3   Watts per square metre = (Power/Unit) x (Units/Workplace)/(Area/workplace)
4   This diagram is not to be reproduced in any form without prior permission of Ove Arup & Partners

Source: Ove Arup & Partners

Partners, which splits information technology development into seven eras, from ancient history to distant future. Ove Arup & Partners predicts that the size of the workstation will increase to accommodate information technology requirements but that power and heat loads will decrease as computers become more efficient and LCD screens more common in the office environment.

Software

All the main commercial software applications are likely to remain in use and will be updated periodically to take advantage of changes in computer architecture and user requirements. The operating systems on which the software runs will reflect the shift towards distributed processing and the extensive use of local and wide area networks. Operating systems will be largely transparent to the user, and expert operating systems may be able to configure themselves to meet the requirements of the user and deal with the wide range of communications options available. As Casimir Skrzypczak says:

> In the past we had dumb terminals with intelligent users. In the future we will need intelligent terminals that can interact with the less sophisticated user[8]

A recent review of emerging technologies by Butler Cox[9] identified a number of application areas that are likely to become significant in the near future:

Expert systems

Research into artificial intelligence (AI) has led to the development of a number of different techniques and tools that can be applied in the commercial environment. In the future, AI based techniques will increasingly be used to create and use very large knowledge bases and to provide easy access to large databases. (A knowledge base contains an area of expertise – a representation of all rules of thumb and basic principles relating to a particular area such as fault evaluation, medical diagnosis or market forecasting). An expert system can very easily be embedded inside another application so it is likely that standard applications such as Desk-

top Publishing (DTP) and Computer Aided Design (CAD) could include expert systems advising on page layout, drawing techniques or likely construction problems.

When working with large or complex databases, expert systems will allow the user to enter complex search criteria in plain English; alternatively the system will manage the data search completely, putting questions to the user rather than vice versa. AI techniques have also been used to develop new programming methods designed for use by ordinary engineers and analysts rather than by specialist engineers. These programming methods (for example, CASE) will become more common in future since traditional methods are increasingly unable to keep up with rapidly changing user requirements. The disadvantage of this type of technique at present is the high cost of the programming workstation – up to $250,000 each – and the high cost of running applications developed in this way.

Towards the end of the decade we may see the development of commercial applications using neural networks. A neural network is constructed from simple processing units, each modelled loosely on the functioning of a biological neuron, whose combined behaviour mimics to some extent that of an animal's brain or nervous system. Neural networks are able to learn how to solve problems by themselves: they are not programmed and, unlike most expert systems, it is not necessary to specify the rules of inference. Furthermore, once the network has been trained on a large set of problems, it is able to generalise the principles it has learned and apply them to similar problems. Neural networks will be particularly suitable for problem solving tasks where some of the data is missing, corrupted or uncertain, such as speech recognition and radar target recognition systems[10].

Neural networks are currently still in the research phase but information technology consultancy Butler Cox predicts that by 1993–1995 a speech recognition system based on neural networks will be able to deal with continuous speech and learn new users, and will have a vocabulary of more than 5000 words. Butler Cox sees systems of this sort being used to produce audio word processors and to enhance the interface between the user and computer[11]. There are major problems to overcome before neural networks become widespread – for example, the lack of formal methodology in network design and lack of audit trail when evaluating the reasoning of the system – but the amount of worldwide research and investment in this area suggests that they will have a role to play in the future.

Groupware

'Groupware' is the generic term for computer software which supports the ways in which groups of people work together.

> Employed on a large scale, groupware systems have the potential to have as great an impact on the work of managers and professionals as data processing had on the work of clerical staff. In particular, groupware will allow a greater emphasis to be placed on personal contributions, it will enable organisational structures to become more flexible and it will improve working practices.[12]

Butler Cox identifies a number of application areas which meet its definition of groupware:

● commitment managers – focuses on the process of negotiating commitments

● computer conferences – support open, screen-based discussion between participants

● issue-based information systems (IBIS) – support structured argument between collaborators

● co-authorship systems – allow people to collaborate on the preparation and review of documents

● procedures processors – automation of routine office procedures for moving documents between people

● message and document processors – advanced electronic mail capable of filtering messages.

Significant benefits can be had from using this type of software but Butler Cox suggests that there may be management opposition to its introduction. Possibly they feel threatened by it, or they consider applications such as computer conferencing frivolous. Technical problems may also need to be overcome since this type of software requires powerful network servers and comprehensive and compatible local area networks.

Hypermedia/multimedia

These are computer-based interactive systems that provide flexible access to pre-recorded audio, pictures, text and video. They are already in use to some extent with optical text retrieval systems and published information databases such as the BBC's Domesday Book, but the technology is still very much in its infancy. CD-ROM, the basis for many systems of this type, is still in the process of defining its standards. CD-WORM systems (Write Once Read Many times) are readily available but the development of robust erasable CD systems is still underway.

The production of a master disk with its sophisticated indexing is still a complicated process, hence most current hypermedia applications are 'publications' of commercial information rather than in house information sources. In the future hypermedia is likely to be used to improve application interfaces with animation and sound, and in training systems where users of interactive video disks are able to stop a film and call up explanatory text and images.

The high cost of workstations able to support hypermedia applications has so far inhibited the corporate use of hypermedia. Butler Cox predicts that this will change as standards become established and as more powerful workstations become available. Within a few years, a hypermedia workstation with video capability should cost only about $500 more than a standard workstation.

In the corporate environment, the introduction of hypermedia applications could also have major implications for network design as multimedia communications can increase communications traffic by a factor of 10, or even 100, compared with text only communications[13].

Summary: information technology and the workstation

The trend in workstations is towards smaller, more powerful units, able to download information from large central databases and process it locally. The keyboard will continue as the main form of input; LCD screens will become more important during the later half of the decade and efficient colour laser plotters will be the main output device.

Operating systems will be designed with the network environment in mind, and users will be able to link up with a range of local and wide area networks without having to concern themselves with communications protocols and the like. Existing software applications will continue to develop and will change to take advantage of developments in computer architecture, and a number of new application areas will contribute to the work environment.

Information technology and the building

The physical requirements of information technology within the building are now well known and a number of recent publications, such as those by Butler Cox[14] and Eosys[15], have attempted to make this information available to all involved in the construction process. New forms of organisation demand buildings and interiors that are able to cope with both an increase in the overall amount of information technology in the building and the introduction of new types of technology in the future. Unfortunately, not all new buildings will be able to meet these challenges. In the future, with an oversupply of office space likely in many cities, developers will find it increasingly hard to let buildings that are not able to accommodate information technology easily.

The network infrastructure – the data cabling – is the key interface between the building and the information technology running through it. In the recent past the state of data cabling in many buildings could best be described as chaotic. Organisations were having to cope with a wide range of proprietary cabling systems which were often incompatible, and the profusion of different networks meant that risers and floor voids were frequently packed with an assortment of cables. The problems this caused when trying to implement new systems or simply manage existing ones during periods of organisational change were huge, and it has not been unusual for an organisation to vacate a building because of the difficulty of sorting out cabling problems within it.

While these problems may continue in existing buildings that have yet to undergo a major refit, they are largely a thing of the past. The increasing use of structured data cabling systems using standard cable types such as unshielded twisted pair has made the provision of data networks within the building a relatively simple operation. With a structured cabling system, the cable has become the 'fourth utility' – it is provided throughout the building with regular outlets. All cables go back to a number of sub-equipment rooms and/or to a main communications room where the networks can be configured or links to mainframes set up. The key to this type of system is that any network service can be provided to any data outlet – it is simply a matter of patching the outlet into the appropriate network controllers. Cable management becomes a process of recording patch changes and network availability – for example, recording how many Ethernet ports are unused on the controller – rather than worrying about the mass of cables in the floor void.

Most computer manufacturers can now support twisted pair cable; the remaining ones will have to do so if they want to remain competitive. But how well will this type of cabling network cope with future bandwidth requirements? At present copper based networks are generally able to meet requirements up to 16 Mbps, which is fast enough for most current applications. However, this is not sufficient for very data intensive applications such as CAD, DTP or dealing operations and in the future more and more data traffic within organisations will be of this sort.

Fibre optics are currently used to solve the bandwidth problem – either within the building backbone or, in some cases, right to the desk. Fibre has considerable advantages over copper in terms of bandwidth, security and freedom from interference, and the ratification of the Fibre Distributed Data Interface (FDDI) standards will mean that fibre will increasingly be used to support 100 Mbps networks within the backbone and between buildings.

Fibre is not without its problems, however, and it will be some time before all its inherent or potential benefits will be apparent. It is currently expensive to install; termination and splicing of fibres can be a difficult process; the cost of the opto-electronics required by the computers to use the fibre is high, and most computers are unable to transmit and receive information fast enough to utilise more than a fraction of the bandwidth available in an optical fibre. Many of these problems will be minimised in the coming years as increased demand and competition reduce the price of components considerably, and as hardware is designed with fibre-based communications in mind.

The increasing use of fibre does not necessarily mean that copper-based networks are on their way out. The lower bandwidths currently available on copper will be sufficient for many applications throughout the 1990s, but research is underway to increase the bandwidth of copper. AT&T has already achieved 80 Mbps over short distances and a copper-based FDDI proposal is being drafted at present. Within two to three years, 100 Mbps over existing copper unshielded twisted pair cable may be possible, but it is too early to say what the distance limitations on the system will be and how expensive the networking equipment and filters needed to achieve this will be.

A well planned and managed structured cable infrastructure obviously has space implications for the building. Fibre backbones require substantially less space in the riser, and fixed underfloor cabling may result in smaller voids. However, space savings will not always be evident since the flexibility provided by a structured cabling system depends heavily on the provision of communications rooms and sub-equipment rooms to accommodate patching frames and networking equipment. These sub-equipment rooms may well be located on every floor of a building and will generally be larger than a normal riser cupboard; therefore the space saved by the more efficient cabling will be more than used up by other network functions.

It is questionable whether sub-equipment rooms should be considered part of the building's core or more realistically part of the lettable space since they are a vital part of the tenant's business communications system. However, such a change in attitude would be contrary to current UK letting practice and is unlikely to occur in the near future.

As businesses become more reliant on their communications infrastructure they will also become more concerned about disaster recovery in the building. Duplicate entry points into the building for cables; duplicate computer and communications rooms and duplicate backbone cabling will all be necessary. This may be expensive in space terms but when an organisation cannot function without its data networks

this space will increasingly be seen as a necessary investment.

Another major cabling issue for the future concerns the integration of cabling systems within the building. Voice and data networks currently have to be on completely separate cable systems (although the voice and data cables are often identical). This situation in the UK is very different from the US where it is possible to run voice and data in the same cable. While there may still be good reasons for keeping the two systems completely apart, regulation needs to reflect the fact that data and voice communications are merging and artificial separations of this sort must end.

The introduction of Integrated Digital Services Network (ISDN) will change this. All communications traffic, including voice, data, fax and video, will become integrated signals perhaps originating from a single device and travelling down the same wires or fibres. The widespread use of ISDN is still some way off but Figure 6.1 gives an indication of the range of services that could be supported by ISDN, particularly once broadband ISDN is available.

Another form of cabling integration which may become more common in the future is between the data networks and the building management system (BMS). Currently the data network and the building management system's data network are completely separate although they may use the same cable type and follow essentially the same routes back to the building control room. This doubling-up of cable systems is the result of historic factors: the BMS and the general cabling infrastructure have generally been provided by different companies; BMS manufacturers have not followed industry standard communications protocols. Fire authorities and insurance companies have been reluctant even to discuss the possibility of systems integration.

While there may well be valid concerns about putting fire and security systems on the general data networks – this would mean that they would be devices on the network just like any other computer – there should be no problem in using the structured cabling system to link the BMS intelligent outstations back to the control room. The adoption of OSI standards by BMS manufacturers and the fact that many of the main computer suppliers are now involved in supplying BMS, either directly or through joint

Figure 6.1
The advance of the integrated services digital network[16]. (Source: Clutterbuck, 1989)

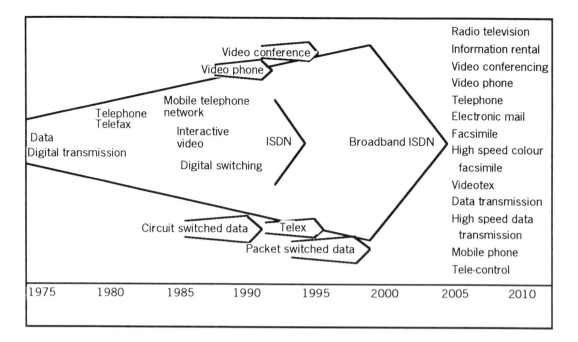

ventures, will also make integration more likely in the future. It should be noted, however, that progress on standards for BMS communications has been slow and it is likely to be a number of years before common communications protocols for BMS are agreed by the major suppliers of these systems.

BMS are already part of all major commercial property developments but they still have their drawbacks. The installation and commissioning process of a major system is often very complicated and ongoing management of the system is labour intensive. A review of major installations in Canada, for example, found the sensors in the system were often not calibrated correctly; line connections between sensors and central management were not functioning; central computer systems were not installed or operated as intended due to lack of training, and local sensors were not corresponding with local controls due to frequent spatial or layout changes[17].

In the future, information technology will be used to make building management systems easier to operate. A single screen will replace the multiple screens made necessary at present by incompatible subsystems, and displays will be more graphic and easier to understand. Expert systems may have an important role to play in monitoring a building's performance over time, learning from experience and fine tuning the operation of the building to meet energy conservation or other performance goals. The amount of data presented to the human operator should be reduced to manageable levels, and intervention will only be required in cases of component failure. Local intelligence in the equipment controllers will allow the building to continue to function even if the central control room goes down.

Advanced BMS should result in users being able to influence their local environment directly – for example, using the telephone to dial up changes in light or temperature – and the building as a whole should be more responsive to environmental and organisational change.

Summary: information technology and the building

Structured cabling has been a major influence in reducing cabling problems to manageable levels. Copper-based systems will continue to be important in the future although they will increasingly be supplemented by fibre optics in the riser and, in some cases, to the workplace. Although structured cabling beneath the raised floor and the use of fibre in the riser does reduce the amount of space required, the savings will be more than taken up by the extra space needed for patching and communications rooms.

Integration of cabling systems within the building will increase. Voice and data will eventually merge to become a single information channel incorporating fax and video and the BMS will be able to utilise the building's structured data cabling. BMS will become easier to use and expert systems will increasingly monitor building performance over time and fine tune the systems without human intervention. This will result in more responsive buildings that are better able to satisfy both the local and the general needs of their users.

The areas discussed in this section – cabling infrastructure, communications, building automation – are often listed, with office automation, as the features of an 'intelligent building.' While sophisticated communications and BMS will become increasingly important to most organisations, it is important not to forget that a building can really only be intelligent if it is able to adapt to the changing requirements of its users, both in terms of space use and technology. While these technologies can assist with this process of adaptation they will be severely limited in their effectiveness if the basic building shell is not designed with adaptability in mind. Guidelines for achieving this are already available to the construction industry, but we still witness the construction of new buildings that are patently inadequate in this respect. These are mistakes that we will have to live with for a long time.

Information technology and the outside world

It is no longer possible for organisations to function in isolation. At the very least voice communications are needed to link into the wider business environment or community but in most cases data links are now also needed to access external information sources or simply to send and receive files between different parts of an organisation.

A wide variety of communications methods are available to users in the UK. These include:

- modem links over ordinary phone lines
- packet switched data networks
- high capacity private circuits (for example, 64 Kbps and 2 Mbps)
- cable (data services offered by cable TV companies)
- television and radio carrier signals (for example, teletext services)
- private networks
- microwave
- satellite

The choice of method depends on location, cost, type of data transmitted and the speed required. The range of choice is likely to remain in the future but the actual process of communications should become a lot easier with self-configuring communications programmes and better interfaces, rendering the process virtually transparent for most users. Even with communications technology as it stands at present we have seen the development of the transglobal corporation. Advances in communications technologies during the next decade will be just as significant, if not more so, and will serve to blur the edges of the work environment. Communications technology will make it possible to work in the office, the home, the community work centre, or anywhere else for that matter, and still be able to link into corporate information systems.

Many of the elements required to make this happen are already in place but further deregulation of communications networks, especially in the areas of satellite services and value added network services, and the adoption of European and global communication standards, are still required. For the purposes of this paper it is assumed that such liberalisation is inevitable. A number of key developments seem likely during the next decade:

Increased use of private wide area fibre networks

As well as services provided by PTTs, a number of private and quasi-governmental organisations are looking to data communications as an additional source of revenue. In many cases spare capacity in existing private networks will be sold to other businesses, or groups will be formed by companies each holding a portion of the communications link. For example, British Rail, who have an extensive fibre network, may go into partnership with a number of cable television companies which are able to provide distribution within metropolitan areas. The 1990 Duopoly Review set out the ground rules for how these private networks will be able to operate and compete with the tariff structures used by the PTTs.

Management of communications by third parties

As the range of communications options and the sophistication of the equipment needed to utilise these options increases, many organisations will find it more cost effective to subcontract communications to an external company. This trend is already apparent with CENTREX PBX services (where the end user has links into a large central PBX and operator services rather than providing such facilities in house) and Packet Switch Stream based private data networks, and it is likely to increase substantially during the next decade. Organisations using this type of service will effectively be setting up a 'virtual private network'. This will function as though it were a completely separate network but it will be achieved through software rather than hardware and has the major advantage that organisations should only have to pay for the services they need when they need them. For example, a satellite ground station is too expensive for most organisations to contemplate but through their network provider they may be able to book the use of one when required.

Satellite communications

Traditional satellite microwave links are unlikely to be used for major two-way data communications in the future because of the inherent problems of the geostationary orbit – the time lags caused by the large distances involved and the interference caused by sunspot and other climatic events. However, satellite and Community Antenna TV (CATV) facilities may be used for blanket off-peak distribution of very large amounts of information to the subscribers of new information services[18].

Satellites will also continue to play an important role in one-way corporate communications such as the transfer of large files between different parts of a company. Line of sight and interference problems with satellite dishes in major cities will mean that the provision of teleports in less crowded areas will become more important. Companies will buy teleport time when required and it will be the fibre optic links to the teleport that will become critical rather than the actual location of the earth station. Cities or areas that provide high speed fibre, copper or microwave links to the nearest teleport will have a competitive advantage over ones that do not.

The rise of the free address workstation

Innovations in communications technology during the next decade will have a major influence on how the work environment is defined. It should be possible to make the provision of voice and data services independent of location. Data services are relatively easy to make location independent. Many corporate mainframes and networks already allow dial-in access via modem, which allows users at any standard terminal access to a wide range of computers and services if they have the appropriate access codes. The challenge for the future will be to make this communications process transparent to the user. This should become possible once the X400 and X500 communications standards become ratified, giving computers a unique addressing system and providing links between a wide range of electronic mail and messaging systems.

Users will probably carry some kind of smart card which will contain information about the computers and network services they have access to. Once this is inserted into the terminal or PC the communications software will manage the communications process and the user will simply have to select from a menu of options. Within the office environment this will mean that a user will be able to sit down at any computer and instantly configure it to his or her requirements. What is more liberating, however, is the fact that there is no reason why this system could not be extended to other places outside the main work environment. The smart card could be used to access corporate systems from the home or a local office centre; it could also manage the billing process so that the parent company is billed for communications traffic undertaken on its behalf wherever it occurs.

Voice communications are considerably more volatile and the early 1990s will see a number of new technologies emerging. Cellular communications have been around for a number of years now, enabling subscribers to make and receive calls in virtually every part of the UK and, once the standards have been agreed, across Europe. However, the quality of communications is not always good and the cost is likely to remain high relative to ordinary telephone charges.

CT2 represented an attempt to lower the cost of portable communications. Systems such as Phonepoint and Callpoint are based around Telepoints located at regular intervals throughout metropolitan areas. Within a reasonable distance of these base stations users are able to make outgoing calls using less expensive handsets. Plans have been announced to develop office based systems utilising CT2 technology which will allow two way communications within a limited area. Problems are inevitable, however, because the system will not be able to support high density usage and it is not possible to 'hand over' calls from one telepoint to another as the user walks around the building. Despite this, CT2 offers the first possibility of local address free voice communications – the user simply carries the portable telephone to whatever workstation he or she is using. To overcome the problems of CT2 in the office environment, CT2 Plus was announced in Canada in 1990. It will allow hand-over during calls and roaming within the office, but its capacity will still be limited.

At the beginning of 1990, Ericsson announced the launch of CT3, an enhanced system of this type which is based on the European Digital European Cordless Telecommunications (DECT) standard. This uses different radio frequencies to CT2 and smaller cells, making it more suitable for high density office environments. CT3 will be used as the basis for A5 PBXs and for links to the cellular telephone network.

All these technologies are precursors to the development of the Personal Communications Network (PCN). The UK leads the world in this area and three licences have already been issued to develop PCNs in the UK (Microtel, Mercury Personal Communications and Unitel). PCN is based on higher frequencies with a shorter range (1 km) allowing radio frequencies to be re-used more often and the network to support more users at the same time. Investment in the infrastructure is underway and PCN services will be available by 1992. Mercury predicts five million PCN customers by the end of the decade out of a total of ten million PCN customers in the UK[19].

Handsets costing £100 to £200 will be able to act as cordless extensions in the office environment. Outside the office they would be able to locate the nearest PCN base station and send and receive calls through it. In the home, the domestic or community base stations could fulfil the same function. If no base station were available the handset would then access the cellular network to make its call. Each handset would be able to receive calls for two separate numbers, home and business, with outgoing calls being billed to the appropriate account.

PCNs are likely to take off rapidly amongst office users in major cities. Domestic use will be much slower to develop but PCN base stations will become part of the infrastructure provided to new communities and housing developments.

Fixed (cable based) voice communications will remain important for data communication via modem and for areas of low population density. Fixed communications may also be able to contribute to the concept of free address workstations with the use of personal numbering systems. Telephone numbers may be associated with a particular subscriber rather than with the telephone itself. As the user moves between locations he or she can use a smart card to inform the central database of the new location. When a call is made to the user it is routed via the central database system which sends the call to the latest telephone address for that user. This system is unlikely to be available until the late 1990s and it will be expensive to introduce because of the central infrastructure required and the replacement of all handsets[20].

The ultimate address free communications system was announced by Motorola in 1990. The company is working on a worldwide digital, satellite-based, cellular personal communications system called Iridium which will enable users anywhere on the planet to communicate both voice and data using portable handsets similar to existing mobile telephones. The system, which will cost $2 billion to set up, is based around 77 small satellites orbiting at 413 nautical miles above the earth. This avoids the time lag problems commonly associated with satellites and ensures that every point on the earth's surface is continuously in line of sight of one or more of the satellites. The satellites are used to set up a cellular system on the earth's surface with each cell approximately 360 miles in diameter. The size of the cells means that the system is primarily designed for use in low density areas and in each country served by the system there will be links to the public switched telephone network (PSTN).

When placing a telephone call on this system, the signal will be transmitted from the caller's portable cellular phone directly to the nearest overhead satellite, which in turn sends the signal to an earth 'gateway' station which verifies the caller as an authorised user. The call is then routed through the constellation of satellites to its destination anywhere on earth[21]. The system will require at least 700,000 subscribers each paying $3500 for the handset and $100 per month air time for the system to break even[22].

Satellite communications of this type are unlikely to have a significant impact on the workplace in the foreseeable future but developments such as Iridium serve to remind us that there are no practical limitations to communications: given time, investment and market demand, the technology can be developed to support any requirements demanded by new types of working practice.

Summary: Information Technology and the outside world

There is already a wide range of communications available and these have contributed to the development of new transglobal organisations. The range of options in the future will continue to increase and key developments will include the increased use of private fibre networks, the use of satellites for high volume file transfer and the rise of third party communications companies which will take over the communications function within many large organisations.

In the next decade communications technologies will have their most dramatic impact in freeing many workers completely from geographic constraints. The free address work-

station will become a technical reality with truly portable voice and data links, even to the extreme of having personal satellite links anywhere on the planet.

Conclusion

During the next decade information technology will provide the tools that will make possible a complete rethinking of the work environment. It is important, however, to remember that information technology is a tool which allows the user to achieve new and better things, rather than a technical development which may not always be appropriate for the user. For example, the potential liberation of the free address workstation must be accompanied by an understanding of its implications for people and organisations: such as the need for increased social interaction and new management techniques able to cope with a dispersed workforce.

References

1 Ove Arup and Partners, *The Changing Context of Major Projects: Information Technology Position Paper*, Unpublished research document, 1990, p26
2 Clutterbuck, D. (ed), *Information 2000: Insights into the Coming Decades in Information Technology*, Pitman Publishing, London, 1989, p. 42.
3 Ove Arup and Partners, *Technological Trends in Information Technology*, Unpublished research document, 1990, p4
4 Butler Cox, *Emerging Technologies: Annual Review for Managers*, Butler Cox Foundation Report 73, February 1990, p1
5 Ibid, p2
6 Ove Arup and Partners, *The Changing Context of Major Projects: Information Technology Position Paper*, Unpublished research document, 1990, p10
7 Ibid, p11
8 Clutterbuck, D. (ed), *Information 2000: Insights into the Coming Decades in Information Technology*, Pitman Publishing, London, 1989, p71
9 Butler Cox, Emerging Technologies: *Annual Review for Managers*, Butler Cox Foundation Report 73, February 1990
10 Ibid, p8
11 Ibid, p10
12 ibid, p3
13 Ibid, p7
14 Butler Cox, *Information technology and buildings: a practical guide for designers*, Butler Cox plc, 1989
15 *Eosys cabling guide for building professionals*, Eosys Ltd, London 1988
16 Clutterbuck, D. (ed), *Information 2000: Insights into the Coming Decades in Information Technology*, Pitman Publishing, London, 1989, p9

17 DEGW Ltd, *The Intelligent Business Environment*, DEGW Unpublished research document, 1990

18 Ove Arup and Partners, *The Changing Context of Major Projects: Information Technology Position Paper*, Unpublished research document, 1990, p.9

19 'Survey of International Mobile Communications', *Financial Times*, 15 October 1990

20 Ibid

21 Press releases and system description for Iridium Satellite Communications System, Motorola, Slough 1990

22 'Survey of International Mobile Communications', *Financial Times*, 15 October 1990

7 Building performance for the Responsible Workplace

William Bordass, William Bordass Associates

Summary

This paper examines trends in the building industry and in users' demands across four main areas: construction methods and materials; internal environmental control; information technology and the management of building performance, and user-responsive information technology.

The Responsible Workplace building will depend on integrated design, execution and management. The 1980s shell-and-core approach militated against such integration. Building shells have excluded the external environment and demanded air conditioning and other high level services. Office scenery is designed in haste without regard for energy efficiency.

Appropriate technology may not be the most advanced. Technology may be used more selectively in a more natural environment rather than as a blanket provision. Robust designs could contain engineering systems that can be changed easily, complementing and assisting natural systems. Central building services may decline in favour of more local and adaptable components.

Building shells need to accommodate diverse and changing types of environments, with variations in servicing requirements. Building floor to floor heights will need to remain generous to accommodate the possible range of demands over the long term.

Building performance should become less energy dependent and more energy efficient. The pace of increasing electrical requirements and heat output from information technology may decline with the development of more energy efficient products. Electronic intelligence can be used for simple low key and user friendly environments.

Introduction

This paper looks at trends in the building industry and in user demand for office buildings, and their potential implications for the Responsible Workplace. It addresses four topics in particular: construction methods and materials; internal environmental control; information technology and the management of building performance, and user-responsive information technology. The focus of analysis is the individual building and the workspace within the building. Many of the issues here apply at the scale of the individual room, wherever it finds itself. Most of tomorrow's workplaces will also be in buildings which already exist, and which will need adapting where appropriate.

This paper identifies some potential incompatibilities between recent technological and economic trends and the likely user demands for a Responsible Workplace. In particular, it raises six key questions:

• How can the regular alteration of buildings to suit rapid organisational change be reconciled with a need to consume the earth's material resources more responsibly?

• Will better constructed, quality assured and healthier buildings necessarily offer better long term performance? They might not be sympathetic to alteration, and maintenance could become expensive once warranties have expired. Suitable briefs and possible solutions to these potential problems will need to be explored.

• Will the electrical requirements and heat output from information technology in the general office continue to grow? There are signs that they may not, and the pace of this change may accelerate if consumers press for more energy efficient products that can be accommodated with less demand upon environmental services in buildings.

● Are sophisticated buildings necessarily the most appropriate containers for sophisticated information systems? Simpler, more robust building shells and adaptable modular services may offer greater versatility, in the same way that roads are more versatile than railways or canals, and able to support a wider range of vehicles and performance characteristics. The designer may currently be trying to do too much. It may be better for a building to facilitate and support future change by others rather than to be fully equipped to meet all future eventualities save the ones that actually occur in practice.

● Will the sealed air conditioned office which became the UK standard in the 1980s be the exemplar for the future? It tends to be less energy efficient and more energy dependent than its predecessors and occupants do not seem to be very happy with it. The Responsible Workplace may often be able to make better use of natural light and air while also having the potential to accommodate more sophisticated services, but only when, where, and for as long as required. This approach may suit new future-proof building designs and also facilitate the refurbishment of older buildings which were originally designed to be more climate-responsive.

● Why is electronic intelligence generally associated with aggressively technological buildings? It is equally applicable to things that are simple, low-key and user-friendly.

While many of the problems are international, the solutions may be more diverse, depending upon culture and climate. Conversely, developments regarded as innovative for the UK – for example buildings with both mechanical cooling systems and openable windows – are more common in some other countries. Perhaps the most pressing requirement is to understand better the real user needs and to change many of the associated industries, technologies and processes to provide the products, systems and services that today's increasingly demanding building users really need.

Construction methods and materials: recent trends

Industrial background

As technology has developed, it has become increasingly cost effective to make things in quantity under controlled conditions using machines in factories, and often with more sophisticated components, than to hand-craft them locally. With rising productivity, labour costs have risen, making bespoke products – such as buildings with their necessary site-specific features – relatively more expensive. Improved plant, computer aided design and manufacturing techniques, more simply and quickly installed components and subsystems, better management, and more prefabrication have helped streamline the building process by doing more of the work in the factory and by bringing more factory-like procedures to the site.

Nevertheless, the change from a craft base to a technology base, from construction to assembly, from reliance upon tradition to reliance upon research is far from complete; and its implications are not even fully recognised or understood. A recent series of interviews in the UK and the USA for the Fenestration 2000 study revealed some major issues for the building industries in both countries:

● insufficient and ineffective co-ordination, innovation and industrialisation

● substantially under-resourced research, development and testing

● resistance to innovation, notably from increasing litigation

● unwillingness to tackle the main problems, which occur at the interfaces between components (and in my experience between professions as well)[1]

The study also noted that some leading construction companies were already increasing their investment in the industrialisation of components and attempting to integrate the total process: R&D, design, fabrication, marketing, service, construction, after sales service and maintenance. Of course, the major Japanese contractors have been doing this for a long time with commercial success, but in a very different environment, and with investors who take a long term view.

The uncertain performance of the product is a particular problem at present where buildings themselves, their components, and the demands placed upon them by clients are all changing rapidly, making the experience of the past no good precedent. In the UK, the evolution of the main contractor's role predominantly into managing disparate subcontractors means that sites can now lack the physical and technical 'hands-on' skills necessary to pull things together at the weak interfaces. Continental European countries, in their different ways, have industry structures in which the technical development of building details is addressed more rigorously, and is more linked to production than to design.

In the UK, professional structures and conditions of engagement and contract can also hinder appropriate solutions. For instance, the appointment of individual members of the design team is seldom fully coordinated and their professional conditions of engagement do not dovetail precisely. The problems are being exacerbated in the current atmosphere of fierce fee competition, which seems to be making effectively integrated collaboration and attention to minor but important details still more difficult. Furthermore, the environmental performance of the fabric is seldom as thoroughly considered as other elements, perhaps partly because it is easier for environmental engineers to get fees for designing building services to overcome the effects of an inappropriate building design than to assist in designing some of the energy consuming services out! This also leads to product gaps where, for example, insufficient design and development effort has been devoted over a long period to improving the overall thermal, ventilation and optical performance of windows. Also, UK methods of tendering and contract tend to discourage any thorough ongoing collaboration between consultants', contractors' and manufacturers' technical staff. Finally, clear follow-through and feedback seldom occurs from briefing to design to construction and via commissioning and handover into use and back again. There needs to be much more feedback and a better, clearer briefing language. Changes are long overdue and harmonisation of European practice in 1992 may be the spur.

Client pressure

In the UK, some experienced clients are becoming dissatisfied with the state of the industry as they see it, and are forcing change themselves. In *Building Britain 2001*[2] the following demands were identified:

- more detailed briefs, including not only space requirements, cost limits and quality aspirations, but sometimes technical specifications and procurement systems

- rapid progress, with designs, firm prices, starts and completions as rapid as possible

- minimum exposure to risk. No surprises. Quality assurance

- durability, reliability and maintainability

- quick rectification of defects, without litigation.

Many clients also like a single point of contact, which has promoted the growth of design-and-build contracts and to a lesser extent multi-disciplinary design practices. Some clients have also looked overseas for designers and for building models. The results, although an improvement in some respects, may be culturally inappropriate: for example North American models for the office block could well be backward-looking in terms of building services, energy dependence, organisational structure, and responsiveness to user needs.

Building Britain 2001 – perhaps not surprisingly in view of its sponsorship by a number of large contractors – concentrates upon procurement and construction, and not on what the buildings themselves offer, apart from minimising call-backs. *Fenestration 2000* picks out some more general client concerns:

- better comfort. Better views out. More individual control. Higher security

- compatibility with changing information technology and communications systems

- timeless, flexible, affordable, dependable buildings

- buildings that are sympathetic to renovation and refurbishment

● longer term concerns about energy use and conservation.

Materials and components

Normal standards of UK building components (windows, for example) have often been lower than in other advanced countries. Owing to low production volumes, higher specifications have tended to be markedly more expensive, and not always as well designed, tested, engineered, or treated on site as they should have been. Often they are assembled from components sourced from all over the place, and their one-off nature has inhibited continuous development based on feedback from in-service experience. In recent years, good quality imports have become available at reasonable prices, sometimes with a packaged service including design and installation, and logical deliveries at assured dates. In several areas (high performance cladding systems, for example) the UK product has been substantially displaced. In others (air conditioning chillers and terminal units, for example) market growth has been satisfied largely by imports rather than by expanding UK manufacture. Again, *Building Britain 2001* saw this as a bad thing, but in a highly cyclic UK construction market it may be economically wise not to make everything locally.

Buildings have historically been regarded as safe if they were not patently unsound and unhealthy. Now growing numbers of health hazards are being discovered: a particular cultural shock in something traditionally regarded as secure. The subject is reviewed in a recent guide to buildings and health produced by Rosehaugh plc[3]. Some hazards – for example radon, asbestos, and legionnaire's disease – have been present for a long time but their effects took a long time to diagnose. Others, and in particular chemical pollutants, have largely entered buildings as new and apparently useful products, and sometimes also as outlets for wastes from other industries. Recent scientific data are beginning to suggest that contaminant levels many times lower than present day threshold values can affect sensitive individuals and have more widespread long term or low level effects, particularly where several pollutants are combined.

Construction methods and materials: the future?

Industry structure

Building Britain 2001 foresaw that making new buildings would increasingly rely upon rapid assembly of dry-fixed prefabricated products and packaged engineering systems. Where site-forming remained essential, processes would be streamlined with the increasing use of robots, as is already happening in Japan. However, its perspective is that of major contractors, yet the building industry also includes many small firms with limited capital who want – and will continue to want – to maximise the value added by their own labour.

Building Britain 2001 predicted that maintenance and refurbishment would become a completely separate industry from new construction, carried out by direct labour, single-skill specialists, or handymen, and on a larger scale by specialist building care firms with increasingly expensive craft skills. On the other hand, since refurbishment, alteration and maintenance is likely to continue to be a growth industry, and one which is probably less cyclic than new construction, in practice it seems unlikely that all the major contractors will wish to exclude themselves from it.

Important trends

Building Britain 2001 identified the following important industrial and technological trends:

● Higher technology and international standards would make world markets for high value added products. Low value materials and products would remain largely local markets.

● UK industries which proved to be underskilled would fail or be taken over.

● Large buildings would be either (a) designed and assembled by large firms or consortia, or (b) built as low-tech shells, to be fitted out subsequently by the client. (b) was seen as a bad thing as it would reduce the market for UK building contractors – at least as constituted at present – and could lead to increased import penetration. However, as a concept it may have considerable validity, separating as it does the long and shorter life components of the building.

● Specialist contractors would become more vertically integrated (for example, cladding) and horizontally integrated (for example, fit-out) combining design, manufacturing and installation skills.

● There would be increasing pressure to guarantee systems, products, and services.

● Computer aided design (CAD), linked to flexible computer aided manufacturing (CAM) would move the centre of gravity of operations from production systems to information systems.

● R&D would be of increased value to the industry, for whole buildings as well as for individual component or system performance.

R&D seems particularly necessary in five main areas:

● Addressing problems of whole building and subsystem performance, both under construction and in use.

● Developing standard products and installation methods which can be relied upon to perform, and which can be tested both before assembly and in the completed building.

● Identifying when one is entering unknown territory, where project-specific R&D will be needed to produce the required result.

● Designing to facilitate future maintenance and alteration.

● Understanding and meeting the needs of users.

Construction materials

Appropriate construction materials are very much driven by the economics of the process, and the relative values of materials, labour, transport and time. The increasing use of lighter, more highly-engineered components suits the economies of production and simple (albeit sometimes specialised) installation, and the trend to prefabrication and packaging is likely to continue. This may substantially affect HVAC systems, with a trend away from central, tailor-made installations to smaller transportable modules connected to simple, flexible main services.

On the other hand, some building materials are so cheap and relatively abundant (for example, sand, gravel, water, clay) that value

added components cannot easily compete with them: we will probably have concrete foundations and concrete floors for some time, although developments will continue to speed up the process and reduce the time and amount of material used, as was the case with composite floors in the 1980s. It would need very radical changes to expectations of buildings generally to rule low cost, heavy materials out altogether. The building industry also likes to add value itself on site, and will therefore wish to develop, streamline and automate its in-situ methods to compete with prefabricated products.

As knowledge of their health and environmental aspects increases, so the use of individual products in construction and within buildings will come under increasingly careful scrutiny, not only for health and pollution risks (during extraction, manufacture, construction, occupancy, alteration and final disposal[4]) but as responsible uses of global resources.

Discussion

Building Britain 2001's arguments have an inevitable ring to them in terms of the economic imperatives, but the results will not necessarily be better for the user in the long run. Higher technology products, the separation of making from maintaining buildings, and packaged systems do not necessarily go hand in hand with environmental responsibility or even user friendliness. The buildings may not only consume more natural resources initially, but ease of assembly, quality assured performance, and design for low maintenance does not necessarily bring long product life and low life cycle costs. There is an often an implicit judgement that the job stops with the handover of the building, or at best at the end of the warranty period. Highly engineered solutions may also lack flexibility and redundancy, decaying ungracefully and having shorter cost effective lives with premature obsolescence and even systematic failure. As Sir Bernard Feilden said: 'maintenance free = impossible to maintain!'[5]. And there is nothing more dead than a high technology product for which spares are no longer available: one either has to replace the whole thing or try to bodge it!

Does this matter? Many people have claimed that we are now in the age of the 'throwaway' building, and that we need to act accordingly. But the replacement rate of buildings is still very low and consuming capital goods does not sit happily either with a climate of global responsibility or with peoples' emotional needs for some stability in their environment. I see three possible avenues of solution for commercial buildings:

• To develop lightweight, low energy, buildings from standard components which can be dismantled, re-erected and finally easily recycled.

• To adopt shell-and-core principles where the building is sensibly located and the shell and core contain sufficient elbow room spatially and structurally to permit a wide range of functional uses without themselves becoming obsolete.

• To develop a more robust architecture which responds not only to indoor requirements but to the external environment, providing the maximum amount of climate-sensitive 'passive' environmental control with the minimum of energy consuming and throwaway components, while also being able to accommodate more intensive servicing systems as appropriate.

I see scope for all three, depending on the site and the clients' needs.

Statutory standards and requirements are dealt with in other papers and will not be discussed here. These are likely to become increasingly stringent on health, safety and environmental issues. Voluntary standards may also become important if they confer a market advantage, as evidenced by the high level of interest in the BREEAM 'Green Label' scheme[6].

Internal environmental control – recent trends

Characteristics of the stock

A recent study of energy efficiency[7] estimates the UK's total office space at 65 sq km including the public sector. According to a Department of the Environment (DoE) study[8], in 1987, total commercial floorspace was 49.4 sq km, of which 37% was in Greater London. The Building Services Research and Information Association (BSRIA) estimates that 30% of Greater London's office space is air conditioned and 60% centrally heated, with 65% centrally heated and 10–15% air conditioned elsewhere. The balance is small offices with local heating, largely electric[9].

Recent trends

The DoE study also states that nearly all new London office space is air conditioned. Both this and BSRIA's national air conditioning figures are probably on the high side, relating to large speculative developments and not to the stock as a whole including the public sector. Nevertheless, the past decade has seen a rapid increase in air conditioning both in new offices and in refurbishments – from about 5% of the total stock in 1979[10] to perhaps 15% in 1990.

The growth in air conditioning has been accompanied by a growth in shell-and-core developments. While it makes clear sense to think in terms of shell, services, scenery and sets, and to keep parts with different lifespans physically separate, too often they are kept operationally independent as well. This militates against an integrated design concept and tends to make offices less energy efficient and more energy dependent than they really need to be.

The *shell* provides a gloomy view of sorts through sealed, tinted glass largely to exclude the external environment and make the servicing easier. Flat, bland and continuous curtain wallpaper helps maximise net lettable area and allows flexible partitioning within.

The *services* can now be inserted to deal artificially with the environmental controls, some of which could have been met naturally. The fact that services also have long, intermediate and short life elements is also not fully recognised, making them unnecessarily difficult, expensive and wasteful to alter.

The *scenery* is designed by others in haste with a view to space planning and to appearance, but without much, if any, recognition of energy efficiency (particularly in lighting), air distribution, and control ergonomics. It can often wreck the original design intentions for both fabric and services.

We must learn to integrate the concept while keeping the components separate. The division of responsibilities seems to be worse in the UK than in the US, where tenants usually use the shell-and-core design team to complete the fit-out: in the UK tenants appear to be deeply suspicious of the developer's or landlord's team and introduce their own, further fragmenting the design and undermining some of the original intentions.

Energy and maintenance costs

In recent years, while heating requirements have tended to fall, energy costs tend to have risen owing to increased electrical consumption. The rise is normally attributed to new information technology and particularly desktop computers, but the indirect effects – in particular more air conditioning and artificial lighting – can often account for more of the increase. For example, when an office is refurbished, and although more insulation, double glazing, and better boiler plant and controls often save on heating bills, tinted windows and open plans cause people to have the lights on more; fan power replaces natural ventilation, and lowered suspended ceilings exacerbate any tendency to overheat, leading to a call for air conditioning even if it was not there in the first place.

Case study information

The BRECSU/EEO Office Case Studies[11] show that offices can now have much lower energy requirements than average. They also suggest that:

- In new buildings, where reasonable standards of heating and insulation are met, reducing electrical costs is usually a higher priority.

- Air conditioning usually doubles electrical costs for building services, although part of this effect is indirect – for example, occupants who require air conditioned buildings may also use them more intensively, and air conditioning permits deeper planned spaces which in turn require more artificial lighting.

- For air conditioned buildings with all-air systems, fan energy consumption frequently exceeds refrigeration energy consumption, often because ducts are too small, operating pressures too high, full-load running hours too long, and system and control design wanting.

- Electrical consumption and heat output from office equipment is not usually as high as people expect: typically one third of nameplate levels, but varying widely from item to item.

- Lighting energy use varies tremendously and nearly always exceeds consumption by equipment in the general office (although not in machine rooms); it offers good scope for further savings, particularly in open plan areas, where lights are often on throughout the working day and beyond. The efficiency of light sources, reflectors and controls has increased markedly over the past decade, while design illuminance levels have dropped to meet the needs of VDU users. While many recently completed offices have installed lighting power of 15–20 W/sqm (and older offices 30–50 W/sqm and occasionally more), good new installations can now be below 10 W/sqm.

- Mainframe computers and their air conditioning can account for a high proportion of the overall energy costs. Often both consume more energy than strictly necessary and opportunities for simple energy saving and heat recovery are seldom taken.

- Simple energy efficiency measures are more likely to succeed than complex ones. It is better to do a few things well than to try too hard and create unnecessary complexity.

- The potential of modern control systems is not always realised, often owing to split responsibilities for their design and commissioning, a lack of awareness by designers of occupants' real needs, and division of operational responsibilities between tenants, landlords and their contractors. Often controls are too complicated, and not sufficiently user-friendly.

- Good management is vital, but often absent. However, the solution to this is not only in the hands of the occupier: designers need to recognise that building management is a scarce resource and that a design aim should be to make buildings more easily manageable.

The case studies also revealed the following. Many offices use far more energy than they need to, while others, although occupied similarly, are comfortable and effective using far less. Also, in the good buildings, the energy saving systems are usually unobtrusive. Indeed, where more assertive methods were used, the results were often disappointing. Further, most of the 'good' buildings offered scope for further cost effective savings. Finally, perhaps the main obstacle to cost effective energy efficiency was that clients seldom asked for it in their brief, and so design teams were not united in their response. So a lot can be done before moving into unknown territory.

Health and comfort

Environmental services should be all about improving the occupants' – that is, people and equipment – and the organisation's health, comfort and productivity. In recent years, while the equipment has become more tolerant of the environment, the people have become less so. Known and correctable clinically diagnosed health and safety problems such as humidifier fever, legionnaire's disease, and in some places formaldehyde, radon and methane, are now fairly well characterised. Less well understood symptoms tend to be collectively branded as sick building syndrome. A recent review article suggests that to improve building performance the following items require attention:

• Outside air ventilation rates. Attention required, although there is not yet sufficient evidence to stipulate minimum safe rates. (Note that the recent dramatic increase in minimum air change rates in the US only returns their standards to a level similar to the UK ones)

• Temperature and air movement. High, uniform temperatures and low air movement may increase symptoms.

• Relative humidity (RH). Not a big problem but low RHs (below about 35%) may sometimes cause erythema (skin rash) and very low ones (around 20%) eye irritation.

• Lighting standards. Symptoms have been shown to be more prevalent in buildings where there is little daylight and the decor is dull and uniform.

• Airborne pollution from occupancy, fittings, furnishings and equipment. Although pollutant levels are usually very low in relation to occupational exposure limits, symptoms may be caused by irritation, sensitisation, or combined effects.

• Airborne pollution from the air conditioning system, especially organic matter from humidifiers and standing water.

• General dissatisfaction – with the job, the employer, the workplace or the environment (which can be a good scapegoat for more deep seated concerns)[12].

The review concludes that sick building syndrome is far more prevalent in sealed buildings, and although air conditioning is not definitely a cause, it is difficult to disprove some link. However, air conditioning may well also correlate with other negative influences, such as deeper plans, more dependency on unseen technologies with less individual control, less humane environments, poorer outside awareness, and stressful work situations. Ill health in buildings appears to be a multivariate problem involving many aspects of the building, the environment and the work, and there may seldom be one single cause or one easy solution[13]. Nevertheless, buildings and their services must attempt to minimise any negative features.

It is possible, and even likely, that the increased technological complexity of modern buildings is in itself potentially alienating and that it reduces peoples' tolerance of adverse conditions. So not only does the new technology require more and better management, but individuals are more likely to complain to management about any deficiencies as their dependency upon the technology has reduced the options they have – or at least perceive to have – to sort out minor problems themselves. Where management is not up-to-the-mark, then a vicious spiral can result.

Internal environmental control – the future

Natural ventilation or air conditioning?

Organisations usually see a straight choice between natural ventilation and full air conditioning for both speculative and purpose built offices. In the UK most now choose the latter, although they typically get twice the building services energy costs, plus higher maintenance and management costs[14]. However, not all of these are directly related to the air conditioning system but to the overall characteristics of buildings which tend to be air conditioned. Apart from improved comfort (anticipated but not always realised), reasons for choosing air conditioning include:

• organisational prestige

• standard requirements, particularly for many multinationals

• deeper plans, partly for alleged organisational needs, and partly to maximise site floor area

• claimed flexibility – seldom achieved except at a high cost – to accommodate changing requirements

• higher rental levels giving a better rate of return for investors and developers

• deterioration of the external environment, and particularly traffic noise.

But perhaps the most important, and most quoted need is to provide an environment for, and to absorb the heat output from, office information technology. But there are counter arguments:

• Some occupants are reacting against deep, environmentally controlled spaces and state a preference for a more domestic environment with greater individual control.

• Electrical consumption and heat gains from office equipment are seldom as high overall as anticipated, although there can be localised high concentrations of heat.

• There are opportunities to plan larger sites and buildings to be their own defences against road noise. Even in city locations, quiet enclosed courtyards are often possible.

• Modern design, engineering, management and control techniques allow buildings without full air conditioning to be more comfortable than their naturally ventilated forebears, particularly those of the lightweight over-glazed 1960s variety.

• Public opinion could swing against buildings which have more environmental impact and use more energy than thought necessary.

On the other hand, in many air conditioned buildings – at least as they stand – surveys may reveal that the occupants would be happier with natural ventilation, but this may refer to the idea and not necessarily the response to the environment that would result if that same building were to be naturally ventilated.

What air conditioning?

Received wisdom in the mid-1980s was that variable air volume (VAV) air conditioning was best. It was often an improvement on earlier constant volume systems, which were unable to respond economically – if at all – to locally varying heat gains; induction systems, which were often noisy, inflexible, taking up perimeter area, and best suited to shallow plans, and ceiling fan-coils with their poor air distribution and water and maintenance overhead. VAV also offered savings in refrigeration energy and fan power. However, VAV also had some drawbacks in terms of a limited controllability range, air distribution patterns which changed with load, low fresh air quantities at low cooling loads, and unexpectedly high fan energy consumption. Today a number of enhancements to VAV are available (fan-assisted is currently in vogue) and alternative systems should also be considered, preferably as considered responses to actual needs, rather than as fashionable imports from overseas. For example, at present low temperature air systems are becoming popular, even though they reduce fresh air volumes and are much more suited to North American electrical tariffs, which are punitive on summer peak demands.

Most office air conditioning in the UK is by large central plant, and although packaged, the equipment is often 'specials'. Although large plant can be more efficient in an engineering sense – for example, thermodynamically – operationally it can be wasteful through the 'tail wagging the dog' effect – for instance, if only a small part of the building is in use outside normal hours – and changing user needs may cause premature obsolescence. In Japan small modular units dominate and can give better operational flexibility. The building industry trends discussed here would seem to confirm the logic of this, and further growth in modular decentralised plant is anticipated.

We have not yet come to terms with thinking probabilistically about air conditioning. While it would be expensive and probably unnecessary to provide services that can instantly cope with all foreseeable conditions anywhere in the building simultaneously, it would be sensible to have the capacity to deal with the likely aggregate of requirements and to be easily reconfigured to suit changing local needs. For example, terminal units could be designed for 90 percentile power loadings, but capable of easy upgrading. Alternatively, primary systems (say, VAV) could be installed for baseload cooling and ventilation requirements, with supplementary sensible cooling systems (for example direct-expansion, fan coils or unit heat pumps) added where necessary. Some design techniques and technical solutions are outlined in a recent article[15].

Improving user satisfaction, health and comfort

A good building is an elusive thing, but it is probably one which satisfies organisational needs at reasonable cost and without unnecessary effort, and which the inhabitants are happy to work in. This brings us back to a good brief, good design, and good management. We can see four key features:

• Adaptability to meet a range of space and servicing requirements

The building should not make it difficult for occupants to do what they want. For example, in addition to the current shell-and-core facilities, offices might accommodate a wider range of choice in internal environmental services, from natural ventilation and lighting upwards.

• More contact with the outside world

People seem to like being near a window, and preferably one with clear glass in it. In Scandinavia and Germany this is now being seen as a right, and is having a major influence on office design, with deep open plans giving way to more diverse buildings with offices of a more domestic scale around a core or 'street' of common facilities. The degree to which similar views and solutions will prevail in this country is not yet clear: cultural and climatic differences make building types and their services – however international they may feel – difficult to export, and new icons are just as likely to prove to be those of false gods as others have in the past[16].

• Better, healthier and more productive internal environmental quality

In all its aspects – heat, light, sound, colour, and air quality – perhaps the most difficult requirement as natural ventilation, however poor the outside air, often seems to be psychologically more acceptable than mechanical systems of any kind. And, of course, delight: a building which both works and feels good to be in will be a much better investment in the long run than one which is functional but unloved.

• More user control

Psychologists have observed that the human factor – for example the openable window – is disproportionately significant to perceived well being. The reasons may include social as much as design and health issues. For example, one writer observes that: 'individuals measure their worth within an organisation as much by the control they possess over their environment (in the broadest sense) as by expenditure, however lavish, from an invisible and unfeeling corporate exchequer'[17]. Not nearly enough is known about the behavioural aspects of both simple and advanced environmental control systems in buildings.

Many of the above requirements are more easily met in 'domestic' or 'club' environments than in conventional images of office buildings. Social and technical trends also appear to be leading us in that direction, and the pace could accelerate with advances in information technology, although there will also be a need for machine rooms of various kinds. For example, simple cellular offices can offer good outside awareness and individual choice but can also be energy efficient: although an extended building form may require a little more heating, it can be more easily naturally lit and ventilated, which can reduce electrical consumption substantially. Summertime overheating can be limited by window size, solar control devices, heat storage in masonry partitions, and, if necessary, local cooling, and by automatically controlled natural or mechanical ventilation overnight. However, as in the Scandinavian 'combi' offices, the cellular space is only part of the overall requirement, and future offices may well consist of a range of managed spaces, occupied according to the needs of the task in hand, rather than the present cluster of individual territories with some – usually not enough – shared facilities[18].

Local control is also practicable in open offices. A recent conference paper[19] gives two monitored examples, but there is less experience of what is acceptable and understanding how best to design and deploy it. It is also not entirely clear how far demands for high levels of individual control are symptoms of bad, inhumane environments rather than essential attributes of humane ones.

Finally, if people find their building stimulating, the management helpful, concerned, and competent; the work fulfilling, and the environmental controls responsive, they may be willing to ignore many potential shortcomings. But if the organisational framework is wrong and the building dreary or alienating, no amount of engineering will solve the problems.

Energy efficiency

There is a widespread perception that services for energy efficient buildings have higher capital and higher running costs, other than energy costs. Case studies do not bear this out: there is some evidence of virtuous circles with good, integrated design, good execution and good management as the main distinguishing features, with energy efficiency as one of the beneficial results of a well briefed, well designed, well built and well managed building. Sometimes energy efficient offices may even be cheaper in first cost, with some of the building services designed-out or reduced in size, and seemingly expensive components becoming a cost effective part of the system as a whole. For example, low energy lighting saves on electrical distribution costs and air conditioning loads, and in marginal cases may even allow air conditioning to be omitted.

A possible middle way

Even on sites where good natural ventilation is possible and internal heat gains are not ex-

cessive, it may be unwise to specify an office which could not readily accommodate some air conditioning, in case future cooling requirements grow, either through internal gains or possibly climatic change. One possibility is a 'mixed mode' design, which can be either air conditioned or naturally ventilated, locally or generally, according to need. The thinking is epitomised at Refuge House[20]: what appears at first sight to be a simple, naturally ventilated building with an exposed ceiling soffit actually has all the necessary cooling services under the floor, but brought into service via the electronic BMS only when and where people want them. Some European countries are much further along this path: '[in Germany] offices with unopenable windows and full air conditioning are now seldom built'[21] Refuge House is perhaps a 'belt and braces' approach, and there is room for development of the concept, particularly designs where cooling systems can be more easily added and removed, either with central services and add-on modules or with local packaged units. It needs to become more reputable to adopt an ad hoc approach to building services, but within a rigorous strategic framework.

Openable windows are not necessarily restricted to out of town sites: not all urban areas are noisy and sometimes the buildings themselves can form noise barriers, creating quiet enclosed courts. Broadgate Square in London is an example, although in this instance all the offices are air conditioned, perhaps necessarily so for most of their particular users.

Comments on individual environmental services

Heating

Better insulation (with the 1990 Building Regulations), better glazing (particularly with low-emissivity glasses), better boilers, and occasionally combined heat and power systems will reduce fuel demands and hence help improve the quality of the outdoor air. Better control systems will both save energy and provide more personal control. Sometimes heat can be recovered simply and economically, for example, from air-cooled condensers to ventilation supply air or from solar pre-heating air intakes (as at NMB in Amsterdam[22]). In a few buildings with high insulation and high internal gains, sometimes perimeter heating may be omitted altogether[23], perhaps with some electric heating available as a contingency. Unwanted air infiltration can cause discomfort in highly insulated buildings and care is required in design, installation and testing to meet reasonable standards.

Ventilation

Better air quality is high on the agenda, although as yet it is difficult to identify the vital issues. Sometimes complaints may be as much about other attributes of sealed buildings (permanent artificial lighting, deep plans, tinted glass, open planning, organisational culture) than about the air[24]. However, the following issues need attention[25]:

● Locating air intakes in the best positions, away from local sources of pollution (particularly loads and exhausts) and unwanted heat. A recent Australian study showed that, at least in the suburbs of Melbourne, this was more the exception than the rule[26].

● Designing for more efficient room air circulation, by mixing or displacement, and extracting polluted air at source.

● Specifying products which do not pollute the air badly.
  – Detailing buildings, plant and furnishings to limit dirt accumulation and to facilitate cleaning.
  – Cleaning all these thoroughly.

Over the past two or three years, there seems to have been a strong groundswell in the building services industry which suggests that the recirculation of air – at least by central plant – should be avoided altogether. Similarly, good systems will be required to extract air from equipment, such as some photocopiers, which are beginning to be regarded as hazardous.

Cooling

Internal heat gains from office equipment are often not as high as anticipated, and can lead to unnecessary specification or over-sizing of air conditioning. Routine independent measurements of the true energy requirements of equipment under typical usage patterns (as for car fuel consumption cycles) would be very valuable for designers and building users. There is also more scope than generally realised for cooling not by refrigeration but by extracting unwanted heat at source. Overnight cooling, using mechanical or preferably secure natural ventilation, is also effective in buildings which would otherwise be locked up and systems switched off. In favourable circumstances (for example, with internal heat gains up to 30 W/sqm or so over a single shift, and high thermal capacity, preferably with exposed ceiling soffits) refrigeration may be avoided altogether or at least much reduced in capacity. Examples of fabric storage systems with mechanical ventilation already exist, particularly in Scandinavia where integrated systems are marketed commercially[27], and automated natural ventilation systems are also being investigated in the UK and elsewhere[28]. For additional and more compact storage, materials are also under development which change their phase at room temperature and store latent heat. Where refrigeration is essential, there is a growing range of equipment which is both more efficient and ozone-friendly.

Relative humidity

Relative humidity (RH) is not a big problem in the UK as far as comfort goes, and recently many offices have disconnected their evaporative humidifiers for fear of health problems such as legionnaire's disease. Few report any ill-effects and several mention improved staff satisfaction. However, recent UK winters have been warm, with interior RHs probably seldom below 30–35%. When there is a sustained cold spell, health and static electricity problems may well recur, particularly if fresh air change rates are also increased, and some emergency humidification may prove necessary. Static electricity is usually best dealt with by specifying appropriate floor finishes, although again good performance is difficult to ensure at RHs below about 30%.

Lighting

In many offices, the energy costs for lighting are higher than for any other individual end use. Not only in the offices themselves, but also in stairs, corridors and reception areas, lighting energy use is often unnecessarily high. Major savings on existing power levels can be made with high-efficiency reflectors, electronic high-frequency control gear (which also eliminates the flicker some people find disturbing) and good controls, including electronic systems where appropriate[29]. Where possible, fittings should be capable of being switched off centrally and from strategic positions such as exits, and switched on and off locally. Central 'On' is usually wasteful, except for safety and security purposes.

In recent years daylight in offices has been neglected[30]. This is partly due to problems of heat gain, glare, and computer screen visibility, particularly in open planned offices with continuous ribbon windows. But recent user surveys are revealing a strong desire for more natural light and outside awareness, and new generations of display screens should become legible under a wider range of lighting conditions, allowing buildings again to be lit to meet peoples' needs rather than to mitigate shortcomings in equipment design. More daylight not only saves electricity, but changing views make the building more interesting and help people orientate themselves. Improving control of solar gain and glare may need innovation[31] in addition to well established (but not so widely used) repertoires of fixed, manual and automatic shading systems.

Information technology and the management of building performance

Intelligent buildings

As information technology becomes more powerful and communications systems converge, there is a lot of discussion about 'smart' and 'intelligent' buildings, including what the terms really mean. One definition suggests the intelligent building is a flexible and adaptable one, with air conditioning; advanced communications networks; an electronic BMS, and a climatically-responsive facade[32].

As already discussed, the second requirement may not be essential, although the facility for air conditioning can often be necessary. The other four points are reviewed below. First, one should consider why the features are there at all. Although the concept of electronic intelligence has become intertwined with virtuoso technical wizardry and high-tech buildings, there is seldom much point in having more technology than strictly necessary to do the job. To be really worth having and not just a gimmick, intelligence needs to be justified because it makes the building better, more useful, more productive, more comfortable, or more cost effective. This is beginning to be recognised in recent studies[33]. In this spirit, high technology systems can equally be applied to simple building elements, sometimes taking over duties which would have been done by thoughtful caretakers 50 years or more ago, for example using natural ventilation overnight to remove excess heat accumulated during the day.

Flexibility and adaptability

Ideally, one would like a building to be flexible enough to take everything one can throw at it without flinching. Seductive images present themselves of either the totally flexible serviced space which can tune itself electronically to suit any function, or a universal support structure complete with services spine, crane and plug-in modules. In actuality, there can be lots of problems. For instance, one may be buying a lot of things one never uses; under-utilised systems may well operate inefficiently; unanticipated demands may undermine the system and, finally, it could all cost too much. The flexible solution itself may even end up providing short term flexibility only, and actually getting in the way of unanticipated longer term change.

An alternative view is for designs to be robust against a range of alternative scenarios and uncertainties. Nutt has identified five overlapping approaches:

1 Loose fit. A deliberately imprecise response to specified requirements.

2 Indeterminacy. Avoiding exact briefs, clear goals, single strategies.

3 Flexibility. But not the common one which only exists on paper, accommodating foreseen changes in an over elaborate manner while lacking adaptability for more radical alteration.

4 Contingency planning. For example through oversizing of space, structure and services space.

5 Least commitment, Avoiding taking decisions today which can be faced perfectly happily later[34].

Essentially these are all 'no regret' policies[35]: one does what is sensible and cost effective in relation to a wide range of future scenarios, while initially not departing too far from the immediate needs but leaving other things to be resolved by others in due course. This is not a soft option: it means a more statistical approach to problem definition. Some decisions, like the building's location, shape, orientation, thermal and loadbearing capacity are irreversible and must be good and precise to start with. Others, such as space utilisation and servicing, are now subject to larger variations in requirements than before, and this needs to be recognised.

Somehow this thinking must be brought further upstream into the physical provision and its management and some established rules must change. One needs to think about buildings as whole systems over their whole life, rather than as different aspects being dealt with if not by different organisations then at best from different pockets. For example, net lettable space excludes plant rooms and risers, so one tries to minimise 'waste space', in turn restricting adaptability, by squashing up plant and distribution systems and confining them to inaccessible corners. By moving to a concept of 'gross lettable space', there could be more interchangeability between plant and occupied area. With a suitable strategic plan, organisations could have more or less plant, and plant space, to suit their individual requirements, and be able to interchange plant space and usable area accordingly. Somehow this forward thinking has to be turned into a selling benefit, and buildings labelled accordingly so that customers can decide.

Advanced communication networks

An office contains a variety of electronic communications requirements, particularly office automation, telecommunications, building services, security and alarms, and facilities management[36]. Today each function usually has at least one, and often several, communications systems. In the future we can look forward to standard universal networks, readily accessible much like an electrical ring main, and to which most devices can be directly attached. Meanwhile, until the standard becomes commonplace, there is quite a lot to be said for keeping business systems, telecommunications, building and facilities management and safety and security largely separate. They tend to be different areas of management and contractual responsibility, with fairly narrow areas of intercommunication. Physical segregation also limits the scope for disasters affecting all systems at once, or one system corrupting another. In the short term, buildings will still need to accommodate a range of changing cable networks in a flexible and systematic manner. In the longer run, as communications facilities and standards improve, the physical demands upon the building are likely to become less severe.

Electronic building management

Electronic building and energy management systems (BEMS) allow one to: control plant more precisely and in an integrated manner; react rapidly to changing requirements; optimise plant operation in order to reduce energy and maintenance costs; monitor centrally and respond rapidly and appropriately; and collect and process facilities management information.

Over the past 15 years, building services controls have evolved rapidly from dedicated single purpose devices to programmable multifunctional ones; first with cumbersome central systems, then with central supervision and distributed intelligence, and now with networking systems. Each advance has taken processing power closer to the individual item of plant, increasing whole system reliability and reducing wiring and commissioning costs, and we are now in an era of intercommunicating pocket calculators rather than hand configured mainframes.

The costs of electronic building management controls are now similar to comparable conventional controls, and for the larger building can even be lower, becoming the inevitable choice. Distinctions are also disappearing as we now approach the point where each item of plant and each light fitting can come with its own dedicated controller, which can either stand alone, respond to local signals, or be linked into supervisory and command systems which can gather information, adjust settings and optimise performance. This modular network approach can greatly simplify installation and commissioning, as each item of plant can be factory commissioned to run by itself: its performance can then be progressively monitored and upgraded on site via the network. Realising the full potential of modular network systems has to date been inhibited by a lack of agreed communications standards, each manufacturer having its own system. However, things are now beginning to come together. For example, several companies are now supporting one common system[37], albeit a fairly low speed and low capacity one which will no doubt be superseded in due course.

Building management systems are also evolving from the prescriptive to the responsive: lighting can adapt automatically to occupancy and to prevailing natural light levels; ventilation systems can operate at full stretch only when the room is occupied; central plant need only run when there is a local need for it. However, there are still major shortcomings in the user interface and in the relationship between central, intermediate and local controls. For example, controls are too often centrally dictated, while individuals are usually the best judges of the services they require – what they are not so good at is anticipation, economic control, and switching off afterwards. So, where possible, auto 'Standby', manual 'On', and manual or auto 'Off' is a good principle. For example, in a lecture room where traditional time controls ran the ventilation for 45 hours a week, monitored occupancy control reduced running times to 26 hours and 'on-demand' push-buttons to three!

At present, however, too many BEMS are disconnected, under-used, or running wild, for three main reasons:

1 The system is incomprehensible, put together by people who did not understand how the building was likely to be used, what the users required, and sometimes not even the design intentions for the plant itself. Controls specification is seldom clear and responsibilities tend to be split between a large number of parties, few if any of whom see the whole picture.

2 The BEMS is not properly integrated into the overall management structure. It must be seen as a management tool and not something which will somehow look after itself. Inappropriate staffing and divisions of responsibility between owner, occupier and maintenance contractor can exacerbate these problems. Frequently the designer sees the BEMS being operated by one all-seeing all-knowing individual at the central console. In practice, buildings seldom get managed like this: responsibilities are parcelled-up and delegated, and the people operating the systems have no feeling for, or responsibility to, the end users, have inadequate training and support, and lack incentives to operate the controlled plant economically or efficiently.

3 The costs of operation and maintenance of the system can be out of proportion to the benefits. It is easy to go over the top and provide over elaborate facilities which are not cost effective to maintain. Things are becoming easier with modern systems with greater local autonomy and more user friendly central supervisors, but strategic clarity is at least as important as remedial technology, and quite possibly more so. Systems are also often programmed to employ advanced, sometimes incomprehensible, control features rather than to give useful management information on how equipment is performing and where things might be going wrong.

So, while BEMS have a growing role their technical capabilities are currently outstripping the ergonomic engineering of control systems generally and the understanding of the behavioural aspects of their use. More effort will be required if their full potential is to be realised.

Adaptive facades

Another element of the intelligent building vision is a facade that adapts to the climate, not in the conventional way of opening and closing windows, shutters and blinds, but by automatically changing its light and heat transmission characteristics, preferably using electronic systems with no moving parts. Some of the necessary technologies exist on a small scale, but they are not yet available at an acceptable cost and with the size, scale, durability and life span suitable for the external envelopes of buildings. For the time being, passive, mechanical and electrical systems are likely to remain with us while new technology first attacks some tricky problems which are not solved very well at present.

The desirability of fully automated systems is also uncertain. For example, modern, well insulated buildings with low-emissivity glass do not lose much heat anyway and variable insulation would only be cost effective if energy costs were to rise very substantially. With a good modern office costing 10 to 15 pence per sqft net per year to heat (and much of this for ventilation air), and with a ratio of window to floor area of, say, 20%, a halving in total heating costs (a generous estimate) with a four year payback criterion would only make available about £1/sqft for a long life maintenance-free device. There may be more scope for saving on lighting and cooling costs with variable transmission and reflection glasses, but if experience with motorised blinds and automatic lighting controls is anything to go by, many occupants will wish to make adjustments to suit their individual requirements, and fully automated control may well give rise to adverse user reactions.

User-responsive information technology

Background

Ten years ago the information technology people told us that their equipment could come out of the machine room and work in a 'normal office environment'. What they did not say was that this same equipment, if applied in bulk, could ruin that environment, requiring a major rethink of office building services and a rapid, and sometimes over-rapid, growth in air conditioning.

The shape of future information technology

But for how long will this trend continue? In the short term, energy consumption and heat gains by office equipment are likely to grow, particularly as numbers increase. Butler Cox[38] foresees a rapid rise over the next 20 years, then a levelling-off. On the other hand, technological advances – and often the application of existing technology in a more energy-conscious manner

– could lead to a fall, quite possibly within the coming decade[39]. This trend could be accelerated if there is consumer pressure for it ('why should we air-condition our buildings to accommodate your equipment: we'll buy somebody else's that is less demanding') and if comparisons of equipment energy consumption begin to be published, either independently or by manufacturers wishing to obtain a market advantage.

Convergence may also begin to reduce the proliferating range of electronic devices. Currently, in addition to a desktop computer and/or terminal, a single workstation may have a printer, a typewriter, a fax, a scanner and a copier, when all it really needs is one paper input/output device (assuming paper stays around for some time yet to come), and such devices are indeed now coming onto the market. Widespread use of computers with voice recognition may also occur; this might increase the demand for cellular offices, which themselves can often incorporate electronic equipment more readily with less environmental stress.

Future cooling loads

Even if heat output doesn't fall, not all of it has to turn into a cooling load, at least not in the general office. In recent studies, we have found that heat output from office equipment over a 24-hour period (apart from mainframe computer and telephone switch rooms) often splits three approximately equal ways:

1 Equipment which has to be on or near the desktop: PCs, terminals, typewriters, personal printers.

2 Equipment which is normally in a separate room or at least near the entrance: large photocopiers, vending machines, minicomputers.

3 Equipment which can be anywhere but could often easily be clustered: minicomputers, file servers, shared printers, communications equipment, central faxes.

If the items in Categories 2 and 3 are put in separate rooms, or at least grouped under air exhaust positions, much of their unwanted heat can be extracted directly without necessarily being a cooling load. These machines are also more likely to be on for twenty-four hours than those in Category 1 and can overheat the office overnight when the windows are shut or the air conditioning is off; if their local exhaust runs overnight too then such problems are also reduced. Local exhaust may also be increasingly necessary to maintain acceptable air quality.

Effect on buildings

The only certain thing is the growth in information technology and the uncertainty of its power demands. So while it would be unwise to design a building not capable of accommodating greater electrical loads and heat output from information technology, it is also quite possible that the current increase in cooling requirements may be a 'blip' rather than a trend, at least in general office areas: the supporting equipment rooms may be with us for longer. This reinforces the view that, to avoid obsolescence and unnecessary energy consumption, the Responsible Workplace should accommodate a range of servicing solutions including natural ventilation where appropriate. When more sophisticated services are required, they do not always have to be a blanket provision, but should operate only when, where and to the extent that they are actually required.

Conclusions for the Responsible Workplace

The building that accommodates the Responsible Workplace will need to be better, healthier, more adaptable, less resource-hungry, less polluting, more climate-responsive and better managed than its forebears – quite a tall order. It will need to be better managed and also be easier to manage. It will not necessarily, or even predominantly, be a new one: some older buildings can be more adaptable and environmentally friendly than their more recent counterparts and are capable of further improvements. The early success of BREEAM[40] suggests that its performance is also likely to be measured and labelled, and that the criteria adopted may extend beyond the statutory.

Better

A good building depends less on lists of particular attributes and technologies (which may turn out to be little more than buzzwords) than on good integrated design, good execution, and good management, with innovations added where necessary to a platform of proven knowledge. Appropriate technology is not necessarily the most advanced, except where this gives real benefits to the user. I would prefer to see robust designs which make the most of natural forces; contain engineering systems that are easy to alter, extend and maintain; operate without undue effort and absorb major changes without undue fuss. To address these issues effectively will require better teamwork and communication, better supported by research, development and testing, and ultimately major changes in the professional and fee structure of the building industry and the related professions including property departments, agents and facilities managers. User requirements and behaviour also need to be much better researched, particularly in relation to control systems and to adaptability: for example, when does a physical feature of the building form a 'useful discipline', which helps to give the user obvious clues about what should and should not be done, and when does it turn into an 'impossible constraint'?

Healthier

The employment and use of hazardous and environmentally damaging materials should be minimised, but through careful risk assessment rather than fashionable knee-jerks. The internal environment needs to be better, and not just in the physical sense but also to raise the human spirit. Suitable features include better design generally, a more interesting experience of the building, more effective ventilation, better views and outside awareness (not only at the workplace but when moving about the building), more individual control of temperature, lighting and air movement, and better maintenance and cleaning. The trend towards sealed and fully air conditioned office buildings may be reversed, with demands for more 'natural' environments with technology used more selectively, for example for specific areas and at particular times of the year rather than as blanket provision. Mechanical and electrical systems will then be used in a more sophisticated manner, in some areas complementing and assisting the natural systems and correcting their shortcomings, rather than supplanting them altogether.

More adaptable

Working practices and the supporting functions and technologies are still changing rapidly, requiring buildings with the flexibility to meet known short term needs and the adaptability to accommodate uncertain longer term change. Office buildings are likely to become more highly diversified, with 'domestic', 'club' and 'high tech' environments in close proximity all within the same shell, which should therefore be able to accommodate a wide variety of mixes. Complex base level servicing will not always be essential, but there must be the potential to obtain the services needed, when and where they are needed, and without undue difficulty. Adaptability requires clear spatial organisation and maximising access both to services and to the exterior. Building shells will need to be generous, particularly in floor-to-floor heights, if they are to meet the necessary range of demands: it will be important not to repeat the mistakes of the 1960s and go for the lowest common denominator. Central building services systems may well decline in favour of those with more local – or certainly locally adaptable – components, many of which can perhaps be trollied-in, connected-up, and moved around with no more difficulty than a washing machine.

Less resource-hungry

It is difficult to define exactly what this means for the selection of materials. For example, is energy intensive (but readily recyclable) aluminium a better choice than polluting (and also energy intensive) plastics, and is timber a renewable green product, or ecologically destructive and short lived unless filled with poisonous preservative chemicals? It depends so much on the assumptions one makes and the ways in which materials are sourced and ultimately reused or disposed of. Better accounting systems will need developing before

many of the questions can be effectively answered[41]. Avoidance of waste is more easily addressed, with many buildings and components becoming functionally obsolete well before they are worn out. A general rule seems to be: the more tightly designed the building, the shorter its life, and so principles of adaptability appear to offer wide benefits. Buildings should also be located where they do not unnecessarily increase the energy used by the transport required to get to them, and preferably where they reduce the transport burden.

Less polluting

Health and pollution aspects of the building materials themselves have been touched upon. The other main source of pollution is fuel consumption, not only at the building itself but by its energy supply systems, and particularly power stations: every five years or so this accounts for as much energy as was embodied in the building's construction[42], including the manufacture and transport of all the materials used. Major reductions in energy consumption are already possible by making simple and effective use of technology that is already available; more sophisticated solutions offer further potential but at higher risk. An important feature in reducing energy consumption and energy dependence is to avoid waste and to make good use of natural light, solar heat and natural ventilation when it is practical and economical to do so.

More climate-responsive

Recent trends in offices have moved from traditional climate-responsive forms, which were designed as coarse climate modifiers, to climate-rejecting, sealed designs where the internal environment is created largely or entirely artificially. A number of issues now seem to be questioning this trend and providing some pointers to the future:

• New communications systems bring into question the requirement for large, deep spaces.

• Occupants are asking for more 'natural' environments, with greater outside awareness, more daylight, natural ventilation, and better individual control, but often with mechanical and electrical systems available on demand for when the natural ones cannot cope.

• New materials, systems and design techniques permit closer integration of natural and mechanical systems with intelligent user-responsive controls, allowing buildings which are not fully air conditioned to provide a higher level of environmental control than hitherto.

• Concern for the global environment suggests that energy efficiency needs to be increased, and one good way of doing this is to use natural ventilation, light and solar heat where possible in place of mechanical and electrical systems.

• The growth in energy consumption by desktop information technology equipment may soon begin to fall, reducing cooling loads in general offices although not necessarily in the supporting equipment rooms.

As a result, deep, sealed, fully air conditioned buildings may well give way to shallower ones with potential for more varied levels of servicing from natural ventilation upwards. The shell which contains these will be typically not more than 12–15 metres from window-wall to window-wall, although with architectural and servicing ingenuity, the necessary principles can be incorporated in complex three dimensional forms of greater overall depth using atria, courtyards, setbacks, rooflights and such. However, any temptation to reduce floor-to-floor heights should be resisted. Four metres or so will be required to provide space for services, including full air conditioning when and where appropriate, and this is also a good height to promote effective natural lighting and ventilation.

More manageable and better managed

Good management will be essential to make use of the building's potential as a Responsible Workplace. The building and equipment will need to be effectively maintained; users will need to be supported in their requirements but also made aware of the potential opportunities and constraints the building provides, and the adaptable services will need to be effectively managed. The selection and location of equipment will have to be considered so that it

complements the concept of responsibility and does not create avoidable health hazards or unnecessary demands for or upon energy consuming services. However, buildings must not become unnecessarily complex, creating avoidable management burdens: designers need to become more aware of management's needs and priorities, while managers must become better able to brief designers.

References

1 D A Button & R Dunning, *Fenestration 2000: Phase 1*, Pilkington Glass Ltd, July 1989
2 *Building Britain 2001*, Centre For Strategic Studies in Construction, Reading University, 1988
3 S Curwell, C March & R Venables, eds *Buildings and Health – The Rosehaugh Guide*, RIBA Publications, 1990
4 Ibid
5 B M Feilden, Statement made at RIBA Conference, York University, 1984
6 *BREEAM Version 1/90, An environmental assessment for new office designs*, Building Research Establishment Report BR183, 1990
7 H Herring, R Hardcastle, R Phillipson *Energy use and energy efficiency in UK commercial and public buildings up to the year 2000*, Energy Efficiency Office, Energy Efficiency Series No 6, HMSO, 1988
8 Department of the Environment, Industrial and Commercial Floorspace Statistics, England 1982–85, HMSO, 1986
9 Ibid
10 Davis Langdon & Everest Consultancy Group, unpublished report, June 1987.
11 *Energy Efficiency Office: Office Case Study Series*, Policy Studies Institute (December 1989), Cornbrook House (July 1990), Hempstead House (July 1990), Hereford & Worcester County Hall (October 1990), At least 9 more to follow. Available free of charge from Enquiries Bureau, BRECSU, BRE, Garston, Watford WD2 7JR Overviews of the cases are found in D Brownhill, *Energy efficient offices: case histories, Building Services 63–64* (June 1990); and Anon, Conference Review: Energy and Global Responsibility, *Facilities* 8 (2) 18–22, February 1990
12 J M Sykes, 'Sick Building Syndrome' *Klimaatbeheersing* 18 (12) 430–439, 1989
13 P McLennan, 'Sick Building Syndrome' an alternative view, *Facilities* 8(4) 21–23, April 1990
14 See for example, *Office Services Charges*, Jones Lang Wootton, 1990
15 P G S Rutten, The adaptability of air conditioning systems, *Australian Refrigeration, Air Conditioning and Heating*, 43–50, December 1989
16 See, for example: A Leaman, 'Flying High: SAS Headquarters' *Architecture Today* 8 69, May 1990
17 B Finnimore, *Architecture Today* 2, 8–10, 1989
18 F Becker, *Managing Space Efficiently* Paper to the Association of Facilities Managers International Conference, London, 8 Nov 1990

19 A Wilkes & A Hedge, *The personal control of environmental conditions*, Paper to Building Pathology 90 Conference, Cambridge, 24–26 September 1990

20 R Bunn, 'Rural Refuge', Building Services 17–21, June 1988

21 T Rakoczy, 'Air handling installations with window ventilation and cooling', *Heizung, Luftung, Haustechnik* 40(3) 154–157, 1989

22 W Holdsworth, 'Organic Services', *Building Services* 11(3) 20–14, March 1989

23 W Braun, *A modern concept for office buildings: energy saving and good indoor comfort are no longer contradictory.* Tenth Air Infiltration and Ventilation Centre Conference, Espoo, Finland, 1989

24 S Curwell, C March & R Venables, eds *Buildings and Health – The Rosehaugh Guide*, RIBA Publications, 1990

25 P E McNall, *Control Technology and Indoor Air Quality Problems*, ASHRAE Conference IAQ 88, Atlanta, Ga, pages 77–83, 11–13 April 1988

26 P Williams, *Indoor air quality and equipment faults in 58 air-conditioned office buildings in Melbourne* Paper to Building Pathology 90 Conference, Cambridge, 24–26 September 1990

27 TermoDeck: 'Passive climate control' *Strangbetong*, Stockholm, August 1989

28 A H C van Paassen & P J Lutte, 'Natural Ventilation and Automation with Manual Overriding are Healthy Solutions', *Symposium: Healthy Buildings in relation to Building Services*, Utrecht, 17–20 February 1992

29 W T Bordass, 'Lighting controls: functions, hardware and guidelines', *Facilities* 6 (12), 8–9, December 1988). Also, A I Slater, *Lighting Controls: an essential element of energy-efficient lighting*, BRE Information Paper 5/87, May 1987

30 Healey & Baker, National Office and Business Space Survey, Healey & Baker Research Services, 1990

31 P Littlefair, 'Innovative daylighting: review of systems and evaluation methods', *Lighting Research & Technology* 22(1) 1–17, 1990. See also: D A Button & R Dunning, *Fenestration 2000: Phase 1*, Pilkington Glass Ltd, July 1989

32 D M Lush, *Building Technology – High-tech designs, flexibility, servicing and communications* Intelligent Buildings Seminar, December 1987

33 *The Intelligent Building in Europe*, Ongoing multi-client study by DEGW, In progress, 1992

34 B B Nutt, 'The strategic design of buildings' *Long Range Planning* 21 (4) 130–140, Pergamon, 1988

35 W D Nordhaus, 'Greenhouse Economics: Count before you leap', *Economist* 19–22, 7 July 1990

36 *Information Technology and Buildings*, CIBSE Applications Manual AM7, 1992

37 R Joseph, 'Catching the right bus', *Electrical Design* 26–28, October 1990

38 Butler Cox, *Information Technology and Buildings: A Practical Guide for Designers*, Butler Cox plc, 1989

39 L Norford et al, 'Electronic office equipment: the impact of market trends and technology on end-use demand for electricity', in T B Johansson et al (eds), *Electricity: Efficient end-use and new generation technologies and their planning implications*, 427–460, Lund University Press, 1989. ISBN 91 7966 065 7

40 *BREEAM Version 1/90, An environmental assessment for new office designs*, Building Research Establishment Report BR183, 1990

41 Frances Cairncross, *Costing the Earth*, The Economist Books, Business Books Ltd, 1991

42 R Joseph, 'Catching the right bus', *Electrical Design* 26–28, October 1990

8 Environmental issues and the workplace

Simon Hodgkinson, Touche Ross Management Consultants

Summary

This paper looks at the pressures of environmental issues on the design and use of the workplace. The priorities for the 1990s will be: protection of heritage, global warming, energy efficiency, transport, and hazardous building materials.

The pace of change is led not by the government but rather by private initiatives which put pressure on the development sector and the built environment. Businesses will increasingly view the environmental performance of premises as part of their competitive advantage. Employees will be more aware of the environmental reputation of firms and the quality of their workplaces.

The public seeks to minimise the impact of development on heritage. The response to these pressures will include the wider specification of environmentally friendly building products; the development of design and product guides for environmentally sensible design; the harmonisation of higher building product standards across Europe, and new information technology for managing buildings and their services for improved environmental performance.

Introduction

This paper is in two sections: the first identifies where the pressures of environmental change in relation to the workplace will come from in the 1990s and how they are likely to evolve. The key drivers of change considered are: public opinion; government policy and legislation; business and new technologies. The second section identifies and describes the key environmental issues and trends that are likely to impact on workplace development and use in the 1990s. The issues considered are: protection of urban and rural heritage; global warming; energy supply and use; transport; hazardous building materials and the demand for healthy and environmentally responsive workplaces.

The drivers of change

The path of environmental progress has, over the last two decades, been littered with good intentions. The Club of Rome Report in the 1960s, the talk of energy efficiency which followed the oil crisis of the early 1970s, the Bruntland Report in 1987 have all to date led to little practical action. It is therefore important to be realistic about the prospects for future action arising from the current concern for environmental issues. This time around the issues have undoubtedly reached new heights in political and business agendas. Yet many people remain sceptical that very much will come of all the talk. So what does it all really mean? Who will drive the change, why and how?

The key drivers of environmental change in relation to the workplace will be:

- *People* with green aspirations, exerting their influence on workplace decisions, as voters, activists, consumers, employees and shareholders.

- *Government* at all levels as legislator, decision-maker, and investor in areas which impact on the workplace.

- *Businesses* which develop, use, and invest in workplaces.

● *New technologies* which will provide many opportunities for achieving improved environmental performance

We begin by considering how the first three of these drivers of change are likely to evolve in the coming years, and how they may impact on workplace decisions.

Public pressures

In December 1988 only 5% of people in the UK rated environmental issues as among the most important in the country. By July 1989 the figure had risen to 35%. By December 1989 it was back down to 18%. Is it all a passing fad? Market researchers and pollsters believe not: the signs are that the environment is here to stay as a critical issue of public concern, and that this public concern will become an ever more important force for political and business change. Their key conclusions are that:

● *Public concern for the environment is consistently high.* In one Mori poll 75% of respondents placed environment above economic growth as a priority[1].

● *The Green Vote will be an important force for change in the 1990s.* Mori has concluded that '. . . there is no doubt that [the environment] is now firmly placed on the public agenda for the foreseeable future'[2]. Mintel has arrived at a very similar conclusion: 'although it is impossible to forecast the timescale or in what order the issues will be tackled it is quite clear that it is now becoming politically expedient to be seen to be actively tackling environmental problems. Expediency will increase as each year passes'[3].

● *Concern is greatest in the south, and among the ABC1 socio-economic groups.* Mori concludes that it is those who have benefited most from the Thatcher years who are the most concerned: 'What more material possessions do they want? Few if any. Far better to take their next instalment of the good life in the form of air purified of car fumes, streets swept clean of litter'[4].

● *Concern is manifesting itself in lifestyle changes.* People are eating healthier foods, taking more exercise, joining green pressure groups, buying green products[5]. Moreover

people are making plans to 'green' their lifestyle in the future – for example, 20% say they intend to make less use of their car in the future[6].

● *The first wave of green consumerism has peaked.* Although green consumerism is not set to disappear, there is evidence of a declining interest in green products. People have been disappointed by their performance and grown sceptical of the claims of manufacturers. The indication is that people will in the future continue to buy green, but only on the basis of clear information and not at the expense of performance and cost[7].

These trends have a number of implications for the workplace arising from people's influence as voters and activists; as employees; as consumers and as investors or shareholders:

Voters and activists

At a general level the green vote will encourage governments to impose ever stronger environmental standards on industry and development. More specifically, people as members of environmental pressure groups, and as residents of areas threatened by insensitive development will exert increasingly strong influence over where development takes place, the quality of the architecture, and its impact on the surroundings – the so-called NIMBY (Not In My Back Yard) syndrome.

Employees

In the 1990s business success will be even more dependent on the recruitment of quality people, especially scientists, professional and managerial staff. These are the very kind of people who are showing the greatest concern for the environment, and are most active in greening their lifestyles. These people will be in short supply and will be more able to choose who they work for. In terms of green lifestyle expectations, two criteria will become more important in the choice of employer:

● *The location of the workplace.* Accessibility to the workplace by other means than the car, and proximity to home will become more important for people who want to drive less. For women with children, working nearer home will often be a key criterion. Proximity to town centre amenities may also become more important.

● *The environmental reputation of the employer.* People will judge the environmental performance of their prospective employer. This judgement will be influenced both by the quality of the workplace environment (for example, aspect, facilities, healthiness, environmental control, use of environmentally damaging materials in the building or furnishings) and by workplace practices (for example, recycling of office waste, energy management practices).

Consumers

The influence of green consumers on the workplace will tend to be indirect. Businesses which sell directly to the public will increasingly wish to present themselves as 'squeaky clean' to their customers: premises are an important part of corporate image. These businesses may not wish to occupy developments perceived by the buying public to have damaged the local environment. By contrast they will see it as good for the corporate image to occupy developments built on reclaimed, derelict or contaminated land.

Investors and shareholders

Despite the rise of ethical investment trusts such as the Merlin Ecology Fund, there is to date little evidence of strong pressure from investors and shareholders on companies to improve their environmental performance. However, the belief is that things will change and that the investment community will in the UK, as in the US, increasingly consider environmental performance when deciding where to place investments.

Government pressures

The pressures of the NIMBY vote and the need to tackle environmental problems at the local, national, and international level have raised the environment to the top of the political agenda. Moreover the political agenda on the environment for the 1990s is now set, although many of the detailed policies and timetables for action are not. The pressures that are likely to emanate from the European Community and the UK government are considered below in turn.

European Community

Under the 1986 Single European Act, European Community member states agreed that the EC should include among its objectives environmental protection to the extent that the pursuance of these objectives at Community level is more effective than action at the level of individual member states. In the 1990s European environmental legislation will become of increasing importance, especially in relation to trans-boundary pollution issues and the harmonisation of standards in industry. With regard to the development sector, the EC has already passed two important Directives: the Environmental Assessment Directive[8], requiring that member states conduct environmental impact assessments of major projects with significant impacts on the environment, and the Construction Products Directive[9], which will harmonise building product standards emphasising environmental and energy criteria.

UK Government

The 1990 government White Paper on the Environment[10] was severely criticised by commentators for its lack of new commitments to action. Yet, what the 1990 White Paper did was to set out clearly the political agenda on the environment for the 1990s, and the Government's preferred policy instruments for implementing that agenda.

Policy instruments

At the time of the White Paper, the government was committed to a market-based approach characterised by four elements:

● The pricing of environmental resources so as to provide clearer signals to industry and consumers about the costs of using them. These would include charges on polluters, higher energy prices and industry levies to finance pollution control measures[11].

● Correcting market distortions through privatisation, by providing, for example, recycling credits.

● Setting new regulatory standards on pollution through the Environmental Protection Act (1991).

- Encouraging voluntary action by business and individuals.

The policy agenda

In broad terms the key aims of government policy in the next 10 years will be:

- Reductions in greenhouse gas emissions primarily through energy supply and energy efficiency measures.

- The control of pollution through the enactment of the Environmental Protection Act (1991) which will enforce the 'polluter pays' principle.

- Protection of urban and rural heritage and wildlife through land use planning, and agricultural policy tools.

- The development of clean technologies.

- Waste management and recycling. In 1990 the government set a target of recycling half of recyclable household waste by the turn of the century.

The following is a list of statements in the 1990 White Paper which are of specific relevance to workplace development in the 1990s. This menu of intentions can be taken to represent the environmental agenda for the 1990s in the UK:

Land use planning
- development of planning policy guidance on planning to conserve energy

- work to improve the operation of Environmental Impact Assessment

- promotion of environmental improvements as planning gain

- review of the balance between economic and environmental costs and benefits in transport planning

- promotion of the reuse of vacant, derelict and contaminated land.

Countryside and wildlife
- integration of environmental considerations with the economic activity in the countryside

- encouragement of landscape conservation and improvement.

Hazardous substances
- reduction in exposure to lead, and the use of dioxins

- phasing-out of PCBs.

Waste and recycling
- promotion of waste minimisation and the development of clean technologies

- promotion of the recycling of building and household waste.

Eco-labelling
- encouragement of environmental labelling of buildings and consumer products.

Towns and cities
- encouragement of the best use of land in urban areas

- reducing pressure on other areas of environmental value

- civilising traffic in towns by not providing new road capacity to facilitate commuting

- fostering good design through design guidance and briefing.

Pollution control
- imposing, through the Environmental Protection Bill, a duty of care on landowners not to contaminate land.

Timetable

It seems likely that the commitment to practical action in relation to many of the key areas of environmental policy will develop gradually over the next decade for a number of reasons. First, on global issues, action is likely to be dependent on international agreements which will take time to reach. Second, the costs of certain policies to the public purse will be high, and commitment to this expenditure will be slow to develop. Third, some policies (for example, petrol taxes) will be electorally unpopular. Finally, the present government is unlikely to implement interventionist policies, preferring to rely on exhortation and price signals – an approach which in some areas (for example, energy efficiency) has been shown to be slow to bring results.

Business pressures

While it is early days yet, the indications are that many UK companies are lagging behind leading European firms and UK public opinion in terms of their perception of environmental issues. The key results of a recent pan-European study by Touche Ross Management Consultants[12] of managers' attitudes to environmental issues shows that:

- Management attitudes across Europe varied widely between countries.

- German, Dutch and Danish managers showed a much greater awareness of the issues than their Spanish, Greek and Italian counterparts.

- 80–100% of German companies had environmental policies and board level involvement in environmental issues.

- Companies in Germany and Holland believe that their own country's policies will continue to be tougher than those at the EC level.

- Of the UK managers who responded, over half do not think that stricter environmental legislation will affect their industry; only one third had environmental policies; only half had board level involvement in environmental issues; 80% said that they intended to improve their environmental performance, and 30% claimed to consider the environmental performances of their suppliers.

The main pressures for change felt by UK companies are coming from the public and from green consumerism. In the UK quite a few firms left environmental issues to the public relations department, whilst abroad this is rarely the case. Pressures from other sources – shareholders, insurance companies and banks – are virtually non-existent.

Despite the slow start it is clear that UK businesses will have to face up to the environmental challenge in order to maintain their competitive position in the European context. Businesses will increasingly develop corporate environmental policies designed to achieve a number of business goals. These would include:

- Meeting new market demands for environmental goods and services.

- Complying with rising environmental standards.

- Reducing operating costs through energy efficiency, waste minimisation and other measures.

- Presenting a green corporate image to staff, customers, and the investment community.

There are many companies in the UK that are already actively developing environmental policies and programmes. These include IBM, Procter and Gamble, BP, ARC, Body Shop, National Power, ICI, RTZ, Shell, Tesco, Safeway, Sainsbury, and Gateway. The environmental policy statements of these companies tend to be broad based. For instance IBM's corporate environmental policy, originally published in 1971, commits to 'reducing to a minimum the ecological impact of all its activities' The company aims to 'meet or exceed all applicable government environmental regulations everywhere IBM operates, and to establish high IBM standards where government standards do not exist'[13]. IBM UK now has an Environmental Council chaired by a Board Director and with representatives from all functions. The Council is charged with developing programmes in all areas, and views environmental management as part of IBM's total quality management objectives.

In respect of its premises procurement and facilities management IBM has a number of environmental initiatives including:

- Environmental Impact Assessments (EIAs) are used to identify and minimise impacts likely to be associated with any new development. Environmental assessments of any new site which IBM intends to acquire, be it land or buildings, are conducted to identify problems which might impact on IBM's intended use of the site, pollution liabilities, or public image.

- The Office Environment Programme which conducts yearly audits of all premises and covers issues such as Sick Building Syndrome, ergonomics, energy management, and environmental conditions – for example, temperature, lighting, ventilation, air quality[14].

Environmental considerations have not to date influenced IBM's locational decisions. However, it intends to take more account of the provision of public transport when making future locational decisions. Moreover, IBM's Environmental Council is 'seeking to question the need for a company car fleet'[15].

In the longer term, corporate environmental policies are likely to place a number of distinct pressures on the workplace for:

● *Green flagship buildings.* Premises are an important component of corporate image. Businesses will increasingly want their 'flagship' premises to present a shining example of environmental friendliness in terms of energy efficiency, the use of building materials, and the impact on the wider environment. Examples of this include the headquarters of NMB Postbank Building in Amsterdam and Rosehaugh plc's headquarters in London. New aesthetics will undoubtedly be developed to make more visible the fact that green principles have been adopted. Key determinants of these aesthetics may include the use of more durable or recycled materials, or showing off energy efficient plant and passive solar design features, for example.

● *Environmentally friendly workplaces.* In order to meet the green expectations of their employees, businesses will seek to locate workplaces closer to public transport, and to residential areas where the recruitment of women is important. They will also improve both the quality of the workplace environment (more individual control over environmental conditions, measures to avoid sick building syndrome, space planning to improve aspect, greater reliance on natural ventilation and lighting), and green workplace practices (recycling of office waste, better energy management).

● *Avoidance of sensitive sites and non-green developments* which may be or have been the object of NIMBY attention, either because they are on sensitive sites, or because they are badly designed, or both. The focus will be on reusing derelict sites and on design excellence.

● *Energy efficiency.* If energy prices increase substantially the running costs of buildings may become a more important consideration for business, and generate a requirement for cost-effective energy efficient servicing strategies.

The pessimistic scenario

Despite the apparent commitment to the environment there is a pessimistic scenario with regard to future action which should be spelt out. It is as follows:

Concern for global warming blows over – just as the oil crisis of the early 1970s did – not because there is no problem, but because the problem was hyped up by the US following the bad harvests of the mid-1980s, and the balloon has finally run out of hot air. So it's back to business as usual. Lip service continues to be paid to concern for the environment, but economic recession, cynicism at the prospect of international co-operation on environmental issues (and after all it is China, India and South America that are mainly responsible for global warming – what we can do is strictly limited), will turn business and government back to the traditional attitude that there is a competitive advantage to be gained from not achieving environmental quality, from doing things in the cheapest (and dirtiest) possible way. In the European context, the UK government acts to stall and find loopholes in the environmental legislation to help protect its own industries, and it is joined in this by the other principal environmental culprits in the EC: Spain, Italy, Greece, and Portugal.

In terms of the business sector, the pressure for greener buildings peters out in the name of economy and profit. Green consumerism turns out to have been a fad for those with enough money to pay for the value added quality of a green label. The design industry, being essentially reactive and not feeling the demand from clients, does not respond to the green building challenge – just as it failed to respond to the energy challenge in the 1970s. Finally, environmental legislation is compromised by industrial interests. What is enacted is a compromise and is ineffective in changing practices.

Issues and trends

From the analysis of the drivers of environmental change and their primary concerns, it is now possible to identify a number of key environmental issues which will impact on workplace design and use in the 1990s, namely: the protection of heritage; global warming; energy efficiency;

transport, and hazardous building materials. The following discussion evaluates the trends that may evolve with regard to each of these issues over the coming decade.

Protection of heritage

The growing force of NIMBYism will ensure that heritage protection becomes an ever more important issue in the 1990s. The concern will be for heritage and culture understood in the widest sense, covering landscape, wildlife, and urban fabric. The question of landscape as heritage is particularly potent in the UK. As David Lowenthal has argued:

> Nowhere else is landscape so freighted as legacy. Nowhere else does the very term support not simply mean scenery and genre de vie but quintessential national virtues[16].

Yet the extraordinary rise in public interest in architecture and its impact on built heritage generated by HRH Prince Charles in recent years demonstrates that the force of NIMBYism is developing a new and important dimension, involving a direct attack on the trend to international corporate architecture. Sue Clifford of Common Ground writes of this architecture:

> the constant bleaching of diversity, detail, craftsmanship and meaning affects us all, emotionally and culturally. It impoverishes the spirit and often our resolve to do something about it...[The aim must be] to reinforce locality and local distinctiveness – to help people to hold on to what is valued in the old and to demand the best of the new and increase local identity[17].

To understand how the question of heritage protection will evolve it is necessary not only to understand these perspectives, but also to look at development control and how agricultural and nature conservation policy will evolve in the coming decade. These issues are considered in turn below.

Development control: from presumption for development to appropriateness of development

In the 1980s planning control was characterised by a presumption for development and arguably by comparatively little regard for the impact of development on the surroundings. In the planning process NIMBYs were often successfully discredited as newcomers seeking to pull up the drawbridge. The indications are that in the future this will change. The 1990 government White Paper gave new emphasis to the role of local people as the rightful custodians of natural and built heritage. It states:

> For most people it is the appearance of a building which will be of greatest importance. A good building can contribute to a sense of pride and of place.[18]

The new onus will be on the developer to prove that a scheme will enhance and not detract from its surroundings. Design briefs will increasingly be used to set out for potential developers the problems and opportunities associated with a site and the planning goals for it, and to 'help an area to be developed with unity of purpose in a way that piecemeal development proposals often cannot'[19]. The 1990 White Paper states that the legitimate concerns of such briefs will include: location in relation to other property; bulk; overall relationship to surroundings, and materials.

The future of environmental impact assessment

The European Directive on Environmental Assessment came into force in 1985 and has been implemented in the UK under a number of regulations. From the viewpoint of development, the key regulation is the Town and Country Planning (Environmental Effects) Regulations 1988. Under these regulations local planning authorities can require environmental statements in support of planning applications for new developments. The Regulations are mandatory for certain types of development (for example, major infrastructure developments, mining, power stations) but discretionary in respect of others, including most of the developments which are the concern of the Responsible Workplace project.

Manchester University's Environmental Impact Assessment Centre has monitored the implementation of the Regulations. Their key findings to date are:

- In the first 16 months of operation of the Regulation, approximately 100 EAs were submitted, only 13 under the category which includes B1 developments. Two of these were the proposals for the Royal Docks and for Kings Cross in London.

- EAs have tended to be commissioned late in the design process and have largely failed to date to impact materially on the design principles of schemes.

- Standards of assessment have been low.

- To date, EAs have not tended to explore alternative locations for development. There has been a problem of scoping.

- To date, EAs have largely been a mechanical exercise which has added little to the decision process.[20]

These findings should not be taken to mean that the legislation will have little impact on commercial development in the future. Likely future developments in the use of EIAs fall into two areas. First, they may be more widely and effectively applied in respect of commercial development. Central government is committed to improving the operation of the regulations[21], and local authorities, in 'greening' themselves, will see EIAs as an increasingly important tool for environmental management. Local residents will become more vociferous in asking that statements be prepared for development proposals in their area. In relation to workplace developments, it seems likely that the improved operation of EIAs will become an obstacle to out of town development on environmentally sensitive sites, and to large developments with major traffic impacts. By contrast, it will favour developments which involve the reclamation and reuse of derelict land, and which are well served by public transport.

Second, the EC is currently looking at taking environmental assessment one step back in the process by extending environmental assessment requirements to 'plans, policies, and programmes'. This will include land use plans and transport policies and could have important longer term impacts on regional and sub-regional locational strategies in relation to commercial development[22].

Agricultural policy and nature conservation

Historically the quality of agricultural land has been of central concern to authorities assessing the environmental impact of developments on green field sites. In the mid-1980s, with the growth of agricultural surpluses and accompanying forecasts that large areas of farmland in the EC might be withdrawn from production in the next two decades, the scarcity of good agricultural land became less of a concern. Advice to planning authorities from the UK Department of the Environment began to make reference to the inherent environmental qualities of potential development sites, and to reduce the emphasis placed on the agricultural impacts of a development.

This trend is not likely to be reversed and changing criteria of environmental value are likely to affect development decisions in rural and peri-urban areas. Greater importance is being attached to nature conservation and landscape protection. The number of Sites of Special Scientific Interest (SSSI) is growing. Whereas development is not entirely ruled out on such sites, resistance from conservation groups and local residents is likely to be increasingly strong, as shown in recent cases concerning Rainham Marshes in East London, and the Cardiff Bay Redevelopment. New designations and approaches to countryside management are being tried: the development of woods and forests on urban fringes is being encouraged and planned by several authorities. The Countryside Commission is hoping to create a sizeable new forest in the Midlands. In Scotland, National Parks are to be created for the first time. The concept of linking up different protected areas into a connected system is gaining ground as a tool of countryside management, and several continental countries are experimenting with the recreation of degraded habitats and the development of 'ecological corridors' linking sites. Developments which disrupt ecological networks of this kind will be unacceptable.

Some recent developments have been permitted on SSSIs or similar sites where there has been a commitment by the developer to recreate a similar site elsewhere or to transplant part of the soil and vegetation to a new location. Generally, however, such schemes represent an unsatisfactory compromise from a conservation point of view. It can take hundreds of years to recreate a complex habitat, if it is possible at all, and the results of transplants have yet to be seen.

Agricultural land is also being re-evaluated from an environmental standpoint in several parts of the country. There are to date 21 'environmentally sensitive areas' within which farmers are paid to maintain or establish non-intensive farming methods with some element of conservation. Their number may have increased following a review in 1991. In 1990, the government announced an entirely new type of designated area – the Nitrate Sensitive Area[23]. Although relatively small, they may only be the beginning of a policy whereby farmers are paid to reduce the intensity of farming in order to cut pollution, especially nitrates leaching to ground water. Farming is placed under new restrictions in these areas and arable production may cease altogether, even on good well-drained soils. In the longer run such areas may be diverted to other uses including recreation, woodland, conservation, and, where appropriate, development.

Global warming

There remains some confusion about the facts of global warming, and whether it will really impact on policy in the foreseeable future. It is therefore worth setting down what is known, and what is predicted with varying degrees of certainty.

According to the Intergovernmental Panel on Climate Change (IPCC)[24] there is unequivocal scientific evidence that:

• There is a greenhouse effect by which certain gases trap the escape of infrared radiation and keep the earth warmer than it would otherwise be. This effect has always operated and is a prerequisite to life on earth.

• Greenhouse gas concentrations in the atmosphere have increased significantly since the start of the industrial revolution. The principal causes are: carbon dioxide from fossil fuel burning and deforestation; nitrous oxides from fuel combustion and applied fertilisers; methane from animals and refuse decomposition, and chlorofluorocarbons (CFCs) in refrigerants, aerosols and foam propellants.

• The effects of rising concentrations of carbon gases are very long lasting. Even if we ceased all emissions tomorrow it would take more than 100 years before greenhouse gas concentrations return to pre-industrial levels.

The IPCC has predicted with varying degrees of certainty that:

• There has been a warming of the earth this century as a result of increases in greenhouse gas concentrations.

• Projected concentrations of greenhouse gases could lead to global mean temperature increases of 0.2 – 0.5°C per decade.

• Global warming may result in sea level rises, and damage to agricultural and natural systems.

The policy implications of global warming

Global warming is a global problem requiring internationally agreed action to stabilise the atmosphere through global reductions in greenhouse gas emissions and mitigate the impacts that will result from climate change. The UK is working internationally with the Organisation for Economic Co-operation and Development, the Intergovernmental Panel on Climate Change, and the EC to develop an internationally agreed programme of action. At the time of writing various targets have been discussed but none agreed. As Prime Minister, Margaret Thatcher committed herself to a target of a freeze on carbon emissions at current levels by 2005 if other nations took similar action. A range of policy tools may be used in the implementation of any target reductions in emissions including:

• the use of alternative technologies and fuels in electricity generation – moving from coal to nuclear, gas, renewables, and Combined Heat and Power

• energy efficiency in buildings, industry, homes, appliances, equipment and transport

• halting deforestation

• reducing leakage of hydrocarbons.

Energy supply and use in buildings

Buildings are directly and indirectly responsible for 50% of the UK's carbon emissions. Non-domestic buildings account for 40% of this; 20% of the UK's carbon emissions. It is widely agreed that energy efficiency in buildings is a key to any policy to reduce the UK's contribution to the greenhouse effect. In 1989 the House of Commons Energy Committee conducted an Inquiry into 'Energy Policy Implications of the Greenhouse Effect' in which it stated:

> the most striking feature of our Inquiry has been the extent to which improvements in energy efficiency – across all sectors of the economy – are almost universally seen as the most obvious and most effective response to the problem of global warming.[25]

The key attractions of energy efficiency building policies are the massive potential for reducing energy use, and therefore carbon emissions; the existence of proven and cost effective energy efficiency technologies with which to achieve these cuts, and the immediate and substantial savings that can be achieved through piecemeal investment – compared to, say, investment in new supply options, which takes years to implement. These attractions of energy efficiency as a policy tool have been expounded for many years, but there have been important obstacles to the take-up of measures in the UK, namely: the need for a very large number of small disaggregated actions; the fact that energy costs are peripheral to the main interests of most building occupants, and that the most cost-effective opportunities are limited because of the slow turnover in buildings and building equipment.

Past experience suggests that strong interventionist policies are needed to overcome these obstacles and bring about substantial energy efficiency investment. It is not clear that such policies will be forthcoming. The 1990 White Paper indicates that the main policy tools will continue to be: promotion and advice; improved fabric insulation standards and energy labelling schemes for equipment and buildings. A carbon tax may well be added to this list when international agreements on global warming targets are reached. In the context of the 1990s these policy tools, in combination with business

environmental policies, may be sufficient to trigger a new attitude to energy efficiency in workplace developments. If this happens a number of new trends may emerge in workplace design including:

- the avoidance of air conditioning wherever possible (as this creates year round heat loads)

- the use of new types of energy efficient heating plant (for example, gas condensing boilers, mini-CHP)

- fabric insulation decisions based not on minimum standards, but on optimal cost effectiveness given rising energy prices

- the use of low energy lighting and office equipment (for example, laptops) both to save energy directly and to reduce building heat gains

- more emphasis on passive heating and renewable technologies.

Transport

The 1980s saw government transport policy play a key role in business locational strategies – new edge of town and out of town development growth corridors emerged along new motorways and bypasses. From an environmental point of view these policies have been disastrous. Motorways and their associated developments have damaged some of Britain's most beautiful landscapes. Vehicle passenger miles have greatly increased as more people have driven to work and staff catchment areas have greatly expanded. This has resulted in increased vehicle emissions and worsening congestion in the South East. What does the future hold for the car, and how will future transport policy impact on workplace development?

The future of the car is influenced by several environmental considerations. The car's contribution to global warming – in the UK road transport represents 17% of carbon emissions – is a prime consideration. Catalytic converters will do little to reduce these emissions. Second, there is as yet no alternative environmentally friendly engine technology which can achieve widespread use in the foreseeable future. Third, there is increasing and vociferous public disillusion with congestion. Finally, there is a ing lack of investment in the public transport infrastructure.

The Government's policy over the last decade was to support the 'great car economy', and the 1990 White Paper showed little evidence of a change of heart. (Studies have shown an inelasticity in demand for petrol. A recent study showed that a 100% tax on petrol would be needed to materially reduce demand. This could not be imposed without severe economic and political repercussions). As a result, the 1990 White Paper contains few effective proposals for reducing environmental impacts associated with the car. Its main proposals are to civilise traffic in towns through traffic calming; continue its town centre bypass programme and consider lowering speed limits on motorways.

However, the White Paper does begin to set the agenda for the future by its intention to: 'study ways of locating development to reduce travel distance and increase transport choice'[26] In fact, the Department of the Environment has already undertaken preliminary studies along these lines, the results of which unsurprisingly indicated that current dispersed development strategies are very energy inefficient, and that greater transport energy efficiency could be achieved by concentrating development in or near medium-sized towns[27].

In practice the results of such research could quite rapidly hold important implications for the location of future developments. The costs of implementation would be low, and the objectives would fall in line with other environmental factors such as a preference for siting development on reclaimed derelict land and in locations offering greater transport choice.

Hazardous building materials

The introduction of the Control of Substances Hazardous to Health Regulations (COSHH) 1988 has placed a responsibility on all employers to monitor and limit occupational exposure to hazardous substances. Although COSHH does not prohibit the use of hazardous substances, an increasing number of both developers and workspace users are responding to it by seeking to omit hazardous substances from building specifications so that no health and safety risk is presented either during the construction process, or when the building is occupied. Rosehaugh plc's development brief,

for instance, discourages the use of man-made mineral fibres, except in sealed condition, asbestos and lead in exposed conditions[28].

Several developers, including Rosehaugh and Stanhope, also have policies to avoid where practical the use of substances which have wider environmental impacts, such as tropical hardwoods and CFCs (generally briefs advise on the use of the lower ozone-depleting CFCs such as R22 or R123 as refrigerants). In practice these are token policies in an industry which is by and large a thoughtless user of raw materials and energy, and which produces a wide range of environmental impacts at all stages of the building materials manufacturing and construction processes. These processes include the extraction of raw materials, causing, for example, destruction of habitat, localised pollution and depletion of natural resources; building material manufacturing processes, many of which are energy intensive and generate polluting wastes; the transportation of building materials, resulting in pollution and depletion of natural resources, and demolition and disposal processes which may result in pollution. Little work has been carried out on these 'cradle to grave' environmental impacts of building construction activity.

At present, however, the limited information available about environmental impacts such as these makes it difficult to make informed environmental decisions: such as choosing between different brands of the same product (for example, a brick) on the basis of comparative environmental performance of the manufacturers; or substituting one building material for another (for example, composite board in place of lump wood timber).

The European harmonisation of building products standards through the implementation of the EC's Construction Products Directive (CPD)[29] will begin to change this. The CPD is intended to provide for the free movement, sale and use of construction products through the unification and harmonisation of standards and regulations. An EC mark of approval will act as a passport for construction products. Under the new CPD, manufacturers will have to prove the fitness of a product for its intended use. The definition of 'fitness' has been extended to include questions on the environment and energy consumption, health and safety. The implementation of the CPD will make available to the UK developer technologies and products of higher environmental performance in their manufacture and in use. This will open up new options for improving the environmental performance in terms of manufacture, use and disposal of building materials and components.

Conclusions

This paper has outlined how a range of environmental pressures for change from the public, government and businesses as users of space will impact on economic activity in general and decisions on workplace design and use in particular. The discussion raises several questions which are dealt with below.

How fast will the pace of change be?

This will depend on several factors, including the health of the economy – a healthier economy will lead to a faster pace of change; the emergence of further scientific evidence on the implications of global warming and other environmental issues; the growth of public pressure for action, and the responses of business and government to the above. However, what is clear is that the timescales being discussed for the implementation of policies on key issues such as global warming and the phasing-out of CFCs range between 5 and 15 years. From the point of view of the design and use of the workplace, all the factors discussed in this paper will, the author believes, impinge on decision making in the short to medium term. Stated another way, progressive developers, designers and users are considering these factors already, or will begin to do so shortly. Reactive developers, designers and users may defer their response on these fronts by a few years.

What will be the limits of private action on these fronts?

It is safe to assume that business will only respond to the environmental challenge to the extent that it serves a commercial interest to do so. There are four key factors which will drive this commercial interest:

● *Changing market for environmental goods and services.* The demand for 'greener' goods

and services will be worth £15 billion in the UK by 1995. The demand for 'greener' buildings and design services is a part of this. Developers and designers who fail to respond to this changing market will risk losing market share. The later they leave their response, the greater the risk.

● *Changing staff and investor expectations.* Staff will increasingly look to the quality of the work environment and also to the environmental reputation of their prospective employer when deciding who to work for. In terms of the workplace this is feeding through as a requirement from corporate building users (especially manufacturing or energy companies with major environmental impacts). Companies will increasingly wish to appear to their staff and investors as environmentally responsible as possible, and this will feed directly into their workplace briefing and procurement practices.

● *Changing legislative standards.* The 1990s will witness renewed legislative vigour at both national and EC levels with regard to environmental standards. This will hold wide ranging impacts for new workplace developments which will filter through in the areas of development location; site choice; heritage protection; energy use in buildings; the use of hazardous and environmentally deleterious materials, and design and management to ensure healthy buildings.

How will the pattern of response differ across Europe?

Although EC legislation will seek to harmonise standards, the process of harmonisation will be slow, and different countries will develop at different paces in different areas. The current pattern of progress on environmental issues illustrates this patchiness. In general terms, as the Touche Ross study and a recent study by ECOTEC have shown, Holland and Scandinavia are more advanced on these issues than southern European Countries such as Italy, Spain, Greece and even France[30]. The UK is strong on some fronts (for example, land reclamation, heritage protection) and weak on others (clean production, energy efficiency in buildings).

What are the key implications of all this for the design and use of workplaces in the 1990s?

In terms of workplace design and use, environmental issues will lead to changing requirements in terms of location, design and use of buildings. The following pressures will apply:

Location
- siting to reduce transport energy use through review of development land use patterns
- better accessibility by public transport and to amenities
- a preference for development on disused, derelict or contaminated land
- avoidance of SSSIs and other sites of landscape value.

Site
- stronger development guidelines defining site objectives, massing and materials to ensure that designs are better integrated with their surroundings
- use of planning agreements to derive environmental improvements
- landscaping strategies directed at creating and enhancing habitat.

Building envelope
- improved energy efficiency of building fabric, and greater use of passive solar gain to reduce energy loads
- reduced 'cradle to grave' environmental impacts of building materials, plant equipment, furniture and fittings
- increased use of recycled and reconstituted materials.

Building services
- greater reliance on natural ventilation and light
- improved energy efficiency of heating and ventilation plant and lighting equipment
- use of mini-CHP
- substitution of CFC refrigerants

- more emphasis on personal control over environmental conditions
- increased use of energy and building management systems.

Building fit-out
- concern for the 'cradle to grave' impacts of visible materials and furnishings
- avoidance of materials and furnishings which pose a hazard to health
- development of a 'green aesthetic' based on minimising the use of materials, and greater emphasis on durability
- interior layouts determined by the concern to avoid sick building syndrome.

Facilities management
- reliance on the principle of 'Best Alternative Technology Not Entailing Excessive Costs' when making procurement decisions
- implementation of building and office environment audits
- energy management programmes
- minimisation and recycling of office wastes
- 'green' supplier policies
- office smoking policies.

References

1 Jacobs E and Worcester, R, *We British: Britain under the Moriscope*, Weidenfeld and Nicolson, 1990.
2 Ibid
3 Mintel, Special Report: *The Green Consumer*, Mintel, 1989.
4 Jacobs E and Worcester, R, *We British: Britain under the Moriscope*, Weidenfeld and Nicolson, 1990.
5 Mintel, Special Report: *The Green Consumer*, Mintel, 1989.
6 Barker, S, in *The Observer*, September 1990
7 'The Environment Survey', *The Economist*, 8 September 1990
8 Council Directive 85/337/EEC: *The Assessment of the Effects of Certain Public and Private Projects on the Environment*, OJ, No L175, 5 July 1985.
9 Council Directive 89/106/EEC: *The Approximation of the Laws Regulations and Administrative Provisions of Member States Relating to Construction Products*, OJL 40/12 11 February 1989.
10 *This Common Inheritance: Britain's Environmental Strategy*. Cm 1200, London HMSO, 1990.

11 The basis of this approach is outlined in: Pearce. D, Markadya, A, Barbier, D, in *Blueprint for a Green Economy*, Earthscan 1989.

12 Touche Ross Management Consultants, *Head in the Clouds or Head in the Sand: UK Managers' Attitudes to Environmental Issues*, Touche Ross,1990.

13 Elkington, J, *The Environmental Audit: A Green Filter for Company Policies, Plants, Processes, and Products*, World Wildlife Fund for Nature, 1990.

14 Ibid

15 *IBM's Environmental Policy*, a talk by Brian Whittaker at the ET90 Futures Conference, 20 September 1990.

16 Lowenthal, D, *Landscape Research Group Conference on Landscape and National Identity*, University of Nottingham, 7–9 September 1990

17 Clifford, S, 'Cultural Landscapes: Particularity and Identity. Aspects of Local Distinctiveness, Common Ground', *Landscape Research Group Conference on Landscape and National Identity*, University of Nottingham, 7–9 September 1990

18 *This Common Inheritance: Britain's Environmental Strategy*. Cm 1200, London HMSO, 1990, p118

19 Ibid, p119

20 McDonic, G, Nelson, P, Lee N & Colley R, papers delivered at the conference on Environmental Assessment, University of Manchester. *Environmental Impact Analysis 33: the First 18 months, Ends Report 180,* Environmental Data Services, January 1990

21 *This Common Inheritance: Britain's Environmental Strategy*. Cm 1200, London HMSO, 1990, p88

22 *Environmental Impact Analysis 33: the First 18 months, Ends Report 180*, Environmental Data Services, January 1990, p19

23 *This Common Inheritance: Britain's Environmental Strategy*. Cm 1200, London HMSO, 1990, p168

24 Intergovernmental Panel on Climate Change, *Policymaker's Summary of the Scientific Assessment of Climate Change*, WMO and UNEP, 1990.

25 *Energy Policy Implications of the Greenhouse Effect*, Volume 1, 6th Report of the House of Commons Energy Committee, HMSO, 1989.

26 *This Common Inheritance: Britain's Environmental Strategy*. Cm 1200, London HMSO, 1990, p87

27 Steadman J P, Barrett M, *The Potential Role of Town and Country Planning in reducing Carbon Emissions*, Open University/ERR, 1990.

28 Rosehaugh Project Services plc, *Environmental Design Brief*, Rosehaugh plc, 1990.

29 Council Directive 89/106/EEC: *The Approximation of the Laws Regulations and Administrative Provisions of Member States Relating to Construction Products*, OJL 40/12 11 February 1989.

30 ECOTEC, *Head in the Clouds or Head in the Sand: the UK Pollution Control Industry*, ECOTEC, 1990.

9 The changing geography of location

Brian McDougall, EAL Property Research Consultants

Summary

Offices have become more footloose. Advances in telecommunications and office automation, transport and business infrastructure improvements, and international migration opportunities are seen as liberating influences on workplace location.

Offices remain highly concentrated across Europe at regional and sub-regional levels, although large urban centres have been declining in relative importance. Manufacturing and office functions are becoming blurred especially for technologically oriented companies. Prestige is no longer only associated with city centres.

Control and co-ordinating functions are being dispersed from headquarters to regional and divisional levels allowing more local management autonomy. Specialist and less location dependent activities are being relocated away from central high cost areas. The function of the back office is changing. Labour, communications and support service inputs for offices are becoming less locally based with improved technology and mobility, and changing working practices. Locational dependency of all types of offices is weaker, except for those marketing final services and those in concentrated markets.

Pressures for change on location in the future include the increasing proportion of office-based work undertaken from home or other remote locations and staff expectations of improved quality in the workplace environment. The economic push to devolve office work is limited by the extent to which new technology can support dispersed working patterns over the short term. Nevertheless, office operations will have much more locational freedom resulting in a selective pattern of de-urbanisation.

Introduction

A significant element of change in the office workplace has been, and will increasingly be, location. Office activities are already widely perceived to have become more 'footloose' and although the scale and significance of current relocation activity is often overstated, there can be little doubt that a number of factors – economic, demographic, strategic, operational, technological, environmental, political and social – are facilitating or prompting office occupiers to consider alternative working or locational arrangements, either in piecemeal or wholesale fashion.

On the positive side there are liberating telecommunication and office automation advances, transport and business infrastructure improvements and international migration opportunities, coupled with some major rethinking of effective company organisation in the context of European harmonisation in 1992. On the negative side, occupiers are having to respond to intensifying business, social and infrastructure pressures which have focused minds on locational issues at both operational and, increasingly, strategic levels. This paper examines these trends and pressures for change in the office workplace from a locational perspective, and sketches out the expected future geography of location for the next 10 years or more.

An office location model

Choice of office location at the national, region or sub-regional level is determined by up to nine key factors. Some are critical to the location decision for different occupiers, most are important only to varying degrees:

- business sector: business sector affinity and associated preferences or norms

- office type: whether it is a headquarters, regional or branch office

- office function: whether it performs a narrow or broad range of front or back office functions and associated internal or external interfacing requirements

- office inputs: the sources and availability of inputs required and the size of property requirements

- office outputs: whether the business services typically produced are internally or externally marketed

- office markets: the extent to which markets or activities for which the office is responsible are concentrated or diversified

- office technology: the extent to which the office can utilise technological advances

- internal influences: for example, staff preferences, management inertia

- external influences: government policy, legislation and the operating environment.

No definitive weighting of the respective importance of these factors is possible which would be equally applicable to all office occupiers. Requirements and preferences vary, particularly at the sub-regional level, according to business sector, operational function, corporate culture, executive preferences and size of firm.

With corporate growth and diversification has come an increase in the complexity of office types. For simplicity of analysis we typically only split these into two types: headquarters and back offices. None the less, size, specialisation and functionality create a spectrum of locational choice, diminishing the usefulness of such a distinction. Functional definitions of the office are more useful in this respect.

The functions of an office are more numerous and may be either very narrowly or very broadly defined. Back offices range from being fairly narrowly defined cost centres carrying out labour intensive and low value added processing operations, to operational support centres encompassing finance, personnel, marketing and administration functions. Front office activ-

ities typically include main and divisional headquarters functions and those operations requiring direct client contact such as sales, marketing and client support. For the purposes of this paper, four types of front office and five types of back office activity are proposed:

Front office
- group front office (headquarters)
- divisional front office (headquarters)
- sales and marketing
- external operational support.

Back office
- internal operational support (for example, finance, administration, personnel)
- research and development
- client servicing and telesales
- general administrative support
- Special administrative support (for example, data centres).

Control and co-ordinating functions have typically remained at the headquarters level in the past, although responsibilities are increasingly being redefined, resulting in dispersal of these activities to regional and divisional levels to allow more local management autonomy. As a result, the functions, responsibilities and importance of back offices are changing.

Required inputs of an office vary considerably between the types of facility. However, there are certain location-sensitive inputs – labour, communications and support services – which will directly affect future office dispersal. While many of these inputs have had to be locally based in the past, this perspective is changing with the introduction of new office technologies, improved mobility and changing working attitudes. Office outputs now only tend to affect locational choice when the facility is responsible for externally marketing the final services of the branch, division or corporation as a whole.

When markets are concentrated, occupiers will tend to agglomerate, particularly when it affects their front office functions. However, paperless transacting and electronic trading reduce the size and nature of such physical locational needs. Related to this, the effective utilisation of technology will reduce the locational dependency of all types of office. While this has already been witnessed to some extent, speed of acceptance, cost and local inability to introduce advances (for lack of infrastructure, topographical or other reasons) may still inhibit more radical locational decision making for some time to come.

Management and staff attitudes and expectations can also seriously constrain or facilitate locational choice. Natural inertia, tradition and senior management preferences, however, could be increasingly outweighed by staff lifestyle and workstyle expectations.

Similarly, the framework within which occupiers must operate exerts an influence on locational choice. Legislation (for example, the uniform business rate), government policy (Green Belt policy, Use Class Orders or local economic initiatives) and the operating environment (European harmonisation) will all influence future locational choice.

These influences, pressures, catalysts and constraints on each of the nine office location variables are considered in more detail below.

Past and present geography of location

Past and present location criteria

The key determinants of office location in the past were the nature of office outputs, whether or not these were externally marketed, and the location of markets[1]. These factors necessitated face-to-face contact, ease of travel and communication and an ability to attract top executives, most of whom were found in larger cities. Companies moving to the periphery or to smaller centres did so for reasons of property availability, labour supply and cost, but they made destination decisions almost entirely on the basis of accessibility, given a continuing need for face-to-face communication with clients, contacts and suppliers.

More recent office location criteria suggest that the focus of occupiers has changed – input considerations now outweigh output concerns – but remains risk-averse and operational in nature and, in many cases, short term in perspective as an immediate response to growing business and labour market pressures. For example, in a major Price Waterhouse/Confederation of British Industry survey of over 50

companies carried out in 1988[2], access to good communications networks was still found to be the single most important location selection criterion. Together with local labour supply and quality of environment, these three factors outweigh all other location selection criteria (Figure 9.1).

In a similar survey of 52 European 'high growth potential' companies, access to good road and rail communications was mentioned by 9 out of 10 respondents[3]. This was followed closely by the quality and prestige of local environment (including the presence of a critical mass of similar types of occupier), airport communications and a suitable labour supply. The result has been continuing high levels of concentration of office activities across Europe at both the regional and sub-regional levels for all types of office occupier, regardless of sector, status and, in the vast majority of cases, function. Nevertheless, the largest urban centres have been declining in relative importance in recent years. The reasons for this are related to business, infrastructure and lifestyles. They include:

• The development of more extensive and integrated road, rail, air communication and telecommunication networks extending beyond the major metropolitan areas.

• Longer distance staff commuting patterns and the growth of the suburbs as a suitable office location. Many companies realise that most of the benefits of a city can still be reaped from a more suburban location, whilst taking advantage of lower occupancy costs, less congestion, increased flexibility and potential for growth, a better working environment, and at the same time offering closer proximity to where managers and staff actually live.

• Further afield, regional centres, which enjoyed a degree of success in attracting light manufacturing and low level service activities, developed many of the attributes and business infrastructure requirements to support office functions. Other peripheral centres were man made to ease development, congestion and growth pressures in the major city centres, for example, Milton Keynes in the UK, La Defense in Paris.

• A blurring of distinctions between many manufacturing and office operations,

Figure 9.1
*Office location criteria
current determinants.
(Source: EAL, sample
base PW/CBI 50
firms EAL 52 firms)*

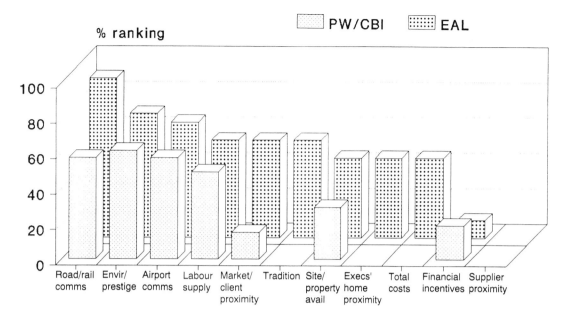

particularly with technology-oriented
companies. Provision of suitable
accommodation to meet resulting property
requirements, such as B1, business park, and
more bespoke office space, has often only
been possible or desirable in less built-up or
new environments.

• Intensifying cost, labour, organisational and
property pressures on occupiers to break up
large office operations and relocate more
specialist or less location dependent activities,
either by function or division.

• Prestige is no longer only associated with a
city centre or capital location.

• Quality of working environment has become
more important and has been redefined by
occupiers and their staff.

• Perhaps most important of all, many more
occupiers now realise the direct implications
for future competitiveness of having suitable,
contented and cost-effective labour skills.

These trends have all contributed to a significant lessening in both office concentration
and urbanisation which is most apparent in the
amount of office dispersal that has taken place
in recent years.

Dispersal of office activities

In the UK, the vast majority of office dispersal
has been from Central and Greater London.

Relocation activity was at its peak during the
recession of the mid-1970s. However, there has
been a significant upswing in recent times
and, more importantly, the number of jobs at
stake has increased dramatically (Figures 9.2
and 9.3). Reasons for decentralisation vary
considerably between occupiers and include
perennial financial, organisational and staffing
concerns (Figure 9.4). However, a discernible
trend has been the significant increase in
occupiers relocating for economic reasons,
either due to labour or office costs. The
majority of companies relocate over relatively
short distances. Almost 50% of moves since
1983 have been to Greater London and almost
90% of occupiers remained within the South
East region. The M25 remains a boundary for
many occupiers. Only one corporate relocation
into Continental Europe has been registered to
date.

Longer distance relocations are a fairly recent phenomenon, many prompted by political
encouragement in an attempt to pump prime
depressed regions. However, selection on
purely commercial grounds would also now
appear to be increasing: 55% of all public and
private sector moves already planned for the
early part of the 1990s are to destinations
outside the South East, most notably the North,
North West and Midlands. More importantly, the
experiences of Manchester and Glasgow suggest that higher status office functions are now
more footloose[4]. At the sub-regional level, the

availability of a suitable site or property is normally secondary to locational choice unless the occupier has a particularly demanding property requirement or timing constraint.

At this stage in the decision process, the Price Waterhouse/CBI survey found that the prime consideration of the typical office occupier was the availability of a suitable size of building and the ability to expand in the future, regardless of specification or precise location. However, the occupier's decision is also tem-

pered by considerations of image, security and the quality of surrounding occupiers. These issues rank well above financial elements, such as rents, rates and incentives, which tend to be taken as given, within certain parameters, once the location decision has been made.

Notably, particularly in contrast to the diminishing office concentration already highlighted, occupiers will often give key consideration to existing local workforce commuting preferences to maximise their potential labour catch-

Figure 9.2
Office dispersal 1964–1991 Central London
(Sources: Jones Lang Wootton and EAL)

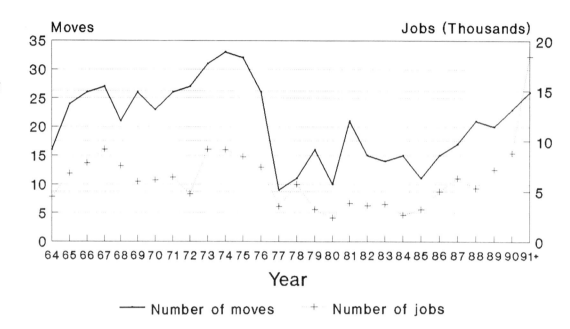

Figure 9.3
Central London 1964–1990 5-year moving averages (Sources: EAL after London Office Bureau and Jones Lang Wootton)

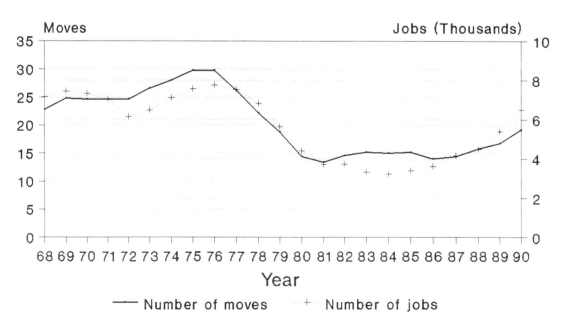

ment and attract staff from other employers. Within any constraints imposed by required building size, specification and working environment, this still tends to channel occupiers towards established areas of high amenity (public transport, shopping, housing) either in traditional city centres, more residential suburbs or out of town developments offering sufficient critical mass.

Future geography of location

Pressures and catalysts for change

There are numerous and often conflicting operational, organisational, economic and general trends that are expected to impact upon future office geography in the UK and the rest of Europe.

Business and social needs

Fundamental business and social elements of change within the office environment present a convincing argument for predicting the longer term demise of major cities as the focus of office activity:

- Business activities are becoming more 'footloose' thereby diminishing the traditional locational advantages of cities.

- An accelerating rate of corporate and organisational change, related to the extent and speed of introduction of technological and communications developments will enable an increasing proportion of office-based work to be carried out from the home or a more remote location.

- Telecommuting and homeworking will therefore allow an increasing number and range of individuals to work from wherever they choose. Current survey evidence suggests the preferences of staff who have the ability to select where they work and live are unequivocally in favour of non-urban locations[5].

- Rising direct and indirect (for example, congestion, absenteeism, shortages) occupancy costs in the major cities.

- Pressures to respond to staff expectations and demands to improve the working environment.

- The social role of the city is gradually being undermined by an increasing preference for more individual, home-based lifestyles.

However, against this, any large scale impetus towards de-urbanisation may be inhibited by the following influences and perceptions:

- *Dual career households.* Both partners often have careers, particularly in the South. The ability of new working arrangements to meet the career requirements of both partners and possibly to enable retention of an established

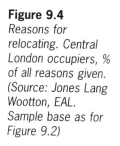

Figure 9.4
Reasons for relocating. Central London occupiers, % of all reasons given. (Source: Jones Lang Wootton, EAL. Sample base as for Figure 9.2)

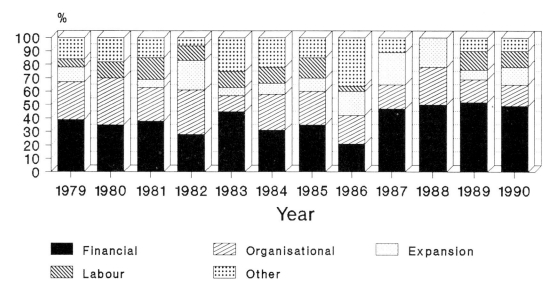

career in the original location may call into doubt longer distance relocation of businesses from established business centres. However, homeworking by one or both partners could overcome this obstacle.

● *Career development prospects.* The percentage of the workforce with degrees is highest in the South East and school leavers' qualifications are highest in the South East (outside London), East Midlands and the South West. While this is obviously a function of current job availability and career development prospects, there may be resistance from staff, at least in the short term, to the prospect of being left 'out of touch', despite increasing lifestyle preference for non-urban locations.

● *North-South divide.* The divergence in prosperity between the North and the South has created barriers to staff mobility and locational choice. Perceptions (and misperceptions) of areas in the 'North', for example between Bristol and Birmingham or Warwick and Coventry, are important in this respect and this is likely to restrict the scope of de-urbanisation, certainly to within the boundary of the divide.

Transport and accessibility

Journey times by road, rail and air between major cities and abroad remain of central importance to office occupiers' choice of location. Large scale (mainly road) transport infrastructure projects such as the M25 in the UK have already demonstrated their regional and national influence. A number of specific road, rail and air transport and other planned infrastructure projects in the 1990s, which can be expected to improve the locational attractiveness of host and in some cases adjacent regions have been identified in Table 1. Areas in the UK likely to benefit most from improved accessibility are:

● Locations on the fringe of the South East region which will be brought into easy commuting and daily business travel distance to London as a result of rail electrification, although at a substantially increased price. The 1989 Central London Rail Study predicts such travel will grow by 30–40% between 1986–2001[6].

● The M11 corridor.

● The M40 extension corridor (Oxford to Birmingham).

● Kent, and most particularly Ashford, as a result of the Channel Tunnel.

● East London and other local areas within conurbations where the introduction of passenger light rail systems and other transport improvements are proposed (for example, Bristol, Greater Manchester, Leeds, Sheffield, Tyne and Wear, the West Midlands, Southampton and Croydon).

The locational impacts of the Channel Tunnel are likely to be largely confined to London, the South East and Northern France, at least in the medium term. Accessibility from elsewhere in the UK is believed to be too restrictive to have a wider impact[7]. Moreover, the vast majority of firms likely to be affected appears to be in the producer rather than service sector.

London is currently one of the best served international gateways of any European centre and this position is likely to be further enhanced with the opening of the Channel Tunnel. However, limited transport capacity means that many of the increased benefits of foreign business may not accrue to London, but to the rest of the South East[8].

Demographic and workforce trends

Availability of suitable labour within a defined local catchment and the ability to transfer staff from current sites assume great importance in occupiers' locational choice. By the year 2001, the population of working age in the UK is expected to rise by only 0.6 million from 1988 levels. This compares with an increase of 2.4 million in the previous 13 year period and an expected overall increase in the labour force of only 0.8 million over the period through increased rates of participation.

Forecasts of future labour supply indicate that far fewer young people will be entering the labour market. Available labour in the UK aged under 25 is expected to fall by 1.1 million over this period. Demand, however, is expected to continue to grow. Almost all of the projected national increase (over 90%) is expected to be among women, who are predicted to make up 45% of the labour force by 2001[9].

Table 9.1 Planned transport infrastructure schemes

Region	Date	Location	Scheme
Scotland	1992	Cumbernauld	M80 extension
		West Coast	A74 upgrading to motorway standard
	1993	Glasgow	Urban rail upgrading
		Edinburgh	Urban rail upgrading
		East Coast	BR electrification
North West	1992	Manchester	Airport improvements
		Manchester	Light rail P1
	1993	Manchester – Birmingham	M6 relief motorway
		Manchester	Northern relief road
		Salford	Light rail P2
		Manchester	Airport rail spur
		West Coast	BR/Channel Tunnel upgrading
Yorkshire & Humberside	1992	Sheffield	Light rail P1
		Leeds	Light rail P1
		Leeds	A1/M1 link
	1993	East Coast	Proposed east coast motorway
East Midlands	1992	Kettering	A1/M1 link
	1993	East Coast	Proposed motorway
		East Coast	BR electrification
West Midlands	1992	Warwick	M90 extension
		Birmingham/Wolverhampton	Light rail proposals
	1993	Birmingham	Airport extension
		Birmingham	Northern Relief road
		Birmingham	Proposed M6 relief motorway
		West Coast	BR/Channel Tunnel upgrading
Wales	1995	Severn	2nd crossing
East Anglia	1992	Stansted	Airport improvements
	1993	Stansted	Bishops Stortford – airport rail link
		East Coast	Proposed motorway (M11–Humber Bridge)
		East Coast	BR/Channel Tunnel upgrading
North	1992	Newcastle	Metro/airport link
South East	1992	Docklands	DLR extensions – Bank, Becton, Lewisham
		Orbital	M25 upgrade to four lanes
		London	Red road routes
		Oxford	M40 extension
		London/Ashford	Road/rail upgrading
		Guildford/Redhill	BR electrification
	1993	Maidstone/Ashford	M20 extension/upgrade
		London	Paddington/Heathrow link
		London	East London River Crossing
		Docklands	Jubilee line extension
		London	Cross-London rail link
		Dartford	Lower Thames crossing
		Kent/Hants	East-West strategic road link
		SW/NW	M3–M40 link
		London/Bristol	BR electrification
		Southampton	Light rail scheme
		Croydon	Light rail scheme
South West	1991	Bristol	Light rail scheme
		Bristol/London	BR electrification
		Severn	2nd crossing
Northern Ireland	1992	Stranraer/Carlisle	A76 Euroroute
		Eastern Seaboard	Rail link upgrade

Source: EAL

In the South East, over 80% of the population of working age already have jobs, compared with 65% in Wales and only 60% in Northern Ireland. In the coming decade, participation rates are projected to rise still further due to labour shortages. By the late 1990s, the South East may have reached the upper limit of possible participation at 85% or more, despite continuing migration southwards, most of which is expected to go, as in the past, to East Anglia and the South West[10].

The regional effects of the falling number of young labour market entrants will be most marked in the North and the Midlands (where traditional manufacturing industry relies on young apprentices) and in the South East. Elsewhere, the service sector may compensate for such shortages by making employment more attractive to married women and older segments of the population. However, this will rely heavily on employers' initiatives to maximise flexibility by offering re-training programmes, together with part time and casual working arrangements.

Employers are expected to pay far closer attention to issues of staff expectations and retention, personal career development, wider local company awareness, business priorities, labour saving productivity improvements and, ultimately, locational optimisation.

Key demographic trends are outlined below, together with likely 'winners' and 'losers' from the impending 'demographic timebomb':

- The youngest populations at present (largest proportions aged under 15) are to be found in the North West, West Midlands and Northern Ireland.

- Over the period 1988–2000, regions worst affected by the decline in under-25s will be Scotland, the North, West Midlands, North West, Yorkshire and Humberside. The UK as a whole is projected to experience a 21% drop over this period.

- In all but three regions (Scotland, North West and the North) these falls will be outweighed by rises in numbers of workforce aged 25 and over.

- Female activity rates are projected to continue to rise in all regions, but in three regions – the South West, Wales and East Anglia – the activity rate for females will grow to be within 10 percentage points of the male rate by the year 2000.

- Overall, the most buoyant regional labour supplies in the UK will be found in the South West (+14%) and East Anglia (+13%).

- Labour shortages across much of Europe could lead to a locational pull towards southern European countries – particularly Portugal, Spain, Greece and Ireland – whose demographic profiles suggest that similar shortages of young staff will not occur.

New technology

Considering the impact of new technology from a functional and locational perspective, it is important to look at the changing structure of large knowledge-based firms. Currently, as a rule of thumb, such firms may devote between 40–60% of employment to headquarters activities and the remaining 40–60% to back office activities. In the back office, the labour profile is often at least two thirds clerical – three quarters of whom may be women – and the remaining third professional and managerial[11]. However, there are serious moves afoot by a number of large companies, particularly multinational, financial and high technology firms, to reduce the size and concentration of their international headquarters activities to no more than 20–25% of total personnel. Other functions, presently accounting for up to one third of their traditional headquarters staff, are being devolved. Advances in information technology, office automation and telecommunications, together with spiralling operating costs and changing market geography, are the biggest driving forces behind this emerging trend. The devolved office, regardless of its location, is being seen much less as a processing outpost and much more in terms of its potential to be a specialised, centralised command-and-implementation centre.

The popular view is that, as the use of distributed data processing, printing, storage and electronic means of communication increasingly becomes the norm in the office environment, this will eliminate the need for face-to-face contact and, hence, a city centre headquarters location. Homeworking, teleworking and workstation sharing are increasing in popularity and the advent of personal communication networks (PCNs) will undoubtedly accelerate this trend. In the longer term, traditional methods of office working are likely to become a thing of the past.

However, much of the infrastructure and operating cost savings required for occupiers to exploit these communications and technological advances aimed at eliminating the need for face-to-face contact and increasing the flexibility of locational choice can only be found in the major metropolitan centres at the present time. Continuing limited availability of infrastructure in many provincial and more remote areas, for reasons of topography, occupier critical mass or required investment, could therefore help to reinforce centralisation, particularly of headquarters operations, for some time to come.

The advent of telephony services based on local cable television networks could facilitate more widespread dispersal of such office activities in the longer term, although current experience suggests that many occupiers remain sceptical of the ability of these networks to meet their needs in terms of capacity, interfacing, privacy and cost.

Internal influences and expectations

The impact of executive and staff preferences on location decisions should not be underestimated. In the past this has generally only extended as far as key executives' commuting preferences or lifestyle expectations. However, the process of consultation tends to be broader now, taking into account the views and preferences of line management and operatives, or at least taking note of internal feedback during the option appraisal stage. The extent of this influence is highlighted by the importance now typically placed on lifestyle criteria at the location appraisal stage by larger organisations. These criteria include housing (size of stock, price ranges, quality); education (availability of schools, quality of students); health (availability of facilities); shopping, sports and recreation facilities; arts and entertainment and more general levels of local amenity. Such criteria often rank in importance on a par with many operational requirements (Table 9.2).

Table 9.2 Internal influences and expectations

Best locations for business	
eg	Accessibility
	Operating costs
	Business infrastructure
	Image and excellence
	Labour availability
	Labour suitability
	Site/property availability
	Other operational criteria

Best Locations for living	
eg	Housing availability
	Housing quality/cost
	Educational quality
	Health provision
	Shopping facilities
	Arts and recreation
	Other local amenities
	Dual career households

Source: EAL

External influences: legislation

One of the most critical pieces of legislation to be introduced which will impact upon the future location of office occupiers is the imposition of a Uniform Business Rate (UBR), introduced in 1990, as a replacement for local authority taxes. Under this system, rating assessments for non-domestic properties are based on their annual rental values as at 1 April 1988 and levies based on a national rating multiplier (the UBR) set by the government (at 45p in 1990). The consequence of the UBR is substantially increased occupation costs, particularly for properties which have experienced high rates of rental growth and in regions which have previously benefited from relatively low rate poundages. Worst affected are offices in the West End and City of London, the rest of the South East, East Midlands, South West and East Anglia, with anticipated increases in occupation costs of 25% or more. The implications of this legislation may be either to increase or reduce cost differentials between property types (for example, between B1 and office buildings) in different parts of the country, prompting many occupiers to re-evaluate their occupation strategies. In addition, cost differentials between the North and South will widen, which will improve the relative appeal of less well-established office locations.

External influences: government policies

Government policy has the potential to influence future location decisions in at least two respects: land use policies and local economic initiatives. The general attitude of the current government towards planning policy is positive. There is a general presumption in favour of development and there is a trend towards planning by appeal. Whilst this need have no specific locational effect, there are likely to be continuing pressures for major development activity to be focused in existing areas of high demand (excluding the Green Belt). In the new climate of a much 'greener' UK in the 1990s, it is difficult to envisage the government permitting any significant compromise of current Green Belt policy. The corollary is that future property supply is likely to be pushed to the Green Belt periphery.

The introduction of the B1 Use Class Order has had less impact on occupiers' property and locational demands than was originally expected. This is primarily a consequence of interpretation, both by developers and local authorities. In all but a handful of examples, existing business park developments have failed to meet the expectations or requirements of occupiers in terms of on-site or near-site amenities, accessibility, critical mass, positive management and building specification[12]. Moreover, the criteria indicated for success suggest that very few schemes are likely to be able to match occupiers' expectations in these respects. Similarly, local authorities have continued to exercise planning controls and have contributed to limiting the effective introduction of the legislation in many instances.

There is also a wide range of regional and local economic and planning initiatives in the UK providing various forms of assistance and grants to inward investors and employers.

Examples of such initiatives include Enterprise Zones, which offer a ten year rate-free period, 100% capital allowances and planning freedom; Simplified Planning Zones, Urban Development Corporations, and EC Integrated Development Operations for prioritised areas, offering direct investment and training assistance. Their major impact is likely to be in influencing the location of 'footloose' back offices, although the relative importance of incentives in influencing office location decisions has already been shown to be negligible.

External influences: operating environment, 1992

Locations likely to benefit most from European harmonisation measures are those centres with a competitive advantage. This would be in the form of:

● *Accessibility*. London is currently one of the best served international gateways of any European centre and this position can only be enhanced by the opening of the Channel Tunnel and airport improvements at Stansted.

● *Language*. English is the dominant European language and the second language of the Japanese.

● *Centres of excellence*. A number of professional and business sectors in the UK, for example insurance, finance, telecommunications and medical industries, could be considered to have a competitive advantage over their European rivals. Locational concentration of certain functions in 'centres of excellence' may follow harmonisation on a sector by sector basis. Again, London is among the best placed to benefit.

● *Labour supply*. When barriers are removed, given the distribution of labour and projected shortages of young people across most of the Continent, there could be an influx of labour from southern European countries to major employment centres across Europe. However in the future, as we have already indicated, businesses may prove to be more footloose than people, offering a potential competitive advantage to Portugal, Spain, Greece and Ireland, and a re-united Germany, in being able to attract office occupiers.

Winners and losers – the future demise of the city?

The pressures, catalysts and trends described above have very conflicting implications for the future geography of offices. At a national level, countries with an established or emerging competitive, business or political advantage will undoubtedly benefit. In the context of the UK, at a regional level planned transport and infrastructure improvements are concentrated in the South and future demographic trends would also appear to favour the South and South West. At a sub-regional level, major cities will benefit from urban transport improvements and any geographic limitations of new technology infrastructure on the one hand, but suffer on 'quality of life' and cost considerations. Table 9.3 summarises potential locational 'winners' and 'losers' in response to pressures and catalysts for change. Table 9.4 sums up the arguments for and against the possible demise of the city at the sub-regional level as the focus of future office activities.

Table 9.3 Locational winners and losers

Pressures/Catalysts	Winners	Losers
Internal influences	'Quality of life': low crime: good health/education facilities; low pollution; low cost of living; good housing provision; family/executive ties.	'Inferior' areas: bad congestion; long commuting; poor housing provision; high living cost; poor race relations.
External influences	Uniform Business Rate – winners Green Belt periphery good B1 interp. locs 'competitive adv.' areas for occs + staff	Uniform Business Rate – losers poor B1 interp. locs
Transport + Infrastructure improvements	The south Urban transport improvement areas	Most areas outside the south
Demographic + workforce trends	Areas with most young people; high activity rates; low participation rates; immigration; Southern Europe; Germany	Areas with lowest growth rates; offset factor; high participation rates; service sector bias
New technology	Metropolitan areas/liveable' areas	More remote/low critical mass areas

Source: EAL

Table 9.4 Future demise of the city?

For	Against
– Business activities more footloose	– Concentration of communications and business infrastructure in cities
– Accelerating rate of corporate and organisational change	– Concentration of future transport and infrastructure improvements
– Speed of introduction of technological and communications developments	– Importance of dual career households
– Appeal of telecommuting and homeworking	– Career development prospects and choice outside the major cities for some time to come
– Rising direct and indirect occupancy costs in major cities	– North–South divide
– Demographic trends and pressures to respond to staff expectations	– Government policies: local economic initiatives
– Social role of the city being undermined	– Future operating environment and centres of excellence
– Government policies: Uniform Business Rate	

Source: EAL

More fundamentally, however, the overriding conclusion we arrive at is that most office operations will have much more locational freedom in the future. In practice, national decisions may be made on the basis of any resulting or perceived competitive advantage. Regional decisions will be made by different types of occupier after taking into consideration input pressures, local business infrastructure and lifestyle expectations. Sub-regional decisions will continue to be made on a sectoral, functional or size of requirement basis. The end result is likely to be selective de-urbanisation in the longer term, but largely on a functional basis.

Sectoral preferences

Locational preferences at the sub-regional level differ significantly between types of occupier. Professional firms, with their continuing reliance on face-to-face contact, continue to be unwilling to compromise on proximity to clients, business contacts and competitors, preferring to be in town and under one roof. As an indication of this, all but two of the 588 office-based premises occupied by the 20 largest UK accountancy firms in 1990 were traditional office buildings[13]. The culture and dependencies of the professional sector make firms such as these followers rather than leaders in the shift towards new types of location for office-based functions.

Most financial services and insurance companies also retain a city centre presence, but have a much higher propensity to decentralise particular functions and back office operations. Indeed, in a 1988 study, as many as 25% of major insurance companies were noted as positively preferring edge of town locations[14]. Other office-based sectors, particularly those with less dense floorspace utilisation or more bespoke property requirements, are willing to be based in edge of town and out of town locations. High tech companies are well known for their preference for greenfield and out of town sites. For example, in 1989, central offices only accounted for 24% of floorspace occupied by major computing and electronics companies in the UK (but half of all headquarters buildings) while campus and business park space accounted for almost half of all floorspace occupied by the sector[15].

Consequently, there will remain a perceived graduated scale of choice for office occupiers considering the location of different types of premises. However, any locational correlation that may exist in the future between types of businesses and very limited locational choice will probably be restricted to a handful of sectors – accountants, solicitors, merchant bankers, financial and commodity traders, media and advertising, senior government –

where the nature of their business, their customer base, size of organisational units and requirements for internal and external interfacing and resources continue to warrant a specific location for all or most of their operations.

Functional preferences

Using the front office/back office definitions described above, Figure 9.5 indicates current functional location preferences amongst major office occupiers on a general basis. As one would expect, there is a distinct bias towards in town and edge of town locations for front office, marketing and after sales activities, but the spectrum of perceived choice amongst occupiers does not yet extend to out of town locations. Such activities are estimated to currently account for around 40% to 60% of total employment. In contrast, many back office activities (operational support, R&D and administrative and processing activities) have already been devolved to peripheral and decentralised locations, particularly where organisational units (for example, R&D and data centres) are of a manageable size and fairly self-contained. Such back office activities probably account for the residual 60% to 40% of office employment at present.

Emerging trends, however, suggest that the functional location preferences of larger office

Figure 9.5
Functional location preferences. Current trends. (Source: EAL)

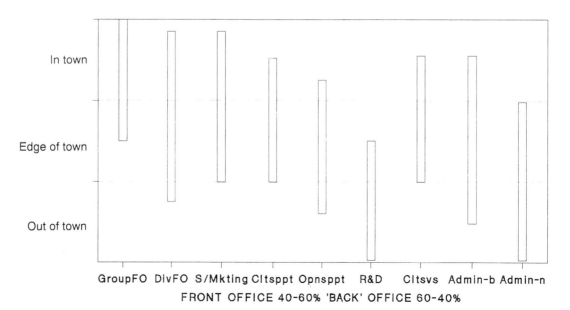

Figure 9.6
Functional location preferences. Possible future trends. (Source: EAL)

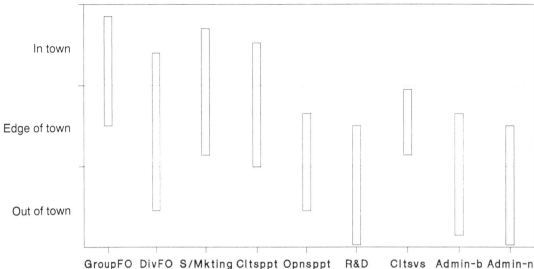

GroupFO DivFO S/Mkting Cltsppt Opnsppt R&D Cltsvs Admin-b Admin-n

FRONT OFFICE 20-25% 'BACK' OFFICE 80-75%

occupiers are continuing to evolve (Figure 9.6). During the 1980s, occupiers were split almost equally between those partially and completely relocating their operations from Central London. However, planned moves over the next few years suggest that many occupiers across a broad spectrum of business and institutional sectors intend to make their operations more divisible, taking advantage of inter-regional cost differentials, slacker provincial labour markets, technological and communications advances and their own more functionally-oriented organisational styles, meanwhile retaining smaller headquarters and client servicing functions in London or the rest of the South East (Table 9.5).

The result is likely to be a structural shift, both in the size and importance of back office operations and in the locational preferences of occupiers for different functional operations. The implications for city centre office markets are enormous. First, front office (and correspondingly mainly city centre) operations in the future may only account for half of current employment levels, seriously reducing the demand for office space in such locations. This will be exacerbated by a redefinition of the spectrum of locational choice for front office activities, with more spatial freedom for divisional and operational support activities likely to result in increased demand for fringe and out of town premises. In the longer term, therefore, the focus of activities remaining in city centre locations may narrow to slimmed down corporate headquarters and showcase operations.

The exceptions to this are likely to include organisations reliant on a large amount of internal cross-selling and constant human interfacing. The continuing major uncertainty in this whole scenario relates to cost. If the supply-demand equation in city centres reaches such an imbalance that occupation costs fall dramatically, our hypothesis may no longer be valid, certainly on such a large scale or within a similar timescale.

Table 9.5 Types of decentralisation

	1963–1978	1979–1982	1983–1986	1987–1989	1990+
Complete	26%	56%	42%	55%	35%
Partial	74%	44%	58%	45%	65%

Note: Pre–1978 data is for Greater London; post – 1978 relates to Central London

Source: EAL after the London Office Bureau and Jones Lang Wootton

The future geography of location

The overriding issues underpinning the future geography of office location must be viewed at three levels: national, regional and sub-regional. At a national level, most office occupiers will undoubtedly have the freedom to locate their back office and, increasingly, a large proportion of their front office operations in any country they choose. Office occupiers will increasingly have to move to where their staff choose to live, or to where the largest pool of labour is, in view of future labour market shortages. Alternatively, they will be able to adopt more readily exploitable working arrangements to accommodate this shortfall and at the same time meet their business needs. Location decisions at national level will be made on the basis of existing and growing business or sectoral centres of excellence; countries and centres of increasing political, financial and market influence; inter and intra-country accessibility, together with a plethora of possible intrinsic business and social attractions: for example, physical, cultural, demographic factors.

At the regional and sub-regional level, we have noted that existing preferences for living and working in major urbanised areas have lessened considerably as a result of lifestyle changes, expectations and concerns. In the UK, people would ideally choose to live and work where there are low crime rates, good health and education facilities and low levels of pollution. Other key factors are relatively low cost of living, housing provision, shopping facilities and, we would anticipate, existing family ties. On this basis, the most 'liveable' towns and cities in the UK are thought to be, in rank order: Edinburgh, Aberdeen, Plymouth and Cardiff. The quality of life in most cities in the South East is perceived to be vastly inferior to the rest of the country[16].

Will the resulting presumption of widespread de-urbanisation therefore happen? Over a number of years, the answer, in my opinion, is affirmative, particularly for cities that are either above a certain mass or of an 'unfavourable' make-up. The latest pattern and scale of relocation activity – and not just decentralisation from London – would appear to go some way to confirming this. The status of functions now being devolved to more accessible parts of the South West, Midlands, North West and even Scotland suggests a strengthening structural shift in occupiers' thinking.

Furthermore, in the new business environment of more positive management of corporate and, most notably, property assets, major 'lead' occupiers' plans to devolve further activities will undoubtedly have a bandwagon effect. This threshold is likely to be breached within the next five years or so.

At the sub-regional level, locational preferences will still be determined to a large extent on a sectoral, functional, status or size of requirement basis. The strongest of these influences will evolve from being sectoral to being more functional in the future. However, the speed of wider acceptance of edge and out of town locations will be determined to no small extent by the quality of supply.

Finally, homeworking and non-office-based working are likely to be possible for and acceptable to a wider range of people, for a larger proportion of their working time. The major impact of this will be on future space requirements, rather than on more direct locational choices. Accountants and management consultancy occupiers already only make provision to accommodate approximately two thirds of their staff at one time in London. The impact on occupiers' location decisions will mainly be determined by the availability of local infrastructure and topography to facilitate related technology. This could therefore be another constraining factor on future de-urbanisation since, as we outlined above, much of the telecommunications infrastructure required to take advantage of the technology that eliminates the need for face-to-face contact is focused on city centres and will continue to be so.

We would anticipate, therefore, that while the future of the office is secure, its functionality, typical size and preferred or optimal location in the longer term is likely to be radically different from the present day for the majority of office-based activities.

References

1 Economist Intelligence Unit, 'A Survey of Factors Governing the Location of Offices in the London Area', report prepared for the Location of Offices Bureau in Daniels, P W, *An Urban and Regional Study: Office Location*, 1975; Economists Advisory Group & Industrial

Commercial Planning Services, *Factors Influencing the Location of International Offices*, client report for the Department of Industry, July 1985

2 Price Waterhouse & CBI Employee Relocation Council, *Moving Experiences*, Volumes I & II, January 1989

3 EAL Property Research Consultants, *Factors Influencing the Location of Offices of High Growth Companies*, private client report, 1989

4 EAL Property Research Consultants, *Property Markets in Europe*, private client report, 1990

5 Henley Centre, *Regional Futures – The Geography of British Prosperity, 1988–1995*, June 1989

6 Department of Transport, British Rail Network South East, London Regional Transport & London Underground Ltd, *Central London Rail Study*, January 1989

7 Price Waterhouse & CBI Employee Relocation Council, *Moving Experiences*, Volumes I & II, January 1989

8 London Chamber of Commerce and Industry, *Employment in Finance and Business Services: Trends and Prospects*, London Economy Research Programme, 1989; SERPLAN, *The Channel Tunnel: Impact on the Economy of the South East Region*, June 1989

9 Employment Gazette, *Labour Force Outlook to 2001*, April 1990

10 Cambridge Econometrics, *Regional Economic Prospects: Analysis and Forecasts to the Year 2000*, January 1990

11 Black, J T, Roark K S & Schwartz L S, *The Changing Office Workplace*, Urban Land Institute, 1986

12 Jones Lang Wootton, *The Decentralisation of Offices from Central London: An Annual Special Survey*, 1988; 1989

13 Property Market Analysis, Occupier Survey, *Chartered Accountants*, May 1990

14 Debenham Tewson & Chinnocks, *Office needs: the Occupiers' View*, August 1988

15 Property Market Analysis, 'Occupier Survey: Computer and Electronics' in *Industrial Market Review*, October 1989

16 University of Glasgow, 1990

10 A view of the regulator's perspective

George Atkinson, Consultant to the Building Research Establishment

Summary

This paper traces the history of the development of the regulatory framework, in England and Wales primarily, for the design and use of the workplace. Regulations are currently operated by various agencies under different control. The regulatory process will change as a result of the influence of: the movement to European rather than national technical specifications; the adoption of proposals for EC directives on the workplace and environmental conditions; further developments in the UK planning process; the greater emphasis on environmental issues, and the potential for information technology to manage and integrate regulatory compliance and surveillance.

There are two distinct approaches in Europe to regulation. In the French model responsibility is held by constructors (practitioners and clients covered by insurance) to comply with regulations; in the German model responsibility is held by national and local authorities to ensure compliance. It is expected that the existing system in the UK will evolve to incorporate elements of both models, with the more open French approach considered the more attractive.

Background

Changes in the character of workplaces over centuries have brought new challenges to regulators. Before the industrial revolution, the workplace and the proprietor's residence occupied the same premises, but as workplaces became noisier, dirtier and more crowded, the distinction was made between residence and workplace and between office and factory. New 'clean' technologies and extensive use of electronic information handling equipment have further broken down barriers between office and light industrial work, a fact recognised under the Town & Country Planning (Use Classes) Order 1987 where the new B1 Business Use Class was introduced to include not only offices, research and development studios and laboratories but also light industry. Similar transformations have influenced the development of business parks, which provide more space for parking and building expansion and include, besides B1 premises, B8 storage and distribution uses and shops, restaurants and leisure facilities, often on greenfield sites. The main elements of the English regulatory system are summarised below. Explanations are given in Table 10.1[1].

Over time, matters controlled, control systems, control procedures and responsibilities for compliance change, as a consequence of fire disasters, structural collapses, epidemics, growing public awareness of an environmental hazard or, possibly, changes in social policies or the machinery of government. In recent years the need has arisen to regulate matters such as environmental noise and pollution, conservation of natural resources, preservation of countryside and buildings of architectural or historical interest and health and safety at work. This need has been reflected in EC as well as national legislation and regulations.

Along with changes in the form and coverage of control systems, technical specifications – national codes and standards prepared in consultation with industry and which incorporate construction R&D information – have been more widely adopted as guidelines for compliance with regulation requirements, and for third party approval of fitness of construction products and equipment, a process to be seen in the Approved Documents issued under the 1984 Building Act. A similar trend is evident in land use legislation with the issue of Planning Policy Guides. This approach to the regulatory process is likely to become more widespread with EC legislation.

Reference to technical specifications as guidelines for the satisfaction of 'essential requirements' in regulations is, as yet, imperfect. It can give greater freedom and flexibility, but requires higher standards of technical competence from regulators and constructors, and places on them greater responsibilities for the quality of their decisions. Superior bodies, such as construction ministries, have to decide whether assurance of the fitness of a design or product is to be restricted to qualified persons and organisations or open to all; and, in the former case, who should be the judge of qualification. Here, implementation of the EC Construction Products Directive should provide lessons.

In Europe, Germany and France approach regulation very differently. Germany depends on detailed administrative specification of procedures in legal documents, backed by a comprehensive set of technical specifications, the regulatory process being administered by a qualified technical service largely responsible for assessing compliance and fitness in use. France, on the other hand, places the onus of assurance largely on building owners and constructors, making responsibilities clear in law and requiring insurance against failure causing damage. Independent technical control by state licensed offices is only required by law where consequences of failure are serious, such as fire or structural collapse in a high rise building. Otherwise, although damage insurance may be mandatory, independent technical control is voluntary but may have benefits in terms of insurance costs. That new products and techniques do not present abnormal risks is a matter for insurance industry and technical controllers. But certification by qualified persons, generally state-diploma architects, that proposals do not conflict with local land use plans may be required.

How far a European dimension will favour the French or German approach remains uncertain. But a number of issues are becoming clear:

- The growing use in regulatory systems of essential requirements, such as the six requirements covering safety and health which are listed in the EC Construction Directive and developed in related Interpretative Documents.

- The use of technical specifications – standards and technical guidelines – as tools in the assessment of performance against essential requirements.

- The responsibility of member state governments to designate bodies and individuals qualified to test, assess and certify against technical specifications.

Matters yet to be considered, or at least agreed, at Community level include identification and limitation of constructors' responsibilities and the feasibility of adopting the 'essential requirement' approach to other performance aspects of a Responsible Workplace, such as the safety and health of workers, environmental protection, conservation of resources, preservation of the countryside and works of architectural or historical importance.

For constructors involved in the design, build and management process a further issue is the extent to which responsible authorities, such as construction ministries, will decide to specify in law tasks and responsibilities calling for particular technical competence, and license qualified persons and bodies as an alternative to regulation by officials.

Introduction to the changing regulatory system

The pressures shaping future workplace design and use to the year 2000 will cover many areas such as location; environmental impact; design and construction; service installations (including quality of the internal environment); uses and users of facilities (including the handicapped); operation of the building (including ease of maintenance and safety of operators); use and conservation of natural resources such as energy and water, and disposal and recycling of liquid and solid waste. This paper reviews the present regulatory situation in England and Wales relating to land use, design and construction of buildings and their occupancy and use. Some matters are regulated somewhat differently in Scotland and Northern Ireland.

A feature of the regulatory system in the UK, as in all other national systems, is that controls have developed under different legislation as a result of different political responses to events, and are operated by different agencies under different superior bodies (see Table 10.1). Again, the degree of discretion available to controlling authorities, and the form of appeals against decisions to permit development, order works, or prevent uses may differ. Superior bodies publish or adopt technical specifications in various forms which give guidance on what may be 'deemed to satisfy' regulation requirements. In the case of the design and construction of buildings and services within buildings these technical specifications often refer to British Standard Codes and Specifications. In matters relating to the location and use of land and communication, guidance is generally given in ministerial documents produced by the Departments of the Environment and Transport, or in documents such as approved District Plans

Table 10.1 An outline of current regulatory systems relating to the use and development of land, and the design, construction and occupancy of buildings in England and Wales. There are some differences in Scotland.

Type of control	Legislation	Responsible body	Superior body	Technical specifications
Use and development of land	Planning laws & regulations GDOs	District council plans committee (1)	S of State [inspector (2)]	Dept. Circulars PPGs Local Plans (3)
Design and construction buildings	Building Act & Regulations	District council [building control officers (4)]	S of State [construction dept (5)]	Approved documents and related BSs (6)
Occupancy of buildings	[There is other legislation relating mainly to particular occupancies eg safety of sports grounds]			
i] **Fire safety**	Fire Precautions Acts	Fire Authority [FPOs (7)]	Home Office [HO]	HO Guides related BSs (7)
ii] **General safety & health**	Health & Safety at Work Act etc & Regulations	H & S Executive [inspectorate]	Dept. of Employment	HSE Reports related BSs

Notes:
(1) Some powers are delegated to officers
(2) Appeals against a district council's refusal to permit development are taken by an inspector acting for the S of S; the S of S may call in for decision development proposals.
(3) Local plans after statutory procedures acquire a near–mandatory status; and although their requirements are not binding, on some matters like designation of Green Belts they have a powerful influence on the S of S's decisions.
(4) For house building NHBC inspectors may have responsibilities.
(5) Determinations of the meaning of a regulation in a specific application.
(6) Certain BSs are noticed in Approved Documents which with other technical specifications, Agrément Certificates etc assist in decisions of compliance with regulations.
(7) The County is usually the Fire Authority and although FPOs [fire precautions officers] only advise and their advice, which increasingly is influenced by related BS codes, takes on a regulatory character.
Under the heading technical specifications are grouped various documents which give guidance and, although not mandatory, are generally accepted as the 'state of the art' in any interpretation by an authority of a legal requirement.

Source: Building Research Establishment

set out in associated Written Statements and Maps.

The regulatory process will change in a number of ways under the influences of: a move towards European rather than national technical specifications as part of the creation of a Single Market; changes in the English planning process, such as the Planning and Compensation Act 1991; greater emphasis on environmental issues as reflected in the 1990 government White Paper; the adoption of and proposals for EC Directives relating to workplace and environmental conditions, and the potential of computer aids to handle and integrate regulatory information and provide regulators and practitioners with convenient means of compliance assessment and surveillance.

This paper suggests that in order to regulate performance against essential requirements, particularly on matters relating to safety, health and environmental protection, a national choice may have to be made between contrasting systems:

● systems based on a proto-French approach where practitioners and their clients have a large degree of freedom, within clear limits, in assessing how best to satisfy requirements but carry liabilities as well as responsibilities against which insurance may be mandatory and, for economic if not legal reasons, competence is assessed by third parties and is the subject of registration or certification.

● systems based on a proto-German approach where requirements are precise, set out in legal instruments and related technical specifications; compliance is checked by national or local authorities which may require certification of products and persons, and it is assumed that failures will not occur.

Despite influences from mainland Europe, it is unlikely that either approach will be dominant in the 1990s. Rather, the existing system will evolve by drawing on the most attractive elements from both but with a bias towards the more open French approach.

A number of Directives issued by the European Commission already affect working conditions in offices and other workplaces. Although directed at the removal of barriers to trade in construction products, the route taken by the Construction Products Directive[2] to promote

'the approximation of laws, regulations and administrative provisions' through the definition of 'essential requirements on safety and other aspects which are important for the general well being' must be regarded as of major importance for three reasons. First, the Directive brings together in a series of technical committees practitioners and researchers from major institutions in EC member states to give these essential requirements a concrete form in Interpretative Documents which summarise current knowledge. Second, through these documents it will be possible to review, update and simplify the technical specifications which are, or should be, the basis of any regulatory process. Third, in a modified and extended form the essential requirements could provide a framework for regulatory systems affecting the location of buildings and environmentally acceptable use of land, and for the maintenance of safe and healthy working conditions – both matters of special importance when considering the future form of the Responsible Workplace (see Table 10.2).

As far as it is known, the concept of applying essential requirements to regulatory systems concerned with land use has not yet been considered seriously. In this paper, the regulatory aspects of land use planning are examined and a possible route to the introduction of a similar approach sketched out.

Table 10.2 Essential requirements as set out in the EC Construction Products Directive

**Essential requirements
[Annex I Construction Products Directive]**

1 Mechanical Resistance and Stability

2 Safety in case of fire

3 Hygiene, Health and the Environment

4 Safety in use

5 Protection against noise

6 Energy economy and heat retention

Source: Building Research Establishment

Regulation under EEC Directive 85/337 on Environmental Impact Assessment[3], implemented in England and Wales through the Town and Country Planning (Assessment of Environmental Effects) Regulations 1988, is only concerned with major schemes. However, the European Commission is preparing a proposal for a directive on toxic and dangerous waste, and building on contaminated land is a matter to which regulators will be giving increased attention during the 1990s. Even on a greenfield site, the land may be contaminated by earlier deposits of uncontrolled waste. If, as is likely during the next decade, there is increasing pressure to redevelop land used by industry or, for example, a former defence establishment or even a large hospital, the risk that the site may have been contaminated will need expert investigation and assessment.

The changing character of business premises

Until the nineteenth century, commercial business transactions took place either in open marketplaces and surrounding inns, in coffee shops, or in the front rooms of a merchant's private house. Government business was transacted in chambers within royal palaces such as Westminster and Whitehall or in the house of a minister. Somerset House[4] was England's first purpose designed government office, and, like its successors the Foreign and India Offices in Whitehall[5], was modelled on the Italian *palazzo*. The *piano nobile*, approached by monumental stairs, accommodated the minister and his senior advisers. Junior clerks were housed in attic rooms or basements, with more senior clerks on the ground or mezzanine floors. The Italian palazzo continued as a model until the end of the Second World War. There were no regulatory controls for public offices other than standards set by the Treasury and Office of Works. Commercial buildings, mainly in London, were subject to controls under the London Building Acts which involved professional agreement between building owners' consultants and a District Surveyor[6] and which were concerned with structure and fire protection rather than environmental matters. This resulted in many quality buildings of somewhat conservative

design and construction, as a Building Research Station (BRS) team found in a survey of pre-war London buildings carried out in the early 1960s[7].

The BRS team, which directed its attention to structure and finishes rather than building services, found that heating, ventilation and electrical installations sometimes dated from the 1900s and were not covered by regulations other than those relating to fire precautions and electrical safety. Little attention was given to energy conservation. Indeed, a number of Whitehall offices were still being heated with open coal fires in the early 1950s. The comparatively primitive state of environmental engineering was demonstrated in Greenwich Town Hall, one of the more modern buildings surveyed. Although heating and ventilation were generally satisfactory, internal temperatures could not be adjusted to frequent external changes and there were complaints that the building was stuffy, although it was neither over- nor under-heated.

It was largely due to height restrictions under the London Building Acts that high rise office buildings did not appear in the UK until the 1950s, despite the fact that the skyscraper had been commonplace in the US since the last quarter of the nineteenth century, first in Chicago and then New York, culminating in complexes like the Empire State building and Rockefeller Center which mixed business and leisure uses. The development of high rise construction was paralleled by innovations in building services, the design of which was largely regulated through design codes of professional bodies such as ASHVE[8].

Although legislation set limits on building heights and often required set-backs to protect rights of light, architectural concepts continued to be a dominant influence on the built form of most pre-war and many early post-war office buildings. Until the Royal Institute of British Architects (RIBA) set up a committee to consider the orientation of buildings in 1931, daylight, sunlight and glazing had not received much attention. BRS work in the 1930s resulted in the development of the heliodon and daylight factors which were to have an increasingly important influence during the post-war years and resulted in the slab block on podium form, of which 2 Marsham Street in London is an unhappy example[9].

Although a RIBA committee had reported on business buildings in 1944[10], little attention was given to user needs until the mid-1960s when a BRS user survey of modern offices looked at space requirements and environmental conditions[11]. This found external noise and summer overheating to be major causes of complaint, and a 1966 report suggested that 'the provision of air conditioning would be likely to result in cleaner as well as quieter offices'[12].

Despite North American and continental experience, and the fact that the 1944 RIBA committee report stated that no building was a self-contained 'type', office buildings were looked on as a separate use class, as demonstrated in a 1963 Ministry of Housing and Local Government Planning Bulletin[13].

In recent years, the widespread use of microelectronic devices in equipment for offices and light industry has eroded many distinctions between office and industrial work and the development of business parks providing buildings for multiple uses has grown. Since 1987, planning legislation has accepted that there are no longer significant differences between offices and light workshops[14]. Nevertheless, the effect of innovations in data processing and new technologies on the location of workplaces and their built form is still a matter of debate and has not as yet been taken fully into account in the legislative process.

The origins of the current regulatory pattern in the UK

Legislation affecting the location, design and use of buildings follows rather than leads events requiring government action, and the regulatory procedures which follow new legislation are invariably based on an existing legal and administrative structure. For these reasons planning, building and worker protection regulation in different countries at different times takes on different forms and is rarely based on a single system of control.

Fire precautions, for example, were a major influence on the series of London Building Acts dating from the Great Fire of London until they were replaced by a National Building Act in 1984[15]. Many North American building and zoning codes have a similar origin. The all

embracing German planning and building legislation, on the other hand, owes its origins largely to 'the Prussian concept of the state's direct responsibility for public order'[16], while the French civil code approach was derived from a concept based in Roman law that someone investing in a building – the *maitre d'ouvrage* – should be protected against latent damage resulting from bad work by his builder – the *maitre d'oeuvre*[17]. Worker protection legislation which now may cover office as well as factory premises had quite a different origin.

Outside inner London, English building regulation owed much to public health reforms in Victorian England and the need to protect a growing urban population against epidemics, through improvements to sanitation[18]. This is demonstrated in the Bill for the Better Drainage and Improvement of Buildings in Large Towns and Cities, 1841; the Public Health Acts 1848 and 1875, and the By-laws as to New Streets and Buildings, 1858 and 1877. Housing and town and country planning have been closely linked since pre-1914 legislation such as the 1909 Act[19].

As a result, in most countries including the UK, three different sets of legislation regulate the location, construction and use of buildings. They are generally administered in different ways and have different superior bodies. For example, land use planning and building regulation is administered by the Department of the Environment (DoE) in England, working closely with the Welsh Office in Wales, and separately by the Scottish Development Department in Scotland; fire precautions are administered by the Home Office in England and by the Scottish Home Department in Scotland; safety and health in workplaces is administered by the Department of Employment through the Health and Safety Executive with some matters under a district council, others under a county council and some a central agency (see Table 10.1).

A leading guide to English and Welsh legislation relevant to the design, layout, methods of construction, and siting of buildings lists some 200 Acts of Parliament[20]. Some Acts, such as the Pet Animal Act 1951 or the Fireworks Act 1951 are unlikely to have any relevance to Responsible Workplaces. There is also a guide to Scottish legislation[21], which shares some features with continental legislation[22].

In England and Wales, the principal legislation

controlling the design and construction of new buildings is the 1984 Building Act and the 1991 Building Regulations made by the DoE under the Act[23]. Land use and the development of building sites is regulated through a number of Town and Country Planning Acts and subsidiary Orders and Regulations. In Scotland and Northern Ireland, where the legislation differs, the principal regulations are the Building Standards (Scotland) Regulations and the Building Regulations (Northern Ireland).

The planning (land use) process

The term 'town planning' was first used in UK legislation in 1909. The aim of 'town' and, after 1932, 'town and country' planning legislation was to place restrictions in the public interest on private action to develop land, erect buildings and change existing uses of land and buildings[24].

Certain developers, such as departments of central government acting in the name of the Crown, are exempt from planning controls although it is customary to consult local planning authorities and, usually, conform to their planning objectives. Under General Development Orders (GDOs), certain groups such as farmers, certain kinds of development such as agriculture and minor additions to dwellings, and certain parts of the country such as enterprise zones may be exempt from all or major aspects of planning controls[25]. Although in the past some planning matters were controlled through building and public health legislation – hence the term 'by-law planning' – almost all matters relating to sites rather than buildings in UK legislation come under planning controls rather than building regulation, unlike legislation in some other countries.

In the UK, permission is required from a local planning authority (usually a district council) to carry out specific forms of development, change the use of land and buildings on the site, or alter the appearance of a building in certain conservation areas, or in the case of buildings that are listed for architectural or historic interest. In considering an application, the planning authority will have regard to town and country and other legislation concerned with land use; to regulations and GDOs made under the legislation; to provisions of its published development plan; to other plans and policies, such as the DoE Planning Policy Guidance Notes (PPGs)[26] and County Structure Plans, and to other material considerations such as advice from English Heritage, the Department of Transport, and police and fire authorities.

County Structure Plans set out broad land use policies on key strategic issues within the framework of national and regional policy guidance, such as the PPGs, and guidance from bodies such as the Countryside Commission, English Heritage, the Sports Council and Regional Councils for Sport and Recreation. Local plans, prepared by district authorities, usually take the form of a Written Statement setting out policies on matters such as housing, employment, transportation, shopping, leisure and countryside, or Maps, which define specific land use changes and areas in which certain policies will apply, and serve to provide the framework against which decisions on individual planning applications are made. On minor issues these decisions may be delegated to council officers but they are usually made by the council's Plans Committee which may refer important issues to the full council. Where the issue is one of more than local interest, the Secretary of State may 'call in' an application for decision.

If a proposal for development or change of use is refused by a planning authority, the applicant may appeal to the Secretary of State, who usually appoints an inspector to recommend whether the appeal should be allowed. The current Secretary of State recently declared that local plans are the vehicle through which a local community can make its own decisions on the detailed pattern of development in its area[27]. Consequently, where there is a formally adopted local plan together with properly substantiated reasons for an authority's decision to refuse a developer's application, the inspector will be guided by the plan and associated documents when dealing with appeals. Furthermore, where a developer has ignored clear statements on planning policies and guidance, the inspector may award costs against the developer; but costs are awarded against the authority where it has acted arbitrarily or has misinterpreted policy guidance.

One way in which exceptions to normal planning procedures are introduced is through amendments to the General Development and Use Classes Orders. Much recent permitted development comes under GDO 1988 and relates to dwellings and temporary buildings but also to most agricultural and forestry buildings as well as development by public authorities. Lists of permitted developments are available.

Changes in planning legislation, outlined in the November 1990 Queen's Speech, give greater importance to the preparation and use of district plans and thus strengthen the powers of local planning authorities where the procedures for their preparation and authorisation have been followed. Consultation papers have been issued on a number of matters including extensions to factory and warehouse buildings to cater for a range of social, welfare or recreational uses (one aim being to encourage the creation of workplace childcare facilities); encouragement of the use of vacant and derelict public sector land; clarification of policies on uses of land for sport and recreation, and changes in planning controls for agricultural and forestry buildings[28].

Two other situations where normal planning controls are relaxed are in designated Enterprise Zones and Urban Development Areas such as London Docklands, the Black Country, Merseyside, Teeside and Tyneside. On the other hand, planning controls are somewhat strengthened in designated conservation areas, defined as 'areas of special architectural or historic interest'. Buildings of special architectural or historic interest also receive exceptional attention under planning legislation, and the DoE recently issued guidance on policies for protection, enhancement and preservation of archaeological sites.

One area where there is firm guidance is development in designated Green Belt areas. Government policy on this issue is clear and well established, with a general presumption against development in Green Belt areas[29]. PPG2: Green Belts, issued in January 1988 by the DoE, gave concise and practical guidance on planning policies. As well as stating that in a designated Green Belt 'there is a strong presumption against all inappropriate development' it states that Green Belts have five purposes: to check the unrestricted sprawl of large built up areas; save the surrounding countryside from further encroachment; prevent neighbouring towns from merging into one another; preserve the special character of historic towns, and assist in urban regeneration.

Although Green Belts often contain areas of attractive landscape, the quality of the rural landscape is not a material factor in their designation or in their continued protection. There is however one exceptional circumstance where development in a Green Belt may be considered: the future use of redundant hospital sites. Guidance stresses the retention or enhancement of site amenity values, with preference for institutional reuse of existing buildings. But the possibility of some new development, for example housing, which should not normally 'occupy a larger area of the site nor exceed the height of existing buildings' is accepted. Already, in parts of the Hertfordshire and Surrey sections of the Metropolitan Green Belt, disposal and ultimate use of large hospital sites and the accommodation of remaining mentally handicapped or mentally ill patients, are matters of local concern. This said, the National Audit Office, reviewing estate management in the National Health Service, found that a number of health authorities experienced Green Belt restrictions in England, probably because the scale of new development was regarded as excessive.

The building regulation process

The 1984 Building Act introduced radical changes in the process of building regulation in England and Wales, not all of which have been implemented. For example, as an alternative to local authority control, the Act allowed 'certification of compliance' by a 'duly approved person' accompanied by 'a declaration that an approved insurance scheme applies' and 'supervision by an approved inspector'. But, apart from housing, which was until recently built under the insurance arrangements of the National House Building Council, this option has never been used, largely because the matter of 'an approved insurance scheme' has not been settled. The concept of certification by an approved person was probably introduced under the influence of the French approach to building control. However, Secretaries of State since Michael Heseltine, who was largely responsible for the legislation, have not as yet taken further initiatives to resolve the key issues of insurance of inspectors and decennial responsibilities of constructors. One initiative under the 1984

Building Act – the expression of technical requirements in functional terms and guidance on the satisfaction through Approved Documents supported by British Standard and other technical specifications – has become established practice[30].

Although the 1984 Building Act makes provision for imposing on owners and occupiers 'continuing requirements' and for regulating 'defective premises', the English system in practice is based on the assumption that, once built, a building will continue to satisfy requirements[31] unless there is a 'material alteration' or change of use. Another feature of the English system is that the local authority has to be notified that work will be carried out and will comply with the Regulations but, unlike many other systems, there is no provision for final inspection and issue of an 'occupancy certificate'.

The concept behind the Requirements listed in Schedule 1 of the Building Regulations 1991 differs only in detail from the concept of 'essential requirements' in the EC Construction Products Directive[32]. Once work on Interpretative Documents is complete, it is possible that these documents will influence the ways in which technical requirements of the Building Regulations are expressed as well as the form

and content of Approved Documents and the technical specifications which support their guidance. Already there is a movement towards further liberalisation and simplification, depending on more extensive use of British Standards and Codes of Practice. Under the Second Stage Review, revised approved documents have been issued[33].

Amendments to certain parts of the Building Regulations 1985 have come into force[34]. Up until then, in contrast to the guidance issued in Approved Documents, the rules for means of escape in case of fire were mandatory[35]. As Table 10.3 shows, fire safety is a complex matter, particularly in the types of premises which may qualify as Responsible Workplaces. Similarly, the concept of a Responsible Workplace may require some fresh thinking on requirements for safety in use, health and the environment, and energy economy.

In February 1990, the Department of Trade and Industry's Deregulation Unit, in conjunction with the Home Office and the Department of the Environment, published a review of Fire and Building Regulations by Bickerdike Allen Partners in which the general thrust of the Stage Two Review of the Building Regulations was supported, and the extension of the scope and application of Part B: *Safety in fire* to all aspects

Table 10.3 Fire and safety and protection: key elements

Objectives of fire regulations	
Prevent Fire Event:	**Manage Fire Event:**
1 Restrict entry: vermin, arsonist	1 Ensure safety in fire of occupants, neighbours, passers-by and fire-fighters
2 Ensure integrity of pipework carrying gases and inflammable liquid; electric cable insulation	2 Minimise damage to structure and contents, and to nearby property through:
3 Avoid ignition by flame, sparks, self-heating and smouldering materials	a detection of smoke, heat and flame
Limit Fire Growth	b warnings to occupants and fire-fighters
1 Storage of inflammable and explosive materials	c direction and movement of occupants to place of safety; easy access for rescuers
2 Use of combustible furnishings and building materials	d control of smoke obscuring escape and movement of fire-fighters
3 Compartmentation	e ensuring structural integrity at least during escape and fire-fighting
Source: Building Research Establishment	f providing facilities for suppression by fire-fighters and/or automatic systems

of fire safety and most building types was recommended. Attention was drawn to the dynamic nature of the technologies of building and fire engineering[36].

Following criticism from a number of interested groups including the National Association of Fire Officers, which was mainly directed at reducing levels of structural fire resistance and increasing compartment sizes, proposals to change the Building Regulations relating to fire safety are being considered by the DoE Building Regulations Advisory Committee and its Fire Advisory Panel[37].

The regulatory process in the 1990s

It is likely that the regulatory process will change during the 1990s, although the nature and speed of change will depend on many political and economic, rather than technical, factors. This discussion considers first the land use planning process which is largely, but not entirely, influenced by events within the UK.

In 1989 and 1990, the DoE published a number of proposals either in the form of draft PPGs or Consultation Papers relating to structure plans (general policy documents at county level covering matters such as Green Belts, economic development, business uses, transport, airports, and leisure facilities); regional planning guidance; the role of planning and of local communities in the planning system; and the countryside and the rural economy. The last includes proposals for more flexibility in the reuse and conversion of agricultural buildings for housing and industry.

Changes have been introduced in the rules governing publication of details of unused and underused land in public ownership, and district development plans will in future be set within a new framework provided in PPGs, and will integrate the declaration of conservation areas into the development plan system and make special arrangements for National Parks and for temporary planning initiatives for Urban Development Corporations and Enterprise Zones. The issue of a White Paper 'The Common Inheritance' in September 1990 was followed by new planning legislation; the 1990 Town and Country Planning Act and the 1991 Planning and Compensation Act; and by an associated

DoE Circular 21/91. The legislation confers new and improved enforcement powers on local planning authorities who, as a result, are actively updating local plans after formal inquiry and adoption, which clearly state what kind of development may take place in a designated area.

Registration of land title in England and Wales was until recently based on legal documents of medieval origin, rather than on surveyors' records as in Australia, New Zealand and many European countries. Registration of title to land was first introduced by the Land Registry Act of 1862, the aim being to maintain a register of land owners whose title was guaranteed by the state. Registration was voluntary, and the register was not open to public inspection. Under the 1966 Act, registration in certain areas was made compulsory on sale, with the aim of extending compulsory registration throughout England as resources permitted.

Until December 1990, the owner's permission was required to consult the register. It is now possible for anyone interested in land on the register to gain information on the land and neighbouring properties. Unlike Norway, for example, where the register is maintained by a district authority and any planning conditions as well as technical matters such as boundary dimensions and drainage levels are automatically entered, the English register is held nationally. Together with arrangements being introduced to encourage the use of vacant public sector land, a greater transparency in land matters should foster improved efficiency and help reduce the speculative element in the use and development of urban land.

While it is highly unlikely that there will be a return to the complex measures introduced by Silkin in his 1947 Town and Country Planning Act which, with associated legislation, introduced the concept of a development charge linked to the granting of planning permission and established the New Town Corporations and National Parks[38], it is possible that the need to maintain the UK's economic standing within the European Community will result in a move away from a speculative to a more efficient and constructive use of land, including greater transparency in ownership and land transactions. The consultative documents on sport and recreation[39] and on planning controls over agricultural and forestry land[40] and, in particular, the importance placed on maintaining up to date planning policy guidance and local district plans and on the need to ensure that planning policies are 'applied in an even handed way regardless of ownership' are all pointers to a change of emphasis on land matters in the 1990s.

It is not yet possible to assess the effect of the EC environmental Directives such as 85/337/EEC: Environmental Impact Assessment[41], which requires assessments of the likely environmental impact of planned major industrial or infrastructure projects. Fortledge lists the kinds of development for which an Environmental Assessment is mandatory and those for which it is discretionary[42].

However, an indication of one likely way in which the European debate on environmental policy will develop is the issue of a communication on the use of economic and fiscal instruments in EC environmental policy drafted by the Commission and discussed at an informal meeting of environment ministers in Rome in 1990. Beginning with the statement that 'the potential impact of economic and fiscal instruments is far from being exploited at present' the communication looks at:

- greenhouse effect and energy consumption – proposing a new tax on energy products with a specific tax on CO_2 to guarantee a reduction in future energy demand

- destruction of the ozone layer – proposing institution of a tax on the use of CFCs

- water pollution with oxygen-demanding substances

- development of a framework for water pollution charges

- road traffic and air pollution

- economic instruments to reinforce existing technical regulations

- household and industrial solid waste

- promotion of economic instruments which change relative prices of prevention, reuse, recycling, treatment, incineration and disposal to exploit potential for prevention and recycling

If the pattern of UK legislation, such as the recent Environmental Pollution Bill, based on the principle of duty of care, is followed regulations dealing with waste disposal will be strengthened and the cost of disposal will treble by the mid-1990s from the current figure of between £10 and £20 a tonne. It is estimated that out of a total 100 million tonnes of solid waste, about 30 million tonnes come from commercial premises – mainly in the form of paper and packaging – compared with 20 million tonnes of household waste and 50 million tonnes of industrial waste, with approximately 5 million tonnes being classed as hazardous. At present it is quite usual to mix recyclable waste and hazardous industrial waste in the same dump. Co-disposal, as this practice is called, is likely to be outlawed under a planned EC Directive. In any case, the new UK legislation will make co-disposal difficult if not impossible. Legislation making waste disposal more costly on the one hand, and a need to recycle suitable kinds of waste on the other, may therefore mean the provision in all but the smallest office premises of special accommodation, for example facilities for compressing and baling paper and packaging waste.

Developments in the regulatory process relating to the design and construction of buildings are more directly matters of safety and health and as such are more closely associated with the process of harmonisation of European standards. The following section therefore looks at the European dimension and the implications of the EC Directives. In considering these European trends, however, attention must be given to the features of construction activities which differentiate them from other activities that are currently the subject of standards development at a European level (see Appendix 4).

The European dimension: objectives and implications of EC directives

The different ways in which European governments regulate land use and the design and construction of buildings have been reviewed in a number of reports[43]. Most include land use and development control within building legislation rather than under a separate group. Some, such as the Danish building regulations, differ only in detail from UK legislation. Others such as Germany and France have very different arrangements and objectives.

Although the effects of EC Directives, particularly the Construction Products Directive, are as yet difficult to predict, there are already signs of change. For example, the elaboration of essential requirements for safety and health through interpretative documents is having an influence on the drafting of building regulations[44]. The Construction Products Directive is a child of the 'New Approach' which is based on sets of essential requirements written in general terms. These requirements are given concrete form in interpretative documents from which the CEN will be mandated to draft European standards and the recently formed European Organisation for Technical Approvals to prepare guidelines for designated national technical approval bodies. These technical specifications will in turn serve in the process of assessment either through third party certification, a manufacturer's declaration, or issue of a technical approval depending on a product's criticality in terms of safety and health.

However, the somewhat complex arrangements for the implementation of the Construction Products Directive demonstrate significant differences from other 'New Approach' Directives such as the Directive for children's toys where there is a one-to-one relationship between technical specification and essential requirement. In the case of construction products, it is the works into which they are built which has to meet an essential requirement. Furthermore, the fact that there may be differences in the application of the concept of essential requirements is accepted in Article 3, which states that 'in order to take account of possible differences in geographical or climatic conditions or in ways of life as well as different degrees of protection that may prevail at national, regional or local level, each essential requirement may give rise to the establishment of classes in technical documents'.

In broad outline, the Directive's list of essential requirements can therefore be equated with requirements in the regulation systems of EC member states although there are basic differences in the way their satisfaction is controlled, particularly between France and Germany. Moreover, the occupancy of the building and the use, operation, servicing and maintenance of its installations are of at least equal importance – particularly in terms of fire safety, health and the environment, safety in use, noise protection and energy economy and heat retention. To achieve the aims of an essential requirement, control over products and their incorporation in the initial construction is but one stage in a process of control and surveillance. As this becomes more widely understood, especially where buildings and installations are more complex, the present regulatory systems may have to be updated to take account of a wide range of responsibilities over a timescale stretching from initial decisions on location to decisions on reuse or demolition and involving many different participants.

Because these require the specialist knowledge, competence and integrity of many different kinds of organisations and persons, the simple system of a single regulatory authority may have to be replaced by a network of persons and agencies, whose qualifications and work practices may be subject to some kind of regulation, possibly involving quality assurance and third party assessment and surveillance with associated responsibility insurance. Here, developments based on the French rather than the German approach would seem to point to a way forward. Among other things, it would require the back-up of appropriate technical specifications and guidelines, and their easy reference through an effective, user friendly data base.

The long term importance of the Construction Products Directive is not just to encourage the free flow of products across national boundaries but, through interpretation of essential requirements for safety and health in concrete form, to develop European standards which in turn will become fundamental influences on the design and construction of buildings and civil engineering works and their regulation. That this will happen is recognised in the full title of the Directive which states that it is for 'the approximation of laws, regulations and administrative provisions relating to construction products'. Although it is not yet possible to assess the effects of EC Directives such as those on Improvements in the Safety and Health of Workers at Work (89/391/EEC); Safety and Health for the Workplace (89/654/EEC); and the Noise Directive (88/295/EEC), it is likely that they will have a similar influence.

One of the early tasks of the European Commission, in consultation with the Standing Committee for Construction, has been the preparation and publication of a series of Interpretative Documents which give concrete form to the essential requirements[45]. Already their potential to provide a new approach to regulation can be seen, for example in the listing of a range of ways through which expression of energy use and conservation may be demonstrated.

Contrasting approaches to the achievement of building quality

Among the EC member states, contrasts in approach to regulation systems are most marked between Germany and France[46] (Tables 10.4, 10.5, 10.6, 10.7, 10.8, 10.9 & 10.10). Both are based on a civil law system which derives from Roman law and a written constitution, and both depend on the technical direction of an elitist professional bureaucracy – in Germany by members of the *Technische Verwaltungsdienst* (higher technical administrative service), graduates of a Technical University[47], and in France through the less direct influence of members of the *Corps des Ponts et Chaussées*, usually graduates of the Ecole Polytechnique.

However, there are marked differences. The Federal nature of Germany has meant that the state (*Lander*) governments are responsible for building law, whereas in the centralised system of French government, building law, in so far as it exists, is shared between ministries in Paris and is still to a large degree administered by their agents in the *departments* and *regions*, although in recent years there has been a degree of devolution with local authorities handling day to day matters.

Probably the most significant difference arises from the basic aims of the two systems. Although, as in most other countries, German building law derives from attempts to mitigate the effects of disastrous fires and pestilence, it was much influenced by the Prussian concept of the state's direct responsibility for 'public order'. The present *Lander* building ordinances, based on a 1960 model, govern matters of urban development and land ownership as well as the actual construction of buildings[48]. They lay considerable stress on assurance of quality, which is defined in the DIN standards issued by the Deutsches Institut für Normung[49]. Stringent production control requirements in the *Lander* building ordinances mean that virtually all building products undergo some form of technical assessment, usually by a third party, through a licensed laboratory. Structural work is usually checked by an independent licensed structural engineer.

The basic aim of French building law could be defined as 'consumer protection'[50]. The legal basis of the decennial guarantee of *solidité* and fitness comes from the 1804 Civil Code argument that a future building owner is a layman in building matters and should be protected against professional constructors – architects, engineers and builders. In modern times, however, a system of checks and responsibilities has had to be introduced, in part to improve consumer protection and clarify responsibilities and liabilities under the 1978 Spinetta law on liability[51], and in part to manage better urban planning and social housing and ensure public safety under a number of legal laws and decrees relating to planning, housing and construction, labour protection and public security.

Because French designers and constructors insure, or are required in some circumstances to insure, against their decennial liabilities, and because in many cases building owners have to take out damage insurance under which repair work is done while the respective liabilities of designers and constructors are determined, the state has less direct interest and the insurance industry and licensed technical controllers – employed since 1978 by the building owner rather than by the insurance company – play major roles. The types of document are more varied with French standards appearing to play a lesser role as technical specifications than do the German DINs. *Avis techniques*, (technical assessments) developed under the guidance of the French government research organisation CSTB, and accepted by insurers as demonstrating that products and procedures used present no abnormal risk, are important. CSTB also undertakes a codification and publication function.

In France, the 1804 Civil Code (*Code Napoleon*) has had a dominant influence on construction. Aimed originally at protecting small building owners, it makes builders and others professionals such as architects having contractual relations with the building owner liable for major defects for ten years. For lesser defects, the period of liability is generally two years.

Over the years there have been changes in details of the Civil Code. For example, in 1967 recognition was given to the fact that not only architects and builders might have responsibility for building quality. Finally, the Spinetta law on liabilities for defects during the Civil Code periods (*construction dommage*) was enacted in 1978 which made further radical changes. Building owners, as well as architects, builders and other professionals involved in the building process, have to insure against serious damage, while the respective insurers argue responsibilities and costs.

Insurance against Civil Code liabilities has been compulsory for architects since the 1940s under the code of professional duties of the Order of Architects. Up to 1978 contractors were not legally obliged to insure, but insurance was a condition of most contracts. The standard 'civil code liability' insurance policy for contractors required that traditional materials and procedures conform to French *normes*. New materials and processes had, up to 1969, to be covered by *Agrément* (approval) certificates or, since 1969, by an *Avis technique*.

One aspect of both systems which differs markedly from UK is the licensing, or at least required nomination, of qualified persons, either as a legal requirement or as a requirement for decennial insurance cover. The following are typical:

Table 10.4   Federal Germany:
The regulation and building control system relating to fire safety

Type of document	Topic covered
Ordinance	Landesbauordnung (general requirements) GarVO (garages) FeuVO heating appliances chimneys etc PrüfzVO (testing etc of building products of which groups 3 materials; and 4 equipment, relate to fire) ÜVO (quality assurance of products eg fire doors) GhVO (commercial buildings VStättVO (public assembly buildings)
Administrative regulations	Guidelines on use of combustible materials in buildings
Recognised good practice	DIN 4102: Fire performance of building materials and components DIN 18081 Fire barriers etc
Guidance	DIN 18230 series on structural fire protection
Recognised laboratories for classification and testing of fire performance of building materials etc	
Issue of test marks delegated by Länder to the Institute for Building Technology (IfBt)	

Source: Building Research Establishment

- independent licensed structural engineer (*prufingenieur*) required to check structural work (Germany)
- nomination by building owner of a 'responsible building supervisor' (*bauleiter*) (Germany)
- approval by a *Lander* building authority of an 'official materials testing laboratory' (Germany)
- registration, in some *Lander*, of architects preparing designs (Germany)
- licensing of technical controllers and their mandatory employment for certain categories of work (France)[52]
- classification and qualification of contractors under decennial insurance by a

special organisation on which government and industry are represented (France). A feature of the French construction industry is that the standard 'civil code liability' insurance policies only cover work undertaken by firms whose competence has been independently assessed and registered. Assessment, classification and registration are carried out by a special body, the *Organisme Professionnel de Qualification et de Classification du Batiment* (OPQCB), a semi-official body originally set up by the contractors' federation (FNB) at the request of the French government to eliminate from public contracts post-war reconstruction firms whose only resource was an accommodation address and a telephone, and on which government agencies, architects, other

Table 10.5 Federal Germany and France: systems of regulation contrasted

The German System

'more control by authorities; less responsibilities by constructors'

Strict control during the construction process:
- Stringent regulations.
  based on full national standards (DINs).
- Checking of designs before issue of building permit where necessary by an independent licensed structural engineer (prüfingenieur).
- Products either tested against DINs and subject to factory production control, or approved by IfBt, the Institute for Building Technology, Berlin.
- Technical site inspection, with much attention given to final inspection to uncover deficiencies.

The French System

'less control by authorities; more responsibilities for constructors'

No technical control by authorities during design or construction:
- Building permits issued against signature of an architect that design meets planning, health and fire safety regulations with possibility that compliance checked by government engineer in first three years after completion.
- Clearly stated guarantees for soundness of and fitness for intended used within specified time limits.
- Requirement for building owner's damage insurance and constructors' responsibility insurance.
- Mandatory requirement for independent technical control for high risk situations and preference for building owner to employ otherwise.
- Importance placed on reception or practical completion as start of damage insurance

Source: Building Research Establishment

professions, as well as builders and subcontractors, are represented at national and local levels. On similar lines, the *Organisme Professionnel de Qualification des Ingenieurs-Conseils et Bureaux d'Etudes Techniques du Batiment et des Infrastructures* (OPQIBI) maintains a list of qualifications of consulting engineers and *bureaux d'études* (technical design offices), issuing certificates of qualification for various categories of work. Architects must be registered and carry responsibility insurance.

• registration of architects signing building and town planning permit applications (France).

The German system, with more control by authorities and less control by constructors and the French system, with less direct control by authorities and more responsibilities for constructors, whilst providing alternative routes for European regulation in the 1990s, share a number of common features:

• licensing by government or a commission set up by government of technical controllers for checking major structural work and, in France, fire precautions, with a requirement for responsibility insurance

• classification and registration of certain participants in the design/construction

Table 10.6   France: guarantees and responsibilities

Type of cover	Nature of damage	Time	Start	Insurance I	II	III
Decennial responsibility	Structure of building and parts firmly fixed structure (structural damage and failure of weathertightness) impropriety ie failure to serve intended use*	10 yr	R	•	•	
Guarantee of proper functioning[1]	Failure of equipment to function properly	2 yr min	R			•
Guarantee of work to specification[2]	All defects	1 yr	R			
Responsibility of component manufacturer	Structural damage and failure of weather-tightness caused by component[3]	10 yr	R	•		
Sound insulation	Failure to meet code requirements	6 mth	1st occup			⊙

R: *Réception des travaux* ie practical completion

I   Insurance of professional responsibilities by designer, builder and component manufacturer

II   Insurance *'dommage'* taken out by owner

(Both types of insurance obligatory under the 1978 law)

III   Voluntary

1   *bon fonctionnement* of equipment

2   *parfait achèvement* ie work as designed and specified

3   the definition of a component has not been easy and there is extensive jurisprudence on the matter.

*   the issue of fitness for intended use appears to cover failure to meet a published site use requirement.

Source: Building Research Establishment

process (France) and nomination of a responsible site supervisor (Germany)

- use of national technical specifications – DINs in Germany; *normes* and DTUs in France – as deemed to satisfy indications of regulation requirements

- certification of new products as conforming to regulation requirements (Germany) or presenting no abnormal risk if properly used (France)

- identification of high risk situations where there are special requirements (Germany) or where second-party checking is mandatory (France)

The regulators' perspective: two scenarios

Earlier in this review of regulatory systems it was shown how the concept of 'essential requirements' is central to the harmonisation of technical specifications for construction prod-

ucts under the EC Construction Products Directive. Moreover, the Directive's list of essential requirements can be equated in large degree to the technical requirements given in regulation systems of EC member states, despite basic differences in the way their satisfaction is controlled and how far they cover the operation and maintenance of building services. It has been shown that the difference of approach is most marked between France and Germany.

In terms of safety in case of fire (ER2); hygiene, health and the environment (ER3); safety in use (ER4); protection against noise (ER5) and energy economy and heat retention (ER6), building occupancy and the use, operation, servicing and maintenance of its installations may have least equal importance as its initial design and construction when handed over to the first owner.

To achieve the aims of an essential requirement, control over products and their incorporation in the initial construction is but one stage in a process of control and surveillance. Present regulatory systems may have to be updated to take account of more complex buildings and installations and a wider range of

Table 10.7 France: categories of buildings and construction works for which control of design and sitework by a licensed technical control office is mandatory

IGH	*Immeubles de grande hauteur* (High rise buildings: the regulations regard a building where the top floor is 28 metres above street level as high rise; but another authority refers to buildings over 50 metres)
ERP 1–3	*Établissements recevant du public: catégories 1–3* (Buildings which can accommodate more than 300 members of the public)
Autres	Other than industrial buildings which present high risks eg with basements deeper than 15 metres or foundations deeper than 30 metres; cantilevered structures spanning over 20 metres and other structures with spans over 40 metres; and works involving excavations over 5 metres below neighbouring buildings

Source: Building Research Establishment

responsibilities, involving many different partici-pants, during the construction, design, use and reuse decision processes. Reference may have to be made to 'approved documents' such as technical codes and specifications, many of which will be harmonised at a European level.

Such decisions need to be based on the specialist knowledge, competence and integrity of many different kinds of organisations and persons, and involve an understanding of 'ap-proved documents'. Therefore, the conventional arrangement of control through a single reg-ulatory authority may well have to be replaced by a complex of persons and agencies whose responsibilities, qualifications and practices will be specified and regulated by an authority rather than by technical details of particular items of construction works and services in-stallations.

If this becomes a basis for a future regulatory process, the direction taken by the regulatory process in the 1990s may well be towards an amalgam of legal specification of responsibili-ties, as in the French system, and the assurance of the competence and quality of management based on third party assessment and surveil-lance with associated responsibility insurance, rather than the creation of technical bureau-cracy, as in the German model. To adopt this option would require acceptance of changes in UK legislation, at least for regulation of non-housing works.

In the final account, the quality of buildings, their location and effect on the environment including surrounding property, their internal arrangement and equipment, and the conveni-ence, safety and comfort they provide will be measured by the satisfaction of users and

Table 10.8   France: documents relevant to building regulation

Regulations (*règlements*)	**Official Texts (*JO: Journal Officiel*)**
Official texts (*décrets* and *arrêtés*) carry technical requirements – usually referred to as *règlements* – which form parts of legal Codes or collections of laws: *Code des communes* (local government) *Code de l'urbanisme* (town planning) *Code de la construction et l'habitation* (construction and housing) *Code du travail* (labour protection)	Full texts or extracts of laws, application decrees (*décrets*), ministerial orders (*arrêtés*), and ...... administrative circulars interesting constructors are published in a loose supplement: *Textes Officiels* with the weekly *Le Moniteur*; together with lists of officially adopted French standards (*normes homologuées*)

Technical documents
1 *Normes–NF* (standards)
2 *Documents techniques unifiés* (workmanship codes)
2 *Avis techniques* (French agréments)

REEF (18 volume looseleaf collection of legal texts, technical documents, and product conformity certificates)
CSTB (*Centre scientifique et technique du bâtiment*)

Source: Building Research Establishment

Table 10.9 France: constructors' responsibilities

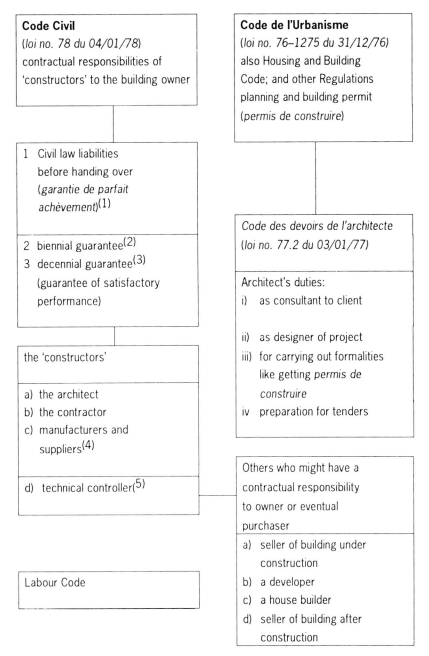

(1)   responsibility for making good defects listed on handing over (reception)

(2)   for *menus oeuvres*, for example, doors, windows, fittings not affecting structure or weathershield

(3)   for *gros oeuvres*, ie structure and weathershield

(4)   responsibility for products designed specially which affect structure or weathershield

(5)   have to be employed for high-rise and public 'assembly' buildings and where the structure is complex (see Table 10.7)

Source: Building Research Establishment

owners. Expectations and user needs change with time and fashion, so do the economics of building operation and maintenance. Performance may deteriorate with losses in efficiency and serviceability. Equipment which fails may not be replaced. New risks arise. Hazards to health and safety, unknown or regarded as of little importance by regulatory authorities when a project was initiated, become matters of major concern.

Quality is not a static feature. To achieve it is like shooting at a moving target. The designer and builder must meet immediate needs and satisfy the requirements of regulatory systems which, however progressive, will be based on past experience. Nevertheless designers and their clients must anticipate future trends, which is no easy task. For example, few designers

aiming to achieve high standards of daylighting anticipated that large areas of fenestration involving lightweight curtain walling resulted in working environments that were unacceptable in terms of excessive sunlight, heat and external noise.

The spiral of quality decay is a recognised phenomenon in the marketing of consumer products. Periodic inspection to check performance is a feature of many regulatory systems and destruction by regulatory authorities of unsafe products is nothing extraordinary. Even though it is impractical to regulate buildings in the same way, for example, as a motor car or a jumbo jet aircraft, a fresh look at the approach to regulation of the performance of buildings over time is likely to be an important element in the regulatory process as installations become

Table 10.10   France: technical control services offered

	Name of service	Scope of service
L	'Legal'	Stability and soundness (*solidité*) of access roads (*viabilité*), foundations, structure, weathershield and services integral with structure – matters in decennial guarantee
S	Safety ('*securité*')	Safety of future occupants: restricted to matters specifically covered in regulations
A	'Assurance'	In additional to L, control over the soundness of installations; but does not include tests to assess performance in operation
A'	'Assurance: type FNPC' *	Service agreed between COPREC and FNPC which additional to A provides for testing operation of installations and control of thermal and sound insulation
E	'*Existants*'	Compatibility of new work with the stability of existing structure
HST	Health and safety of workers on construction site	
	'*mission thermique*'	Conformity with requirements of energy conservation regulations
	'*mission acoustique*'	

*   FNPC; *Fédération Nationale des Promoteurs Constructeurs*

Source: Building Research Establishment

more sophisticated, and as user requirements and risks to health and personal safety are better understood.

Appendices

Appendix 1
Use Classes under the Town & Country Planning (Use Classes) Order 1987

This Order introduced a new Use Class, B1 Business, which combines many office uses formerly in Class II with light industrial uses formerly within Class III of the Use Classes Order 1972. It is for this reason that it is useful to consider as a single class of building not only conventional offices but a wide range of other kinds of workplaces. The introduction of the B1 Class took account of the fact that in a business or science park, for example, it was unrealistic to distinguish between office premises, recording studios and microcomputer assembly workshops.

A separate issue not covered by the Order is that of new uses for agricultural buildings which may be at present exempted.

Appendix 2
EEC Directives, including proposals (as at December 1990), which may have an effect on the regulatory process

1 EEC Directives relating to public works and supply contracts

- Public Works Directive 71/305/EEC; amended by 89/440/EEC (coordination of procedures for award of public works contracts; generally affects contracts for works over £3.3 million; implemented in UK by HM Treasury in July 1990)

- Public Supplies Directive 77/62/EEC; amended by 89/295/EEC (coordination of procedures for award of supply contracts by central, regional and local authorities and similar bodies; implemented in UK by HM Treasury in January 1989)

- Utilities (Excluded Sectors) Directive (adopted by Council of Ministers in September 1990, extends public works and supply contracting to utilities – energy, transport, water and telecommunications – sectors; in force by January 1993: a 'remedies' Directive to ensure compliance is being drafted)

2 EEC Directives relating to safety and performance of products and equipment

- Defective Products Liability Directive 85/374/EC (implemented in UK mainly through the Consumer Protection Act 1987)

- Construction Products Directive 89/106/EEC (due to come into force in June 1991)

- Electrically Operated Lifts Directive 84/529/EEC; amended by 86/312/EEC and 90/486/EEC (mainly concerned with technical performance, inspection and certification of passenger lifts; implemented in UK through Electrically Operated Lifts Regulations 1986)

- Electromagnetic Compatibility Directive 89/331/EEC (safeguards against intolerable electromagnetic disturbances caused by devices; not yet implemented in UK)

- A Directive relating to the use of the 'EC Mark' is being drafted and views on it were sought from Member States in November 1990

3 EEC Directives relating to the environment

- Environmental Impact Assessment Directive 85/337/EEC (requires assessments of likely environmental impact of planned major industrial or infrastructure projects; implemented in UK through Town and Country Planning (Assessment of Environmental Effects) Regulations 1988/1990; a proposed European Environmental Agency has yet to be set up).

- A Directive on Toxic and Dangerous Waste is being drafted.

4 EEC Directives relating to the workplace

• Improvements in the Safety and Health of Workers at work 89/391/EEC (the 'framework' Directive which applied to public and private sectors and will be given flesh by further Directives; to be implemented by December 1992)

• Safety and Health for the Workplace 89/654/EEC (first of the 'follow-up' Directives giving detailed technical requirements affecting design and maintenance of public and private buildings; to be implemented by December 1992)

• The use of Work Equipment Directive 89/655/EEC (second of the 'follow-up' Directives giving detailed technical requirements affecting tools, machines and installations; to be implemented by December 1992)

• The use of Personal Protective Equipment Directive 89/656/EEC (third of the 'follow-up' Directives giving detailed technical requirements; to be implemented by December 1992)

• Manual Handling of Loads Directive 90/269/EEC (fourth of the 'follow-up' Directives listing employers' obligations to avoid workers' risks of back injury)

• The use of Display Screen Equipment Directive 90/270/EEC (fifth of the 'follow-up' Directives covering workstations)

• Machinery Safety Directive 89/392/EEC (covers work equipment to be implemented by December 1992)

• Noise Directive 86/188/EEC (concerned with protection of works from risks related to exposure to noise at work; implemented in UK by Noise at Work Regulations 1989/1990)

• A Directive on Minimum Safety and Health Requirements at Temporary or Mobile Works Sites has been submitted by the Commission to member states

5 EEC Directives relating to professions

• Professional Qualification Directive 89/484/EEC (draft Regulations issued covering professions of Chartered Builder, Chartered Building Services Engineer, Chartered Engineer, Chartered Surveyor, Chartered Town Planner, Chartered Librarian and other professions. Architects are covered by 85/384/EEC, implemented in October 1987)

• A Directive aimed at opening up design and other construction related services is being drafted

6 Other EEC Directives

• Provision of information in the field of technical standards and regulations 83/189/EEC (defines the types of standards documents and liaison between standards bodies)

• Compliance Directive 89/665/EEC (defines procedures for surveillance of public procurement contracts)

• Up to date information of European legislation affecting construction is to be found in DoE; *Euronews Construction*. Table 10.11 is reproduced from the May 1992 issue.

Appendix 3
EEC Construction Products Directive: essential requirements

The products must be suitable for construction works which (as a whole and in their separate parts) are fit for their intended use, account being taken of economy, and satisfy the following essential requirements where the works are subject to regulations containing such requirements. Such requirements must, subject to normal maintenance, be satisfied over an economically reasonable working life. The requirements generally concern actions which are foreseeable.

1 *Mechanical resistance and stability.* The construction works must be designed and built in such a way that the loadings that are liable to act on it during its construction and use will not lead to any of the following:

• collapse of the whole or part of the work

• major deformation to an unacceptable degree

- damage to other parts of the works or to fittings or installed equipment as a result of major deformation of the load-bearing construction

- damage by an event disproportionate to the original cause

2 *Safety in fire.* The construction works must be designed and built in such a way that in the event of an outbreak of fire:

- the load-bearing capacity of the construction can be assumed for a specific period of time

Table 10.11   European legislation – progress: May 1992

Title	EC reference	State of play	OJ reference
Public Procurement			
Works Directive	71/305/EEC	Implemented	L185 – 25.08.71
Works Directive	89/440/EEC	Implemented – 21.12.91	L210 – 21.07.89
Supplies Directive	77/61/EEC	Implemented	L13 – 15.01.77
Supplies Directive	80/767/EEC	Implemented	L215 – 18.08.80
Supplies Directive	88/265/EEC	Implemented – 21.12.91	L127 – 20.05.88
Compliance Directive	89/665/EEC	Implemented – 21.12.91	L395 – 30.12.89
Utilities Directive	90/531/EEC	Adopted – 17.09.90	L297 – 29.10.90
Utilities Remedies Directive	COM(90) 297	Adopted – 25.02.92	Not yet printed in OJ
Proposed Services Directive	COM (91) 322	Common position 25.02.92	Not yet printed in OJ
Proposed Utilities Services Directive	COM (91) 343	Proposal made November 1991	Not yet printed in OJ
Mutual Recognition			
Architects Directive	85/384/EEC	Implemented – 21.10.87	L223 – 21.08.85
1st General Directive	89/48/EEC	Implemented – 17.04.91	L19/16 – 24.01.89
2nd General Directive	–	Common position February 1992	Not yet printed in OJ
Safety in use			
Hot water boilers	COM (90) 368	Proposal	Not yet printed in OJ
Electromagnetic Compatibility Directive	89/336/EEC	Implemented. Proposal for amendment	L139 – 23.05.89
General Product Safety Directive	COM (90) 259	Common position reached – 15.10.91	C156 – 27.06.90 (text later revised)
Machinery Safety Directive	89/392/EEC	Implemented	L138 – 29.06.89
Used Machinery proposal	–	Proposal October 1991	Not yet printed in OJ
Machinery Safety Directive	91/368/EEC	Adopted – June 1991	L198 – 22.07.91
Health and safety			
Construction Sites	COM (91) 117	Common position reached – 19.12.91	C112 – 27.04.91
Workplace Directive	89/654/EEC	Adopted – 30.11.89	L393 – 30.12.89
Display Screen Equipment	90/270/EEC	Adopted – 29.05.90	L156 – 29.05.90
Use of Personal Protective Equipment	89/686/EEC	Adopted – 30.11.89	L399 – 30.12.89
Manual Handling of Loads	90/269/EEC	Adopted – 29.05.90	L393 – 30.12.89
Use of Work Equipment	–	Adopted – 30.11.89	L156 – 21.06.90
Construction Products Directive	89/106/EEC	Implemented – 27.12.91	L40 – 11.02.89
Marketing and use			
Asbestos	91/659/EEC	Adopted – 31.10.91	L363 – 31.12.91
Pentachlorophenol	91/173/EEC	Adopted	L85 – 05.04.91

Source: DoE: Euronews Construction, May 1992

● the generation and spread of fire and smoke within the works is limited

● the spread of fire to neighbouring construction works is limited

● occupants can leave the works or be rescued by other means

● the safety of rescue teams is taken into account.

3 *Hygiene, health and the environment.* The construction work must be designed and built in such a way that it will not be a threat to the hygiene or health of the occupants or neighbours, in particular as a result of any of the following:

● the emission of toxic gases

● the presence of dangerous particles or gases in the air

● the emission of dangerous radiation

● pollution or poisoning of the water or soil

● faulty elimination of waste water, smoke, solid or liquid wastes

● the presence of damp in parts of the works or on surfaces within the works

4 *Safety in use.* The construction works must be designed and built in such a way that it does not present unacceptable risks of accidents in service or in operation such as slipping, falling collision, burns, electrocution, injury from explosion.

5 *Protection against noise.* The construction works must be designed and built in such a way that noise perceived by the occupants or people nearby is kept down to a level which will not threaten their health and will allow them to sleep, rest and work in satisfactory conditions.

6 *Energy economy and heat retention.* The construction works and its heating, cooling and ventilation installations must be designed and built in such a way that the amount of energy required in use shall be low, having regard to the climatic conditions of the location and needs of the occupants.

In broad outline, the Directive's list of essential requirements differ little from the list of requirements set out in Schedule 1 of the Building Regulations 1985. Despite differences in scope and arrangement, much of the building legislation in the Community has similar requirements, if the fact that there may be differences in climatic conditions, ways of life and degrees of protection at national, regional or local level is accepted.

Appendix 4: *special features of construction*

A regulatory system for construction should take into account its special features such as are listed below:

● Statutory authorities regulate design and construction in many ways and stages during the process, and their requirements may be of a detailed, prescriptive or of a functional and general character, and may be followed by examination and, possibly, formal approval of the resulting work.

● Buildings are mostly 'one-off' products, erected on a piece of ground which has unique features and which may vary in quality every few metres. Testing of prototypes is rare. Even when standard designs are used, details have frequently to be modified to satisfy site, regulatory or client requirements.

● Buildings last for decades, often for centuries, and parts of a building may have to be replaced at various times, receiving varying degrees of care, maintenance and repair during their life. Yet the technical requirements of building regulations implicitly assume that a building will remain for ever as built; and the law tends to place all but timeless responsibilities for good performance on the original designer and producer.

● The consequences of a defective design, selection of an unsuitable component or material, careless installation, inappropriate maintenance or repair, and misuse during occupation may remain latent for many years, and only show up and cause trouble following an exceptional 'overload' like a windstorm or explosion, or be identified as a result of change of ownership or use.

● When defects are discovered, remedial work is unlikely to be easy for more than one reason: it may be difficult to determine the cause of failure and a false diagnosis could well aggravate the problem; and neither the original work nor the changes resulting from the remedial work are likely to be recorded systematically.

● By tradition and convention, design and construction are generally considered as separate activities, each practitioner – directly or through a third party – having a separate contractual responsibility to the building owner. Furthermore, design work is often split between different practitioners, and may be more or less completed before the organiser of the production process – the builder – is chosen, responsibility for the process being split between many subcontractors.

● Supervision and inspection on construction sites is not usually systematic. Site testing of work in progress is rarely undertaken except when sub-standard work is discovered. When it is, rectification is likely to be costly and building completion delayed.

● Manufactured materials, components, assemblies and mechanical equipment may have been tested and quality assured in the factory; but once brought on the building site they are likely to be handled, stored, assembled and installed under adverse weather and other conditions, and even when quality assured components are used and care taken in their handling and installation, they may prove incompatible with their neighbours, the resulting chemical or mechanical interactions being a source of trouble.

● Environmental and user conditions vary within a single building, thus the identification of defective components may prove troublesome, and, as the building is likely to be occupied, remedial work difficult to organise.

● Construction workers move from site to site, and many change employers from one job to the next. Types of work change as a scheme progresses, as do the size and skills required from the workforce. Employer relations change, as do the coverage, expertise and quality of inspection and supervision. The level of work quality required from an individual operative is unlikely to be defined clearly.

Because responsibilities of participants in the process of design manufacture, assembly and supervision are complex and sometimes ill-defined in contract, when latent defects are discovered it may be necessary for an owner to start litigation to recover the cost of resulting damage. Court procedures then take precedence over unbiased and open fact finding. Consequently, feedback to other designers and producers is restricted.

● While in traditional construction a degree of robustness and structural redundancy were the norms, this may not be so under new, possibly cost-competitive conditions. A better understanding of how structures perform has enabled designers to work closer to 'limit states' for reasons of efficiency and economy – and, possibly, as displays of technical skill.

● Where new materials and new techniques are introduced for greater efficiency and/or lower costs, the traditional safeguards which protected practitioners of average competence are weakened. It may not matter in offices where the partners and managers are experienced and their technical and professional staff possess above average skills, and where there is effective quality management. But, in the hands of less competent or experienced practitioners, serious problems may result, even when products of good quality are used. Finally, it is not always easy for a client who builds infrequently to identify which firms are experienced, or possess above average skills for a particular task.

● It is an essential requirement of a work of construction that it has adequate strength and stability to withstand safely any likely overloading to which it will be subjected during its service life. Loadings used in a design should anticipate the possibilities of exceptional events such as windstorms, floods, earthquakes, explosion and building fire, estimation of the likely risk and the effects on a structure being matters for decisions shared between the authorities and professions through building regulations and codes, and the building owner and his advisers.

● Standards represent a knowledge, based on research and practice, of loadings, user requirements, reactions to loadings, and performance of products and systems, resulting in the drafting of consensus documents in which this experience is codified. While structural engineers, and more recently environmental and building services engineers, give much thought to the development of design codes which take risk into account, it is not easy to introduce this knowledge into regulatory systems which do not distinguish between levels of competence and experience among practitioners. Yet to do so through some form of classification and certification of practitioners means a potential restriction on an open and competitive market for services.

● Third party monitoring of the process of design and construction to ensure that work in progress, and the completed scheme, satisfy both design specifications and the assumptions on which they are based is beginning to be accepted. But, to date, little has been done to monitor the effectiveness of the methods adopted by authorities to achieve the objectives of their building regulations and other legal requirements, despite the fact that it is an essential precondition for their harmonisation and simplification.

Appendix 5
Essential requirements applied to land use and environmental protection

This brief list, based on the list of essential requirements set out in the Construction Products Directive, suggests that a similar procedure of development, through Interpretative Documents to policy guidance documents, could be adopted in the regulatory field of land use and environmental protection.

1 *Mechanical resistance and stability.* Covers land subject to subsidence, flooding and, where appropriate, seismic effects on which construction works must be designed and built to minimise risk of collapse and damage to neighbouring works.

2 *Safety in fire.* The use of land should be such that the risk of the generation and spread of fire and smoke and of explosions is limited, including spread to neighbouring works and more widely throughout a community.

3 *Hygiene, health and the environment.* The use of land and any activities on it should be such that it will not be a threat to neighbours or the wider community, in particular as a result of any of the following: the emission of toxic gases; the presence of dangerous particles or gases in the air; the emission of dangerous radiation; pollution or poisoning of the water or soil; faulty elimination of waste water, smoke, solid or liquid wastes.

4 *Safety in use.* The layout and uses of any development shall not present unacceptable risks of accidents from the movement of vehicles, aircraft ,etc.

5 *Protection against noise.* The layout and uses of any development shall not present unacceptable levels of noise such as might threaten the health of members of a community and prevent the enjoyment of sleep, rest and work in satisfactory conditions.

6 *Energy economy and heat retention.* The layout and uses of any development shall not present unacceptable use of energy having regard to the climatic conditions of the location, the location itself and needs of the activities taking place.

References

1 There have been a number of attempts to review regulatory systems nationally and worldwide. For example, the Swedish Institute of Building Documentation has published a third edition of A Survey of Building Regulations Worldwide covering entries from 44 countries. Table 10.1 is an attempt to summarise the main elements of the current regulatory system in England and Wales. No similar international review of regulatory systems relating to land use and development control is known.

2 The Construction Products Directive (89/106/EEC). See Appendices 2 and 3.

3 Environmental Impact Assessment Directive (85/337/EEC). The issue is discussed by C A Fortledge in *Environmental assessment: a practical guide*, Gower Technical Press, 1990

4 Summerson, J, *Architecture in Britain 1530–1830*, Pelican History of Art series, Penguin Books, London 1953 pp 258–260

5 Toplis, I, *The Foreign Office: an architectural history*, Mansell Publishing, London 1987

6 Knowles, C C and Pitt, P H, *The history of building regulation in London 1189–1972*, Architectural Press, London 1972

7 *NBS Special Report 33: A qualitative study of some buildings in the London area*, HMSO, London 1964

8 Banham, R, *The Architecture of the Well-tempered Environment*, Architectural Press, London 2nd Edition 1984

9 See Building Research Station *Urban Planning Research Symposium Report*, Building Research Station, Watford 1965.

10 *Post-war Building Studies No. 16: Business Buildings*, Royal Institute of British Architects, HMSO, London 1944

11 Langdon, F J, *Modern offices: a user survey*, HMSO, London 1966

12 Ministry of Technology, *Building Research*, 1966, p.7

13 Ministry of Housing and Local Government, *Town Centres. Current Practice* HMSO, London 1963

14 The Town & Country Planning (Use Classes) Order 1987

15 Knowles, C and Pitt, P H, *The History of Building Regulation in London 1189–1972*, Architectural Press, London 1972.
British fire legislation on means of escape – 1774–1974, Report BR 088, Building Research Station, Watford 1986

16 Cibula, E, *Building Control in West Germany*. Current Paper CP10/70 Building Research Station, Watford 1970

17 Atkinson, G, *Building law in Western Europe: How responsibility for safety and good performance is shared*
Building control in France. Current Paper CP6/71 Building Research Station, Watford 1971

18 Harper, R H, *Victorian Building Regulations. Summaries of the principal British Building Acts and Model Bye-laws 1840–1914*. Mansell Publishing, London 1985; also: Building regulation and health. Report BR 097. Building Research Station, Watford 1986

19 Cherry, G, *The politics of town planning*. Longman London 1982

20 *Building design legislation; a guide to the Acts of Parliament and Government Orders and Regulations with effect on the design of buildings in England and Wales*. Special Publication 22: CIRIA, London 1982, (updated to April 1987)

21 *Scottish Building Legislation* Special Publication 24: CIRIA, London 1985

22 Department of Health for Scotland: *Report of the Committee on Building Legislation in Scotland*. HMSO, Edinburgh 1957

23 Building Act 1984 Chapter 55. HMSO, London 1984
Department of the Environment: *Manual to the Building Regulations 1985*. HMSO, London 1985

24 Cherry, G, *The politics of town planning*. Longman, London 1982

25 Departmental Circular 22/88: *General Development Order Consolidation* HMSO, London 1988

26 Planning guidance is given in a number of DOE documents:
Planning Policy Guidance 1 (revised): General Policy and Principles, March 1992 (For a review of this important PPG, and of *The Town and Country Planning Development Plans (England) Direction 1992*, see *RIBA Practice* May 1992);
Planning Policy Guidance 18: Enforcing Planning Control, 1992;
Planning and local choice. 1989;
Planning permission and the farmer. 1989;
Structure plans and regional planning. 1990;
The countryside and rural economy. 1990; and in a number of Departmental Circulars including:
16/87: *Development involving agricultural land* HMSO, London 1987;
9/88: *Unitary development plans*. HMSO, London 1988;
18/89 *Publication of information about unused and underused land* HMSO, London 1989

27 *Planning Policy Guidance: Sport and Recreation*, October 1990

28 Consultative paper: *Planning controls over agricultural and forestry buildings*. October 1990

29 Departmental Circular 12/87: *Redundant Hospital Sites in the Green Belt*. HMSO, London 1988

30 Institution of Structural Engineers: *Building Regulations, Approved persons and approved inspectors*, April 1986

31 *Manual to the Building Regulations 1985: Schedule 1: Requirements* HMSO, London 1985

32 See Appendix 3: Construction Products Directive: Essential Requirements

33 *Guidance document for the Building Regulations 1991 and Approved Documents 1992*, by Simon Polley, Building Regulation Consultancy Service 1992, reviews the revised Regulations and Approved Documents.

34 'Flexible friends: Building Regulations 1990'. *New Builder*, 29 March 1990

35 Technical Memoranda TM16: *Fire precautions: sources of information on legal and other requirements*. Chartered Institution of Building Services Engineers 1990

36 Department of Trade and Industry: *Fire and building regulation*, HMSO, London 1990

37 'Staying firm on standards', *New Builder*, 18 October 1990

38 Cherry, G, *The politics of town planning*. Longman London 1982

39 *Planning Policy Guidance: Sport and Recreation*, October 1990

40 Consultative paper: *Planning controls over agricultural and forestry buildings*, October 1990

41 Environmental Impact Assessment Directive (85/337/EEC)

42 Fortledge, C A, *Environmental assessment: a practical guide*, Gower Technical 1990

43 A *Survey of Building Regulations Worldwide*, Byggedok, Stockholm 3rd edition 1989. For earlier reviews: Atkinson, G (consulting editor): *Construction Industry Europe*. House Information Services Ltd, London 1974; and Atkinson, G 'Some European systems for regulation and control of private design and construction with particular reference to fire safety', *Structural Survey*, Vol. 9 No 1 (Summer 1990).
Accounts of arrangements for construction product certification, assessment and testing, technical building control, and standards have been published in *Building Technical Files*: No 22: Federal Republic of Germany (July 1988); No 23: France (October 1988), No 27 (October 1989); No 24: Belgium (January 1989); No 25: Denmark (April 1989); No 26: The Netherlands (July 1989); No 27: The Republic of Ireland (October 1989);

No 28: Spain (January 1990); No 29: Italy (April 1990); and No 30: Portugal (July 1990). *Building Technical Files* are published by Building (Publishers) Limited, London

44 Atkinson, G, 'The 'New Approach' construction products directive. Its longer-term implications for European architects and structural engineers', *Structural Survey*, Vol. 8 No 2 (Autumn 1989)

45 BR 177: *The Construction Products Directive of the European Communities. Draft Interpretative Documents: Protection against noise.* Building Research Station, Watford 1990; BR 179: *The Construction Products Directive of the European Communities. Draft Interpretative Documents: Hygiene, health and the environment.* Building Research Station, Watford 1990; BR 180: *The Construction Products Directive of the European Communities. Draft Interpretative Documents: Energy economy and heat retention.* Building Research Station, Watford 1990; BR 181: *The Construction Products Directive of the European Communities. Draft Interpretative Documents: Mechanical resistance and stability.* Building Research Station, Watford 1990; and BR 182: *The Construction Products*

Directive of the European Communities. Draft Interpretative Documents: Safety in use. Building Research Station, Watford 1990

46 Atkinson, G (consulting editor): *Construction Industry Europe* House Information Services Ltd, London 1974

47 Cibula, E, *Building Control in West Germany* Current Paper CP10/70 Building Research Station, Watford 1970

48 Cesselin, E, *La Règlementation de la Construction en Republique Federale d'Allemagne* CSTB/NOREX, Paris 1987

49 *Building Technical File: No 22: Federal Republic of Germany* Building (Publishers) Limited, London (1988)

50 *Building Technical File: No 23: France.* A detailed report on the French system of technical building control, its merits and limitations is to be found in No 27 Building (Publishers) Limited, London (1989)

51 Ibid

52 Atkinson, G, 'Some European systems for regulation and control of private design and construction with particular reference to fire safety' *Structural Survey* Vol. 9 No 1 (Summer 1990)

11 Case studies of organisations and their workplaces

Introduction

Pressures of change and the workplace

A series of themes of change from the trend papers were used to structure research into how a set of innovative European organisations made decisions about their office workplaces. Pressures of change are affecting organisations in complex and sometimes contradictory ways.

Organisational structures seem to be becoming more flexible, less hierarchical. The location of work may be more varied and less constrained by a nine to five routine in the office. Users of the workplace may expect higher standards and more control over their environment. Information technology will continue to lead the pace of change for organisations, but may become less problematic in the ways it can be accommodated within buildings. Energy consumption by information technology may decline. Businesses may want premises that are less environmentally demanding and damaging.

These sometimes conflicting ideas were developed into a series of propositions which were investigated with the case study organisations. They covered the following areas:

- information technology and telecommunications
- organisational structure and relationships
- productivity
- human resources
- comfort and welfare
- use of time
- the environment and green issues

How have pressures of change in these areas affected organisations' expectations for the workplace?

Decisions about the workplace

Every organisation has to make some similar decisions about the workplace:

- means of procuring space or form of tenure
- location and site of the workplace
- configuration of the building (the size and depths of floors)
- methods and level of environmental servicing
- forms of control of the workplace environment
- issues of space layout
- means of security and access
- furnishings and settings

How are pressures of change affecting this range of decisions?

Selection of case studies

These questions were examined through case studies of organisations that demonstrated leadership, innovation, or a particular interest in terms of how they themselves are adapting to change. Organisations were selected not because they had particularly unusual, well known or architecturally significant workplace buildings. They were selected because as organisations they evidenced striking qualities of change in one or more aspects.

A database of over 1,000 organisations which represented qualities of change of interest to us was prepared, out of which a group of organisations was selected for case study research.

The selection of case study firms is not a representative sample. It is a small group of companies in the UK and the rest of Europe that are interesting examples of how organisations are changing in many dimensions. The case studies reveal how these changes influence and affect their decisions about workplaces.

The case studies therefore provide one set of ideas and examples from which guidance and specification for Responsible Workplaces can be drawn. They provide a rich, complicated source of example and ideas.

In the following section, the key themes arising from the case studies are reviewed, followed by the individual case studies.

Table 11.1 Pressures for change most often considered very important (in rank order where 1 = most often)

Pressure of change	UK cases (11)	non-UK (8)	Total (19)
Organisational structure/relationships	2	1	1
Information technology /telecommunications	1	2	1
Productivity pressures	3	2	2
Human resources	4	2	3
Time pressures	5	3	4
Comfort/welfare	6	3	5
Green/environmental	7	3	6

Source: DEGW   and   Building   Research Establishment

Table 11.2 Workplace decisions most often considered very important (in rank order where 1 = most often)

Workplace decision	UK cases (11)	non-UK (8)	Total (19)
Location	1	2	1
Servicing	3	1	2
Open/enclosed offices	2	2	3
Security/access	2	2	3
Settings/furniture	4	2	4
Procurement	3	4	4
Forms of environmental control	4	3	5
Floor size	5	2	5
Site	4	4	6
Depth of space	4	4	6

Source: DEGW   and   Building   Research Establishment

Summary of findings

Case studies with 19 organisations (11 in the UK, 8 in the rest of Europe) were completed*. They show that:

- The most important pressures of change for organisations are to do with *information technology/ telecommunications and organisational structure.*

- The workplace decisions that are most important are to do with *location, servicing*

* One organisation requested that the case study should not be published.

Table 11.3 Ranking of issues in degree of importance for future workplace decisions(in rank order where 1 = most important)

Issue	UK (11)	non-UK (8)	Total (19)
Adapting the workplace to changing organisational needs	**1**	**1**	**1**
Making the office workplace more responsive to user's needs	2	2	**2**
Making the office workplace more productive	3	2	**3**
Using information technology	4	3	**4**
Comfort and welfare of staff	5	4	**5**
Designing the workplace to respond to time pressures	6	5	**6**
Green issues at the workplace	7	5	**7**

Source: DEGW and Building Research Establishment

the workplace, *layout* (enclosed or open offices) and *security/access*.

- In the future, organisations believe that the issue of *adapting the workplace* to changing organisational needs will be their most important workplace decision

The ranking of pressures of change, workplace decisions and future concerns for the workplace are shown in Tables 11.1, 11.2 and 11.3.

Pressures of change

Information technology and telecommunications

IT is fundamental to organisations, a basic requirement that all workplaces must accommodate satisfactorily. The restructuring of organisations is being supported by information technology which allows improved communication and increased productivity. IT has become the repository of work and is now widely used for all organisational tasks from the routine to the creative at all levels.

IT is enabling some innovative companies to support working patterns that radically alter traditional notions of the design, use, and management of the workplace. IT provides the infrastructure for wide ranging changes in the relationship between time and space at the workplace. The case studies show that such changes do not necessarily depend on particularly advanced information technology, nor do they require workplace environments that are very highly serviced or sophisticated. Key to work pattern innovations using IT are ways of using labour flexibly across a variety of locations.

- IT continues to have a major impact on change in working patterns
- IT is less problematic in terms of its accommodation in the workplace

- the workplace need not be highly technologically specified or served to support advanced IT use

- some organisations are using IT to introduce new ways of using space over time

Organisational structure and relationships

Organisations are restructuring to manage with less hierarchy. They are working more with groups and teams. A priority is placed on increasing internal communication. Restructuring results in centralisation of some key functions and decentralisation of responsibility for work tasks. The use of information technology is intensified.

- more contract work

- use of consultants and outsiders

- formation of alliances and joint ventures

- closer relationships with suppliers

Organisations are trying to be more open and participative, but they are not dispensing with the requirements of effective leadership. Organisations are:

- managing with less hierarchy

- working with more groups and teams

- increasing internal communication

- introducing more flexible employment (especially in UK, less so in Europe)

- combining more participation and maintaining effective leadership

Pressure to achieve higher productivity

The increasing use of teams and groups is designed to improve productivity. This necessitates the bringing together of groups and departments to one location and ensuring their effective means of communication both electronically and spatially. Cultural change is often a prerequisite to improving productivity. Workplaces are designed to encourage increased group and shared working patterns:

- more open plan and shared space

- not compromising on quality of environment

- use of IT to increase communication and support team work

Some firms are using information technology to support increased utilisation of space over time by means of sharing space and facilities on a wider level wherever possible.

More organisations examine the utilisation of the workplace as an asset, charging both internally and externally for the use of space and facilities, and trying to understand the relationship between use of space and overall productivity.

Organisations expect buildings to be efficient, allow easy subdivision and not waste space with unnecessary circulation routes.

Issues of pressures of time were closely related to productivity.

Human resources, comfort and welfare at the workplace

As organisations move away from rigid hierarchy, the welfare of valuable human resources is being ensured in new, less status-oriented ways. Staff participation in human resources policies is increased. The provision of a high quality and efficient working environment is recognised as crucial. But quality of working environment is defined in new ways that sometimes refer back to traditional workplaces or to domestic environments:

- provision of high levels of daylight

- use of natural ventilation

- opening windows

The amenity of the workplace also includes the technology, tools and policies that support work lifestyles that are not bound full time to individual desks in the office:

- car phones

- terminals at home or laptops

- policies to support men and women working flexibly around childcare responsibilities

The amenity of the workplace also includes the attractions of the site, landscape and environment, and its location near excellent transport and shopping facilities.

The organisation wants a healthy workforce:

- avoiding sick building syndrome

- no-smoking policies, help for those giving up smoking

- staff satisfaction surveys

- health maintenance policies such as stress management

Organisations do not want expensive gimmicks at the workplace.

Green or environmental pressures

For a minority of case study organisations green issues are vitally important. But most organisations have dealt with green pressures within the wider framework of strategic decisions about their organisational priorities and needs of their workplaces.

For many, green issues are focused through the problem of energy efficiency, and thereby related to the goal of not wasting resources and minimising costs. Several organisations have integrated these goals into the design, management and use of their buildings, particularly in Germany.

Others have related green issues to the provision of a healthy working environment: the naturally ventilated and highly daylit workplace is seen as both green and healthy. The green building is not a sick building. It must also be a building that avoids widespread air conditioning and is not very deep in plan. The green workplace is also recognised as one that avoids the use of non-sustainable resources (tropical hardwoods) and maximises the use of materials that have low energy life cycle costs (but these are not well understood).

There is widespread recognition that the true costs and benefits of green policies for buildings and workplaces are not known.

Workplace decisions

Location and site decisions

The requirement to be in a metropolitan or capital city was essential for many organisations who need immediate contact with clients, a high degree of access to major transport facilities, and proximity to a pool of talented labour. The capital city location seemed less vital in some European countries, particularly in Germany where the federal structure encourages decentralisation.

Organisations can be attracted by the virtues of a special site or a building that provides a beautiful landscape, attractive shopping nearby or an architectural feature that is outstanding. But all of these features must also enable the optimisation of some critical organisational priority: the regrouping of divisions or the accessibility to staff, for example.

For large complex organisations locating in downtown areas may be a problem in terms of finding suitable sites and buildings: edge of town or out of town sites become more feasible. There may be a relationship between the scale of the organisation and its relative autonomy from the need to locate in central city areas.

Degrees of building servicing and forms of environmental control

Many organisations are providing a high level of power supply and cabling to support intensive use of information technology in ways that do not require particularly high-tech building specification. There are big variations in servicing solutions apparent both within and between European country case study examples.

- work requirements of high information technology use can be achieved in buildings with relatively low technical specification, depending on:
  - narrower depth building plans
  - use of natural ventilation
  - focus on servicing in zones of priority need

- green issues are affecting servicing decisions for some organisations, especially in Germany

- green issues are convergent with heightened user concern to control services at a local or individual level

- green issues are convergent with cost pressures to minimise servicing requirements

Open or enclosed offices: issues of layout

The conflicting needs of privacy, identity, and communication are handled both in highly enclosed and totally open plan layouts.

In totally open plan environments, privacy can be provided by ensuring that areas of quiet are provided away from busy circulation routes. Furniture is designed to absorb sound and to screen desks and group areas. Meeting rooms and special working areas can be enclosed for confidential meetings and quiet work. The needs of smaller group identity are provided by forms of semi-enclosure which break up large open spaces. Open layouts are also highly adaptable for sharing space: group areas can be identified in which work settings can be provided for a group of people without providing individuals with their own desks.

In highly enclosed offices, shared open areas may also be provided to provide the space for communication and group work. In Germany the Combi-office layout is overtly designed for this purpose.

Organisations are selecting degrees of openness and enclosure to fulfil the requirements of their working tasks, less as a mark of status. In the UK there is a tendency towards the provision of greater open plan areas to encourage and support more group work and communication. In the rest of Europe the high degree of enclosure that is favoured is supplemented by additional shared or group space.

Security and access

Providing wide access to the workplace for staff to work diverse hours of the day and week has become common. As organisations become more flexible in structure, with various forms of employment relationships, correspondingly new ways of regulating access are required. Few firms, however, have instituted completely 24-hour access. Most limit access around a period of core hours, or allow access to limited numbers of staff at other times.

Ensuring that visitors have limited and controlled access has become a priority. Visitors are more strictly controlled than previously and limited to selected areas of the building. Even staff may be excluded from areas of the workplace for reasons of project security.

Threats to security are monitored with video, closed circuit television, and other electronic systems. Some very high-tech security systems have not been used because they are too complex to implement or too expensive to use.

Furnishings and settings of the office

As organisations are more likely, at least in the UK, to use leased speculative space for their workplaces, the issue of furnishings and settings of the office achieves greater significance as an area of choice and control in the creation of the workplace. Furnishings and settings are used to define corporate image and culture across a range of workplaces that may be otherwise unremarkable. Furniture is used to maximise the utilisation of space and to achieve highly specific patterns of work, integrating information technology services and equipment, and providing for highly varied work activities. Furniture is critical to the design of group and team working spaces. Staff are likely to participate in the selection of furniture. Furniture is recognised as being a very important expression of the relationship between the workplace, the organisation and the individual user.

Procurement and tenure decisions

In the UK organisations are keen to make their property decisions as commercial as possible. They will work with developers on speculative buildings to have them tailored to their needs, and avoid locking up large capital sums into property. In other European countries there is a tradition of organisations developing buildings themselves to suit their particular requirements: the results are more likely to be buildings highly specified to the individual requirements of the organisation, more responsive to their unique characteristics.

Size of floor and depth of space on typical office floors

The size of floors preferred by organisations relates broadly to the needs of communication between working groups or departments. Organisations generally want to keep departments together on single floors and provide for critical adjacency requirements among them. In organisations with large staffs in departments, large floor areas may be required.

The size of floor has to be considered in terms of shape or configuration as well. The needs of communication can be optimised in floor configurations that are open in terms of layout and plan, to maximise visibility. The size and shape of floor is also obviously constrained by the organisational requirements for types of building servicing (natural or artificial) and by the predominant patterns of enclosure or openness.

Outside of the UK, many organisations have maintained a more traditional pattern of narrower depth buildings with natural ventilation. This often coincides with a high degree of enclosed offices or the combi-office in Germany. In the UK, developer buildings have increased floor sizes and depths which coincide with a need for higher servicing levels and complete air conditioning. Even where large open floors have been used, they may be subdivided into identifiable smaller group areas.

AWK, Koblenz, Germany

Company	AWK	Case study workplace, architect	AWK Koblenz offices, designed by Kersten Martinoff Struhk.
Sector	Advertising	Location	August Horch Strasse, Koblenz, W5400 Germany
Country	Germany	Area	3,360 sqm (36,168 sqft)
Number of staff	500	Type of project	Owner occupied building, built in 1982
Number of staff in case study workplace	120	Use of information technology	About 70 per cent of staff have terminals

Source: DEGW and Building Research Establishment

The organisation

AWK is a family owned advertising company. In the early 1980s the company realised it needed a new office building that would express its concern to promote a high level of communication among staff and to create a healthy work environment. AWK has also been concerned with green and environmental issues and wanted its office building to reflect these views.

The use of information technology in recent years has not greatly affected the organisational hierarchy, but it is expected that it will allow more delegation of decision making and a greater degree of democratisation.

There has always been a high level of input from staff and the unions involved at the AWK workplace, although final decisions are made by management. Their concern is how to attract and keep scarce staff. Policies for running the

Figure 11.1
Plan of AWK offices.
(Source: DEGW)

FT 15 30 45 60

M 5 10 15 20

Figure 11.2
Layout of typical working area, AWK offices. (Source: DEGW)

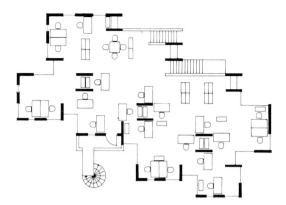

facility seem both generous and informal by United Kingdom standards, for example, staff may bring their pets, such as dogs, to work, and are provided with a staff canteen.

Impact of the organisation on the workplace

The AWK office at Koblenz stands in the great tradition of the Centraal Beheer office building designed by Herman Hertzberger, an office designed to serve a strongly articulated organisational principle: to allow ease of communication among and between working groups and individuals. The result is a building 'more reminiscent of the kasbah than the office' (Figure 11.1). The space is designed to be open plan as far as possible but is arranged in group areas. There was also a requirement to allow all workstations to have access to natural light and to opening windows (as is commonly the case in Germany). These two requirements of group communication and individual identity while providing access to light and air have driven the architectural plan form.

The 'office for a hundred individuals' is created by distributing spaces for small groups (two or four people) around a central double height 'living room'. Shafts are sliced through the building bringing light and air into the centre of the space (Figure 11.2). The group area is usually open, but may be enclosed.

A domestic office

Since the original plan was built in 1982, there has in fact been some adaptation to allow smaller private offices as well. There has also been an increase in the amount of support space. It was intended that the office should appear not to be hierarchical (although the organisation is in fact hierarchical) and to create a domestic, familial quality in the spaces. The key design feature is the ease of visual communication across floors which are broken up into bays for small working groups: combining psychological intimacy and yet encouraging a sense of the whole. The standard working group space is a module of 4.8 metres by 4.8 metres in which are contained four workstations.

AWK manage what they think of as an economic energy policy. The lake adjacent to the office is used as a heat sink in the summer and in the winter warm air is brought into the building overnight when there is cold weather. The building has its own power generator and they manage to produce sufficient electricity to sell off the surplus back to the main grid. The building uses natural materials as far as possible and was designed with well insulated walls which provide a high building mass to absorb heat generated by the use of the office, thereby reducing heating requirements.

Office with a human face

John Worthington has written of the AWK building:

> It is a building conceived from the inside, with a concern for the individual. AWK has a human face rarely found in office design. The building creates a framework within which the organisation can stamp its character. It is a glimpse of the office of the future, when technology is subordinated to the individual

('With a human face', *Architectural Review*, May 1987, pp. 41–46)

Bertelsmann AG, Gutersloh, Germany

Company	Bertelsmann AG	Case study workplace, architect	Offices at Gutersloh
Sector	Publishing	Location	Gutersloh, Germany
Country	Germany	Area	NA
Number of staff	43,700	Type of project	New build, owner occupied
Number of staff in case study workplace	NA	Use of information technology	Most staff have terminals

Source: DEGW and Building Research Establishment

The organisation

Bertelsmann is a book and magazine publisher, also involved with printing, paper production, and the electronic media.

The organisation has become less hierarchical and more geographically dispersed and decentralised. Strategic planning, book keeping and cost management have all been dispersed. The style of management has become more democratic, individuals are more responsible for their own output. Management is based on trust and requires motivation. While managerial work remains largely individual, there has been an increase in team and group working.

Health and environmental concerns

Health and environmental issues are a concern of staff and management. The company is attempting to reduce the use of cars by encouraging staff to use bicycles and by arranging for a bus service to their site.

Impact of the organisation on the workplace

The office is in a suburban location, almost a greenfield site. The company owns the land and the building. The building is composed of two pavilions linked by a glass passage. One bay is 30 metres by 30 metres, the other 22 metres by 22 metres.

The workplace is designed to reflect the high levels of managerial staff employed: there is very little open plan space, almost everyone has their own enclosed offices. As other publishing support functions have been dispersed and decentralised, only managerial staff are employed at these offices. The enclosed offices are about 6 metres by 3.6 metres. Only five per cent of staff, mostly secretaries, are in open plan areas.

In response to health and comfort concerns the building is naturally lit and ventilated as far as possible. High levels of daylight have been provided throughout. Staff are able to individually control their office environment. The company is aware of sick building problems and checks the quality of the air in the office. There are relaxation facilities for the staff and healthy food is served in the staff cafeteria.

The main effort of green policies has been in the area of energy management, but attention has also been paid to the use of materials in the building (avoiding tropical hardwoods and other anti-social or toxic materials). Energy is being recycled through the use of heat pumps.

Dent Lee Witte plc, London, England

Company	Dent Lee Witte plc	Case study workplace, architect	Riverside Three, designed by Sir Norman Foster and Partners
Sector	Change management consulting	Location	Hester Road, London SW11 4AN
Country	United Kingdom	Area	297 sqm (3,200 sqft)
Number of staff	30	Type of project	Tenant in building designed and used by Sir Norman Foster and Partners. Interiors planned by Facility Group Interiors Ltd
Number of staff in case study workplace	30	Use of information technology	16 networked terminals used by 30 staff

Source: DEGW and Building Research Establishment

The organisation

Dent Lee Witte is a young and growing change management consultancy specialising in helping organisations plan and implement change. They offer services of strategic and business planning; organisational development; corporate communications; learning environments; and technology assimilation.

Increasing size and growth led Dent Lee Witte to the need for more efficient management structures allowing for greater employee participation, involvement and improved internal communications. Their offices needed to reflect and support their patterns of team working and respond to quality of life issues raised by their staff.

Absence of hierarchy, encouraging participation

The organisation is trying to be as free of hierarchy as possible. All staff are either consultants or support staff. Much of their work takes place at their clients' premises which has allowed them to plan their office in a way that avoids using the desk as a personal territory. This strategy has been supported by a high

level of use of information technology which is encouraged for all in the organisation. Many staff have car phones and fax machines at home (their car phone bill is higher than the office phone bill). Many staff also use computers at home. Information technology supports flexible working patterns: about 30% of staff time is spent in the office; 60% of staff time is spent at clients' premises.

Staff have been highly involved in designing and reviewing their own human resources policies, including policies towards maternity leave, health insurance, and company cars. Their staff are 60% female.

Impact of the organisation on the workplace

As Dent Lee Witte grew they recognised a need for simple space that could easily accommodate flexible patterns of team working, a high level of use of technology, and provide high standards of air quality, lighting and fittings. The office had to reflect their desire for non-hierarchical space for teams that could easily respond to change over time. 'The workplace should represent the high quality feeling we want to convey in our work to our clients'.

[]

Figure 11.3
*Riverside Three,
London. (Source:
Dent Lee Witte)*

Figure 11.4
*Plan of typical floor,
Riverside Three.
(Source: DEGW and
the Building Research
Establishment)*

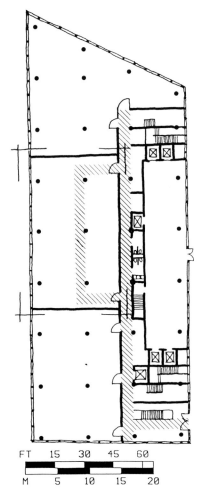

Figure 11.5
*Layout of Dent Lee
Witte's offices.
(Source: DEGW and
Building Research
Establishment)*

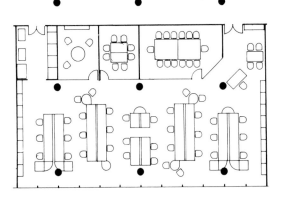

High quality site

The organisation moved to leased space in the building designed by Sir Norman Foster and Partners for their own use in Battersea in 1991 (Figure 11.3). An urban location with access to stations and the airport was considered important, but the critical requirement was the quality of the site and its environment.

The Riverside Three building offered excellent amenities of views of the River Thames and the Albert Bridge, a quiet road and easy parking. The offices have sliding glass doors giving onto a generous terrace above the river.

Dent Lee Witte were concerned that the building should offer the right specification for them: a raised floor for the cabling for their information technology, high levels of daylight from windows into the space and excellent air conditioning.

Flexible team working in shared space

Within the office, project work takes place in shared group areas. There are no personal desks. The office is entirely open plan except for two meeting rooms (25% of the total floor area) which are also used for lunches and quiet working (Figure 11.5). A small proportion of the open area is dedicated to support staff. The office space is used on a task oriented basis, the use of desks geared to the particular needs of project teams at any one time. The desks are arranged in a series of linked workbenches to support team groups of 6–8 people across the length of the office.

Dent Lee Witte selected Herman Miller's Relay office furniture system to provide flexible project team working in shared open space. Of their 30 staff, they expect about one third to be in the office at any one time during a normal working day, although a seat is provided for everyone. The Relay system provides desks that are adjustable in height to allow work to be undertaken standing up.

There are also mobile pedestals (known as 'puppies') that can be moved easily from one place of work in the office to another (Figure 11.7). A mobile end-table may also be added to desks to create additional work surface or meeting areas. Translucent mobile screens are used to define working areas and create some degree of privacy, while 'bollards' are also used to create zones of working areas around the workbenches.

Figure 11.6
Dent Lee Witte, Office interior.
(Source: Dent Lee Witte)

Figure 11.7
Dent Lee Witte office interior, the mobile 'Puppy' pedestal.
(Source: Dent Lee Witte)

Digital Equipment Corporation, Espoo, Finland

Company	Digital Equipment Corporation	Case study workplace, architect	Office of the future and headquarters offices, Espoo, Finland, architect: Olli Parviainen; part interior design: Riitta and Arto Kukasnie
Sector	Electronics	Location	Espoo, near Helsinki
Country	Finland	Area	600 sqm (6,500 sq ft) (size of original Office of the Future site)
Number of staff	500	Type of project	Refurbished office space
Number of staff in case study workplace	430 staff in the main headquarters building	Use of information technology	45 terminals for 60 staff (all shared) in the original Office of the Future site

Source: DEGW and Building Research Establishment

The organisation

Digital Equipment Corporation (Digital) in Finland have instituted a series of innovative managerial changes that have ultimately reshaped their approach to the design, use and management of their offices. The resulting offices challenge the conventional use of the space and time of the office.

Managerial changes that have driven this approach include: decentralising decision making to form many smaller business units across diverse sectors of activity; moving towards less hierarchical team working with more distributed

power; and deepening relationships to suppliers so that they become insiders to the organisation (a process known as vendorisation). All of these changes have been pushing towards improved levels of communication and better group and team working relationships. They have all been supported by the advanced and extensive provision of information technology developed and used by Digital themselves.

Organisational innovations in Finland

The Finnish organisation of Digital has always been rather non-hierarchical. They define themselves as a learning organisation. This is reflected in people rotating jobs and in the use of information technology to communicate across the organisation to all locations, both nationally and internationally. Work has always been organised in teams in open offices. Digital believe they benefit from close contact and in sharing their learning about their customers.

In 1985 Digital proceeded to link everyone in their organisation by network in Finland, to push the use of information technology to its fullest extent and to dispense with the use of paper for office work as far as possible. Information technology was to be used both to save money

Figure 11.8
Digital Equipment Corporation office interior. (Source: DEGW and Building Research Establishment)

Figure 11.9
Digital Equipment Corporation, mobile phone installation. (Source: DEGW and Building Research Establishment)

Figure 11.10
Digital Equipment Corporation, office interior. (Source: DEGW and Building Research Establishment)

Figure 11.11
Digital Equipment Corporation, office interior. (Source: DEGW and Building Research Establishment)

Figure 11.12
Digital Equipment Corporation Headquarters exterior. (Source: DEGW and Building Research Establishment)

and to change working habits. Videotext bulletin boards and electronic mail have largely substituted for paper as far as their internal communications are concerned.

An office experiment by the sales team

In 1986 Digital sales teams collaboratively redesigned themselves a refurbished office space in a small building near their headquarters in Espoo: the Office of the Future. The sales staff were dissatisfied with the traditional approach to the design of their office, and felt that architects would be unable to adequately express what they wanted to achieve for their office. 'The architects were too conservative'.

The result was a startling departure from the conventional office: office furnishings were replaced by domestic furniture, mobile cellular phones replaced the desk top telephone, and the very relationship between one person and a desk was entirely replaced by a range of informal work settings that could be used by anyone. The lounge chair, the sofa, and the swinging chair became symbols of an entirely new way of working.

Key to the functionality of the plan was the ubiquity of networked computers accessible by all staff, a minimal reliance on paper work and files, and the installation of a mobile and portable system of telephones. All telephone calls were made with mobile cellular phones. Underlying the technology, however, was the desire to free up the work process, to enable staff to work wherever they needed to work, and to work with whomever they needed to work with. Driving the process of change was the desire to enhance the processes of communication at work, both electronically and through space and time.

The sharing of desks and work settings by about 60 staff in the initial experiment resulted in a saving of about 45% of space they would have used in a traditional office layout. 35 working places (desks or other settings) were provided for 60 staff. The space of the early experimental office had to be open and to allow good visibility for the sales group, they therefore avoided long or narrowly shaped space. The space had to be attractive, to feel spacious, and be easy to walk around in.

The end result was an environment of diverse work settings, some special workstations for computers, equipment and drawing areas, and many terminals sitting on low tables, high tables, and on every available surface. Sofas and swing seats were arranged in small groups. A coffee bar served as an informal meeting point at the start of the day. Two meeting rooms with glass walls were provided for private meetings or concentrated phone calls.

The impact of the organisation on the workplace

As the success of the early Office of the Future was recognised, Digital decided to institutionalise the office design concept throughout its headquarters offices in Finland. The office was to be seen as 'a concept of the organisation'.

Free address planning has been implemented for all staff for whom this is suitable, including sales, design and consultancy staff. For all other staff some of the principles of space planning, communication and organisational methods evolved in the earlier experiment have been extended as far as possible. These include: entirely open plan offices, no enclosed offices for anyone (including even the most senior directors and executives); a fairly free arrangement of desks and a wide variety of furnishings; a strong dependence on networks, information technology and electronic communications; a high level of home based terminals (for about two thirds of staff); and mobile and car phones wherever these are appropriate.

Conventional office exterior

What is perhaps most surprising on visiting the headquarters offices at Espoo is how utterly conventional they look from the outside. The headquarters building is in fact a 1986 three-storey pre-let building designed with some of Digital's requirements in mind but then modified only in the interior to implement the concepts of the Office of the Future. The image of the office exterior is bland and unremarkable, indicating nothing of the radical approach to the working environment that may be found inside.

Digital also occupy space in a multi-tenanted complex nearby called the Innapolis Center where the same planning principles have also been implemented, this space is used by Digital's Intelligent Building and Networking Group. This particular building offers a much higher external image than the 1986 headquarters, and was designed to be space planned in the conventional Scandinavian Combi-office style: small enclosed offices on the perimeter space with group open plan areas in the central space of the floor. It is significant that Digital's tenancy in the building is the only one so far that has been designed to be entirely open plan.

Digital headquarters building at Espoo

The headquarters building is planned in three zones across an 18-metre span building depth. The central zone is reserved for small meeting rooms, vending areas, cores and other kinds of support spaces. Some of the central zone

Figure 11.13
Digital Equipment Corporation Headquarters, plan of typical floor. (Source: DEGW and Building Research Establishment)

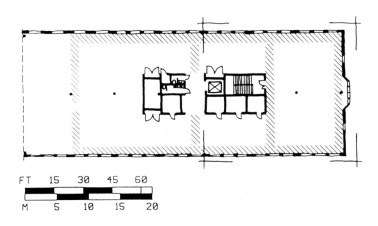

FT   15   30   45   60

M   5   10   15   20

space is also used for working areas. The dimensions of the building plan were originally selected to maximise the access to daylight, so that the depth of space from glass to central core is only about seven metres. (In contrast the space occupied by Digital in the Innapolis building is clear space of up to 18 metres glass to glass in a triangular configuration, avoiding any interruption of the open floor space). The narrow depth of the perimeter open space zones in the older building is rather restricting on the layout of the space, especially for groups and teams to work together.

On the ground floor of the headquarters building is a reception and customer demonstration area. In the customer demonstration area is a mass of equipment displayed on mobile kidney-shaped desks of varying heights connected to flexible coiled cables descending from the ceiling. On the same floor are a series of client meeting rooms and presentation areas.

The building, like many in Scandinavia, offers high levels of staff amenities. These include: staff cafeteria, gymnasium, sunbeds, showers, and photographic dark rooms, a bar and social club, sauna rooms and a swimming pool. The saunas and pool are used for client entertainment but can be used by staff on Fridays for group and unit meetings.

Facility management: vendorisation

A novel approach to deepening relationships to suppliers has resulted in a wide range of what were previously outsourced services being offered by external suppliers within the office. Such services include: car hire, stationery supplies, mail, and copiers.

Figure 11.14
Layout of typical working area. (Source: DEGW and Building Research Establishment)

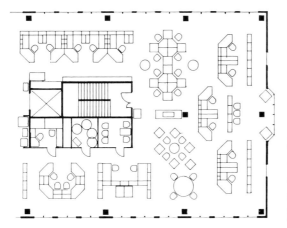

A new way of working across space and time

For the office areas that have fully implemented the Office of the Future concept, the way of working has changed radically. The major change has been the move to a free address system in which no one individual 'owns' his or her desk. For those staff that are frequently out of the office, or who are highly mobile within the office (attending frequent meetings, for example), desks have been reduced to around 50% of the actual numbers of staff. Staff who need desks all the time, such as administrators, are allocated their own desks permanently.

All mobile staff are equipped with portable phones that are held in chargers until picked up when the staff arrive in the office. In many of the working areas, the phone charging position is placed next to a personal mobile pedestal unit, forming a miniature home base for the individual. Typically, in this area of the office staff display family photographs, identify themselves, or otherwise personalise the individual space. The mobile pedestal may be pulled to the selected working position, if required. However, every working position, of whatever kind, is always provided with a terminal on which all files can be accessed, and through which communication may take place on the network. The workplaces are also often provided with a pedestal in which may be found a kit of pens, notepad, and other useful office implements. The kit of work tools belongs to no-one individually and is re-stocked for use every day.

The atmosphere of the office is open and casual. Staff who are only 'touching down' in the office merely stop at one of the higher level desks to access a screen for information. Others form small groups working together. Individuals making important calls walk to find a quiet secluded corner of the open office in which a few minutes of privacy may be found. Others are holding meetings in the glass walled meeting rooms. The absence of banks of filing cabinets is striking: where has all the paper gone? The reduction of paper based work and the variety of work settings provide an entirely new appearance to the office: more open and less cluttered, a space for moving around in and communicating rather than handling a paper process.

Edding AG, Ahrensberg, Germany

Company	Edding	Case study workplace, architect	New office headquarters, designed by Struhk and Partner, Braunschweig
Sector	Manufacturing	Location	Ahrensberg
Country	Germany	Area	5,200 sqm (55,974 sq ft)
Number of staff in case study workplace	100	Type of project	New owner occupied building
		Use of information technology	I terminal per staff (100%)

Source: DEGW and Building Research Establishment

The organisation

Edding manufacture, develop and market felt marker pens. They control 80% of the German market and have a world-wide distribution. They are involved in the research and development of innovative products.

The organisation had maintained staff in two office buildings and felt the need for a greater level of communication between organisational units as well as a need to decrease levels of paperwork. The company wanted a new building to provide better working conditions.

Information technology has already been used by Edding to increase the autonomy of individuals' work, thereby eliminating direct overseeing or detailed control of work tasks. Everyone in the organisation uses information technology. Higher levels of interaction and more team working have been encouraged informally.

Figure 11.15
Plan of typical floor. (Source: DEGW and Building Research Establishment)

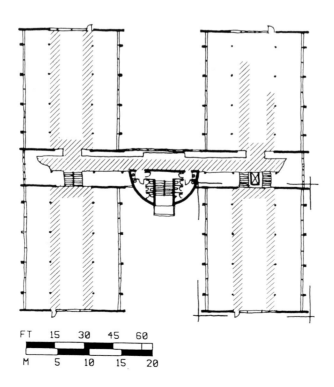

Impact of the organisation on the workplace

Edding worked with a consultant to determine the relationship between their organisational

Figure 11.16
*Layout of typical working area.
(Source: DEGW and Building Research Establishment)*

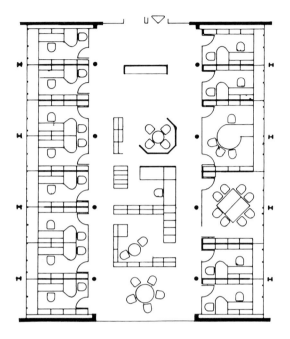

Figure 11.17
*Edding headquarters building.
(Source: Edding AG)*

needs and the design for their new office building. The design of the office building was selected out of three submissions.

Research into the needs of the organisation suggested that departmental groups would be best served by floor sizes that would allow sixteen offices on each floor with adjacent shared open space. Everyone has an identical enclosed office so that the problem of moving people around the building has been simplified. (Previously only heads of departments had enclosed offices and others were in shared group rooms for three or four people).

The size of the floors and the depth of the floor space across the building (from glass to glass) allowed for the provision of both enclosed offices and shared open plan areas in the central part of the floor. It was intended that the provision of these Combi-style offices would encourage more communication, interaction, and team work. But staff have not yet got used to the shared open areas in the centre of each floor and they are not as yet being fully utilised.

The provision of high levels of natural light and ventilation to the enclosed offices was a major design consideration. The central shared areas of space are ventilated through the ends of the building.

At the time of moving into the building the working groups did not yet fill the floors, so there was an excess of space on several floors, resulting in groups feeling somewhat isolated from each other. Staff were also surprised that they do not have more privacy in the new building, because the doors of the offices are left open and the offices are exposed to the group areas. All the support space required by individuals is in the central shared group area.

Enfield Borough Council, London, England

Company	Enfield Borough Council	Case study workplace	Homeworking by staff in Revenues department
Sector	Public sector, local government	Location	Residential housing in vicinity of the Borough
Country	United Kingdom	Area	200 staff of which 59 are home based
Number of staff	10,000	Type of project	Homeworking organisation
Number of staff in case study workplace	The Borough employ 60 homeworkers in the Revenues department	Use of information technology	All homeworking staff use terminals at home

Source: DEGW and Building Research Establishment

The organisation

Enfield Borough Council is responsible for a wide range of community services, and is the largest employer in Enfield. The Borough has been trying to economise in its provision of services and to become more client oriented, providing 'one stop shopping' for the public wherever possible. As part of its drive to improve efficiency the utilisation of assets, buildings and space has been addressed.

Homeworking

The Department of Revenues was under particular pressure in 1990–1991 to implement policies for revenue collection as a result of the new local community charge tax paid by all adult individuals. This required additional staff to administer. Homeworking was introduced as a means of minimising the impact of additional staff on premises costs. The use of homeworkers also enabled the Borough to draw in new kinds of workers, particularly mothers with families who can only work from home, or those with disabilities, who would otherwise not have been available for employment. The homeworking staff work flexible hours within a range of 28–36 hours per week. The actual working times are notified to the Council in advance. A home-based supervisor delivers work to homeworkers several times a week. Training is provided either on a one-to-one or group basis.

Homeworkers are locally-based staff usually carrying out data processing and administrative tasks from their homes, using a computer installed by the Council. The terminal is linked by telephone to a mainframe computer at the Council's headquarters.

Homeworkers are selected by interviews that carefully screen the suitability of candidates for working at home and the suitability of the home environment for working in. The home must be in the local area to enable easy collection and distribution of work. A career path for homeworkers has been established and homeworking staff benefit from the same systems of pay and conditions of employment as office based staff. A regular social evening is organised for the homeworkers and they receive a magazine.

A pilot homeworking scheme with 10 staff was completed in 1989. By 1991 Enfield employed 60 homeworkers within a seven mile radius of the Council offices. Nearly all the staff are women.

Impact of the organisation on the workplace

Once a homeworker has been recruited and their home deemed suitable for homeworking, a computer terminal is installed. The home must provide sufficient space for a desk and chair and key safety requirements must be met. The homeworker is provided a contract with clear policies describing the health and safety aspects of the work, such as the siting of the terminal, and the exclusion of young children and household pets from the working area. The home working area must provide for adequate data protection (lockable drawers to the desk). General insurance for theft and accident is provided by the Council.

Glaxo Pharmaceuticals UK Ltd., London, England

Company	Glaxo Pharmaceuticals UK Ltd.	Case study workplace, architect	Headquarters, designed by Skidmore Owings & Merrill, interiors by Aukett Associates
Sector	Pharmaceuticals	Location	Stockley Park, Heathrow, London
Country	United Kingdom	Area	16,257 sqm (175,000 sqft)
Number of staff	Glaxo Holdings and subsidiaries employ about 12,300 people in the United Kingdom.	Type of project	Lease of space in speculatively developed business park
Number of staff in the case study workplace	Glaxo Pharmaceuticals UK Ltd employ about 800 people in the headquarters buildings	Use of information technology	High level of use, it is available for anyone who wishes to use it.

Source: DEGW and Building Research Establishment

The organisation

Glaxo discover, develop, manufacture and market pharmaceuticals world-wide.

Glaxo have introduced a wide ranging programme of cultural change within their organisation which is designed to restructure the company to respond creatively to changing market pressures in the 1990s. Their operating environment has changed in response to the restructuring of the National Health Service, their major customer. The company has undertaken a major effort to launch several new products over a short period of time. The relocation of the business headquarters to Stockley Park was affected by new thinking on the culture of the business: the design of the new buildings was expressly tailored to suit ongoing cultural change.

Programme of cultural change

A programme of cultural change has been introduced to improve corporate communications laterally throughout the company.

Changes have been designed to break down functional barriers between parts of the organi-

sation, to make the organisation output rather than input oriented. In some parts of the company the levels of hierarchy have been reduced. Pilot programmes of homeworking and flexible working practices have been introduced.

The core staff at Glaxo is 50% female. Issues of new patterns of work have been of particular interest to women in the company. Team working has been increased. Management styles have become more democratic but with a strong emphasis on leadership qualities: 'openness does not reduce the need for effective leadership'. Cultural change is increasing productivity as well as making the workplace more fun.

Impact of the organisation on the workplace

Glaxo moved only six miles from Greenford to Stockley Park, near Heathrow Airport. Yet even such a short distance move was disruptive for many staff, all the more so because of the lack of adequate public transport within the M25 motorway box around London.

Figure 11.18
*Glaxo
Pharmaceuticals UK
headquarters at
Stockley Park.
(Source: DEGW and
Building Research
Establishment)*

for the critical links among the directorates. The buildings should maximise formal and informal interaction at all levels within the company to enable the organisation to respond to the rapidly changing marketplace. This requires buildings that are highly adaptable to change, permitting adaptable workplace layouts and a capacity for high levels of churn. The need for a professional image to the buildings was recognised alongside the high requirement for external security.

Impact of information technology

Glaxo have occupied three buildings on the business park designed by Skidmore Owings and Merrill (Figure 11.18). The buildings have large floorplates 2322 sqm (25,000 sqft) to 3716 sqm (40,000 sqft) wrapped around a central atrium naturally lit through a glazed roof (Figure 11.18). The depth of the floors is typically 18 metres from the external window perimeter to the internal face of the atrium. Each building has three floors.

The objectives for the new buildings were to create a new focus for the company, a cohesive environment for sales and providing opportunity

The use of information technology is recognised as vital to the ways in which the company will work in the future. All professional and senior staff now have terminals, and anyone who needs a computer can have one. Minicomputers are blocked together in groups of eight on networks, avoiding the use of a mainframe computer. Glaxo are moving towards the use of more powerful personal computers linked by local area networks, supported by voice and electronic mail networks. The sales force work at home some of the time and use mobile laptop computers connected to the office by modem

Figure 11.19
*Plan of typical floor.
(Source: DEGW and
Building Research
Establishment)*

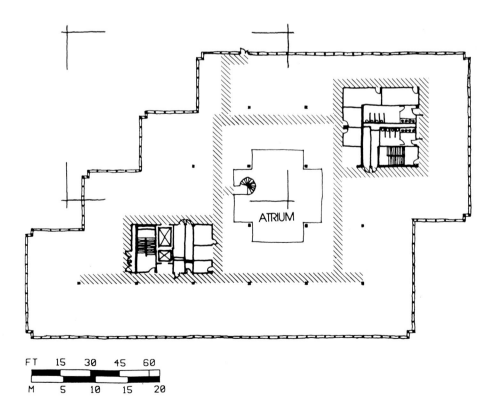

links. All the new furniture for the offices was designed to support the use of information technology and electronic mail is widely used.

Figure 11.20
Layout of typical working area. (Source: DEGW and Building Research Establishment)

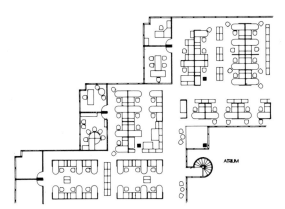

ATRIUM

Move away from hierarchical space layout

The new offices are planned with more open space and less enclosed offices than their previous headquarters (Figure 11.20).

The design of the new offices was reviewed by a group of staff who argued that the layout of the offices did not adequately respond to the changing culture of the organisation. The interiors were thought not to reflect the development of team working patterns. A new business based layout was prepared to replace what had been perceived as overly hierarchical space planning. People working in different departments were brought together to encourage higher levels of lateral communication. An executive dining room was axed and replaced by cafeterias that now serve all staff whatever their rank.

Greenpeace UK, London, England

Company	Greenpeace UK	Case study workplace, architect	Greenpeace headquarters, designed by Feilden Clegg Design
Sector	Environmental pressure group	Location	Canonbury Villas, Islington, London N1 2PN, England
Country	United Kingdom	Area	1,858 sqm (20,000 sqft)
Number of staff	85	Type of project	Rehabilitation of old laboratory space into offices and warehouse
Number of staff in case study workplace	85	Use of information technology	About 1 terminal for every 2 staff.

Source: DEGW and Building Research Establishment

The organisation

Managing growth and change

Greenpeace are an international independent environmental pressure group campaigning against issues of abuse to the natural world.

A massive growth in membership from 20,000 to 400,000 led to rapid increases in the numbers of staff and resulted in major and ongoing organisational changes in the late 1980s and early 1990s. Greenpeace have had to move away from informal 'ragged trouser philanthropy' to a much more professional managerial approach. Staff have grown from 15 to 85 in the last few years, and new managerial skills were needed at the top for the organisation. As public and media interest has grown the profile of the organisation is much higher. Political factors have grown in importance in their work as the organisation changes from responding to problems to raising the agenda for solutions to environmental issues.

An environment for passion and efficiency

Since 1987 Greenpeace have improved staff pay and conditions to avoid the 'burn out' syndrome that was common among volunteers and paid staff. Now they are prepared to pay for the top skills and management expertise to run the organisation. Consultants are also brought in for particular campaigns as needed. As the organisation has grown they have moved away from informality towards a simple hierarchy. The new Greenpeace headquarters was designed to provide 'an environment for passion and efficiency'.

Impact of the organisation on the workplace

As Greenpeace matured as an organisation they recognised that the working environment would have an impact on improving morale and help them to attract and retain their professional staff. The building was designed to care for staff: providing enough space for their books, supporting them with appropriate technology. The building was never intended to be a landmark of green design, but rather an economical attempt to deal realistically with environmental issues within a constrained budget of time and resources.

A green and economical approach to design

Their old offices had not addressed the green agenda at all. Yet the cost of implementing a green design approach had to be balanced against the overall economic requirements of the organisation and the costs of implementing their campaigns. The new offices were planned to be environmentally rational and sensible, to

Figure 11.21
*Plan of typical floor.
(Source: DEGW and
the Building Research
Establishment)*

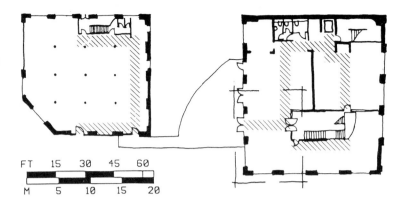

reflect what they are trying to achieve generally. There was extensive employee involvement in the design process.

Greenpeace has always located close to the media and political centre of the capital. Their new office location was intended to provide easy access to public transport (a five or ten minute walk to a London Underground station) and to be in an area provided with pubs and cafes for staff to use.

The new building is a radical refurbishment of an old laboratory building (Figure 11.21). Open plan spaces in semi-defined areas for campaign groups were designed to promote flexibility, collaboration and communication (Figure 11.22). However, some senior managers have installed tall book cases to create more privacy. Some staff did not like being overlooked from the open stairwell. A range of meeting rooms have been provided, which are intensively used, as well as a staff cafeteria.

Figure 11.22
*Layout of typical
working area.
(Source: DEGW and
Building Research
Establishment)*

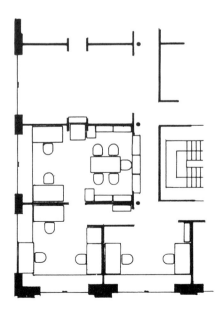

There is a central staircase that serves as a heart for the building encouraging informal meetings and encounters. The building had to bind together an organisation which was growing fast and had spread into three inadequate and unpleasant offices. It also had to reflect the new level of management confidence felt by the organisation.

Design strategy to minimise energy use

The basic approach of architect Fielden Clegg to the environmental aspects of the building was to minimise energy use and enable the efficient use of energy. The conversion provided a passive solar design with high levels of natural daylighting. Natural ventilation is supplemented by simple mechanical ventilation with heat recovery in the deep plan areas of the floor (the depth across the building is 21 metres). The mechanical cooling can be left on at night to bring down the internal temperature. High standards of insulation were used with double glazed low emissivity glass. The top panels of glass in the windows are coated to reduce light transmission and reduce glare, while internal and external louvres eliminate sunlight above about 45 degrees. The tall windows are controlled manually and provide high levels of cross ventilation. There are also ceiling fans operable directly by users.

To reduce greenhouse gas emissions, insulation standards are high and electrical consumption minimised. Metal halide uplighters in the office areas are controlled by external photocells which switch off the lights when the light level exceeds 1000 lux.

A combined heat and power generating unit provides both heating and power for the building. In contrast to electricity generating plants which operate at a 30% efficiency, a combined heat and power plant is 85–90% efficient as the heat energy is also used to supply hot water for perimeter radiators. The generator supplies all the lighting and power needs of the building.

Environmental selection of building materials

Building materials, fixtures and fittings with low environmental impacts were selected as far as was economically viable. Materials and components that were focused on included: windows and frames, use of pvc, paints, carpets and furnishings. Douglas fir softwood was selected for windows, but designed for use without preservatives. In place of a pvc membrane on the roof a bitumen/polyester felt was used. Organic paints from Germany were chosen for the interiors. Linoleum as opposed to vinyl was selected for floor coverings as well as natural carpets without polypropylene base.

Health Education Authority, London, England

Company	Health Education Authority	Case study workplace, architect	Headquarters at Hamilton House, designed by Shaw/ Sprunt
Sector	Public sector (health)	Location	Mabledon Place London WC1 England
Country	United Kingdom	Area	3,251 sqm (35,000 sqft)
Number of staff	about 200	Type of project	Refurbishment of existing offices
Number of staff in case study workplace	about 200	Use of information technology	One terminal per staff with electronic mail.

Source: DEGW and Building Research Establishment

The organisation

The Health Education Authority leads and supports the promotion of health in England, provides information and advice about health to the public, supports and develops the capability of other health educators in health and other sectors and advises the Secretary of State on health education.

Changes in the National Health Service in the forms of delivery of primary health care and the re-organisation of regional and district health businesses has presented major challenges to the organisation. The Authority is raising its profile, making a contribution to the national strategy for health and developing business interests in Europe as well.

The structure of the organisation has evolved from a line management to matrix form. Flexible working times have been introduced for junior staff and self managed jobs for senior staff. The organisation is working more on a basis of autonomous projects using the Authority's mission and value statement as a guide.

Figure 11.23
Plan of typical floor. (Source: DEGW and Building Research Establishment)

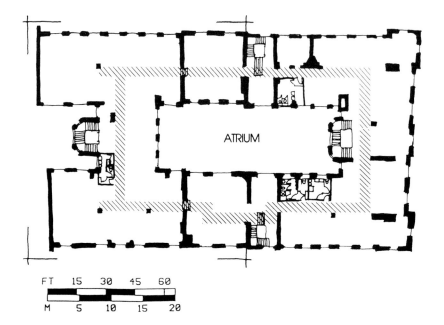

Impact of the organisation on the workplace

The workplace for the Authority seeks to reflect the values of the organisation as far as possible: the provision of a healthy working environment for staff; the efficient co-location of related functions in space; a good physical and electronic system for communications; and the accessibility of the office for their field staff. (The office is located close to two British Rail main line stations).

Figure 11.24
Layout of offices: high degree of enclosure. (Source: DEGW and Building Research Establishment)

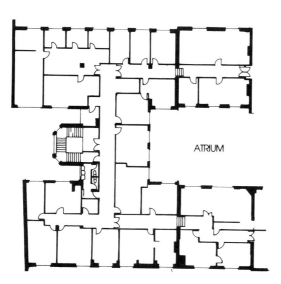

ATRIUM

The leased office space provides office floors of 13,000 sq ft (1,207 sqm), of which they occupy two and a half. It was important for the Authority not to have to spread across too many floors to enable them to be cohesive and to promote internal communication. An atrium brings daylight to the interior of the space. The depth of the floor from the outside windows to the atrium is 10 metres which allows for two enclosed offices and a circulation route (Figure 11.23).

The office space is largely cellular with a few shared group rooms (Figure 11.24). Meetings can be held in the enclosed offices by other staff when they are unoccupied by their usual users. Open plan space was not wanted because of the noise and distraction it was felt would be caused by open circulation routes.

The high level of provision of information technology (one terminal for each staff member) and its networking enables staff to work in various office locations. Some staff work at home part of the time, and are requesting fax machines at home. There is the possibility in the future of more homeworking and the use of computers at home.

The staff have an occupational health group and health promotion group. Many of their staff are devoted to green and environmental issues. A recycling policy for the office has been implemented and a rack for the storage of bicycles which many staff use to get to work.

IBM UK, Newcastle, England

Company	IBM UK Ltd	Case study workplace, architect	IBM branch office Newcastle, Taylor Tulip & Hunter Architects
Sector	Electronics	Location	Newcastle Business Park
Country	United Kingdom	Area	348 sqm (3,750 sqft)
Number of staff	18,139	Type of project	Leased space with rentalised fit -out
Number of staff in case study workplace	150	Use of information technology	One terminal for each staff

Source: DEGW and Building Research Establishment

The organisation

IBM UK manufacture, market, and service information handling systems, equipment and services. IBM is restructuring its business beyond its traditional area of hardware products to diverse solutions including software and other services. Re-organisation has involved changing the basis of the marketing organisation from regions to industry sectors with a strengthening of the services orientation. The rate of computer industry growth has slowed in the 1990s as a result of higher levels of absorption of information technology. For IBM,

growth is now focused on refining products and services. More authority is being delegated down the organisation. Managers are expected to take more decisions.

Impact of the organisation on the workplace

The workplace for IBM must now respond closely to financial and competitive pressures. The workplace building must be 'lean and mean' and low cost in use.

For a new marketing branch office in Newcastle, England, IBM selected a speculatively

Figure 11.25
Plan of typical floor. (Source: DEGW and Building Research Establishment)

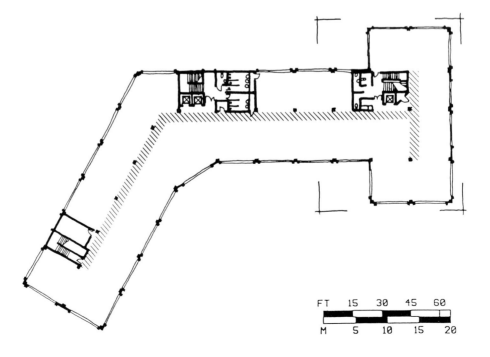

```
FT    15   30   45   60
M      5   10   15   20
```

developed business park building on the edge of the city centre (Figure 11.25). IBM worked with the developer on the fit-out of the space and was able to take advantage of tax incentives as part of a rentalisation of the fit-out

Figure 11.26
Layout of typical working area. (Source: DEGW and Building Research Establishment)

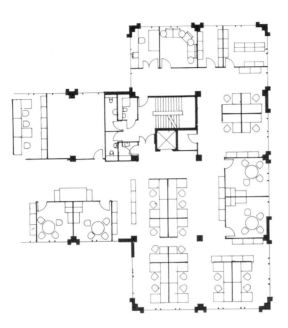

costs. The selection process for the office includes a careful analysis of the costs, layout potential, ease of subletting parts of the space, and its overall flexibility. As part of a broader cultural change, IBM is 'no longer hooked on building Rolls Royce buildings'.

Nevertheless, the workplace must provide a very good working environment for the individual. IBM believe that a high quality environment will increase the productivity of staff. Sales staff are supported with technology and equipment to help them work efficiently with their clients outside the office or at home. IBM UK have implemented a project called Space Morale and Remote Technology (SMART) that has led to the re-planning of sales offices away from individually 'owned' workplaces towards higher proportions of shared space (Figure 11.26). Re-planning has required higher expenditures on information technology to support working in several locations (car phones, terminals at home and at clients' premises, for example). This has enabled IBM to save up to 30% of space occupied in offices where sharing has been introduced while at the same time supporting the productivity of staff who spend much of their time outside the office.

Independent Television News Limited, London, England

Company	Independent Television News Limited	Case study workplace, architect	ITN Building, designed by Sir Norman Foster & Partners
Sector	Television news broadcasters	Location	200 Grays Inn Road London WC1 England
Country	United Kingdom	Area	23,225 sqm (250,000 sq ft) and 6,503 sqm (70,000 sqft) storage
Number of staff	1,000 (200 journalists)	Type of project	Joint venture with Stanhope Properties Plc (developers) prelet to ITN. ITN was able to influence the brief for the developer.
Number of staff in case study workplace	1,000	Use of information technology	One terminal per person

Source: DEGW and Building Research Establishment

The organisation

ITN is an independent television news company providing news services twenty-four hours a day with worldwide bureaux. News gathering is the prime activity. The news organisation can be thought of as a means whereby journalists are the clients for services provided by others in the company to enable them to work effectively.

By early 1991 ITN had grown from 300 to 1000 staff spread through offices in several locations. The new headquarters building was designed to bring together the dispersed organisation, to resolve the resulting fragmentation, and create a togetherness that is a vital requirement for their success.

ITN have recognised that the future of the news business requires frugality, their position as a news organisation will be more severely challenged in the 1990s. ITN wanted to be leaner and fitter in order to better fight the competition.

The news organisation is in fact an information network of great scope and complexity.

Information is brought together from worldwide bureaux and from independent journalists and must be processed into news programmes twenty-four hours a day. The finely tuned timing, consistency and flexibility of the news making activity had to be supported in the architecture of the building and in its management and use over time.

Impact of the organisation on the workplace

The new ITN headquarters had to be located in central London to be close to the commercial and political centre of the capital and the nation. ITN needed a building that was a prestigious landmark, and were pleased that the location is within walking distance of the City of London with good local shopping for staff.

The brief for the site required clear floors of about 30 metres by 50 metres to allow for large studio spaces and to avoid the splitting up of working groups across several floors (Figure 11.27). The site on Grays Inn Road had

Figure 11.27
*Plan of typical floor.
(Source: DEGW and
Building Research
Establishment)*

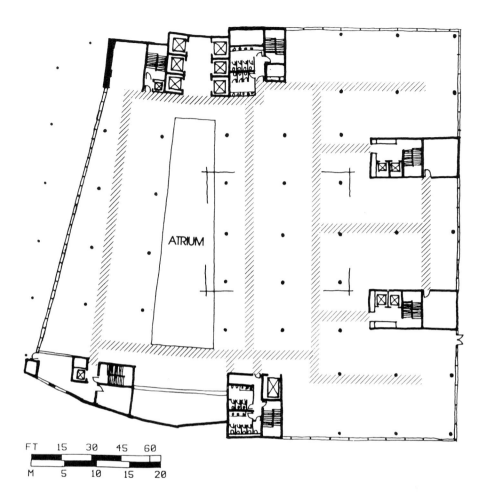

FT   15   30   45   60
M   5   10   15   20

previously been used as the headquarters of a newspaper, and it was provided with deep underground floor space that has been used effectively by ITN for television studios and associated support facilities such as archiving and vehicular access.

Joint venture with developer Stanhope

The commercial development know-how of leading office developer Stanhope Properties Plc was brought to the joint venture and helped to create an efficient building plan and form. Stanhope provided clear guidelines for spatial efficiency in the design that were incorporated by architect Sir Norman Foster and Partners. Although the building was designed according to market-led principles of spatial efficiency that would be expected of any new speculative office space in London, the joint venture also allowed ITN to tailor the building to their particular needs.

130,000 sqft (12,077 sqm) of the 250,000 sqft (23,225 sqm) building is available as sublettable space for other tenants. The floors of the building were designed to allow subletting of either whole or part floors to occur efficiently, with good access to the building cores (staircases and toilets) for potential subtenants.

The office space is arranged on floors around a large glass covered atrium that allows daylight deep into the heart of the building, even down as far as the several floor levels below ground. The atrium has fans to draw out heat and circulate the air.

The joint venture has resulted in a highly specified speculative office building, that might have been designed for a standard office user, yet which is occupied by an extremely unusual user with far from standard requirements. It suggests that the clever design of adaptable and efficient spaces with developer know-how will enable highly diverse users to be accommodated.

Figure 11.28
Atrium of ITN
Building.
(Source: DEGW and
Building Research
Establishment)

Figure 11.29
A transparent
building.
(Source: DEGW and
Building Research
Establishment)

Figure 11.30
Studio equipment ITN
Building. (Source:
DEGW and Building
Research
Establishment)

Transparent image and high security

The desire to bring the organisation together and make it highly streamlined and competitive led the thinking for the new building. The Chairman of ITN wished the building to be transparent, to reveal the organisation to the public, although some staff felt vulnerable and exposed by such transparency (Figure 11.29). Security systems are very tight, including guards with Semtex sniffing technology and the use of identifiable access cards for all staff, yet this has not prevented the building from achieving an open appearance.

Design for communication of working groups

The design of the building provides the short lines of communication between journalists and the technical staff, tools and support they require, such as graphics and video editing. By bringing together the most appropriate groups and teams, ITN was able to save working time and even to eliminate some groups entirely.

The support services are grouped around two major news rooms for ITN and Channel 4 and are linked laterally through the building. New programme making technology has been installed which would have been impossible in their pre-existing premises (Figure 11.30). This will enable them to operate with fewer staff.

Working groups of 10 to 12 people are arranged on large open floors that give directly onto the atrium (Figure 11.31). From most positions around the atrium it is possible to observe activities across several floors, providing a high degree of organisational transparency. The workstations are provided with a central feed for power and communications.

For many groups, individual workstations are allocated to particular roles or functions, rather than to individuals. For example, a workstation will be dedicated to a 'news editor' and will be occupied by three 'news editors' successively over the course of the working day or week. The workstations were designed to suit the high levels of information technology required, and are made in-house. They are provided with two pedestals that are commercially manufactured. Spare desktops are kept in-house to enable workstations to be easily and quickly reconfigured.

The major working areas of news making now resemble financial dealing rooms: massive levels of information technology in a high density layout encouraging communication throughout the space. Internal communication for news

Figure 11.31
Layout of typical working area. (Source: DEGW and Building Research Establishment)

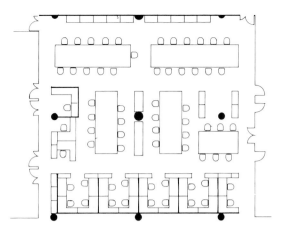

making is facilitated by all workstations being designed to be available for the use of anyone with the appropriate password for access. The creative use of information technology is essential for news workers. Smaller and quieter terminals have helped to create a less cluttered workplace environment: people can talk when using the equipment now.

Apart from on the administration floor, there is only about ten per cent of the office space that is fully enclosed.

Cabling infrastructure

ITN required exceptionally high capacity for cabling. The building is provided with its own communications system, run through special ducts, connected to rooftop transmission and reception points. A raised floor is provided to all levels.

The joint venture development of ITN's headquarters combines an efficient approach to the development of a base building that has also allowed the organisation to design and fit out the space to accommodate complex technological and organisational requirements.

Instituut voor Milieu en Systeemanalyse (IMSA), Bilthoven, Netherlands

Company	Instituut voor Milieu en Systeemanayse	Case study workplace, architect	Proposed new offices, designed by Alberts and Van Hout (design not yet complete).
Sector	Environmental consultancy	Location	Bilthoven, Utrecht
Country	Netherlands	Area	1,100 sqm (11,840 sq ft)
Number of staff	25	Type of project	Proposed new built offices designed for own use
Number of staff in case study workplace	25	Use of information technology	Currently 10 terminals for 25 staff, but expect to reach 100% shortly

Source: DEGW and Building Research Establishment

The organisation

The Instituut voor Milieu en Systeemanalyse (IMSA) is a small growing research and consultancy organisation that specialises in the field of sustainable environmental policies for industry and government worldwide.

IMSA are emerging from what they see as a pioneering phase of growth and are seeking a new 'biography' of themselves, a new kind of organism. IMSA recognise that the workplace sends messages about an organisation to its clients and to the public. Clients want to be educated by what they learn from IMSA's offices: 'These messages cannot be broadcast in a concrete building with air conditioning in a business park'.

An informal culture for work

Consultants at IMSA run their own projects in teams supported by a separate financial management structure. They are expected to work on a variety of projects and not to become over specialised. Staff may work at home if they wish and self-manage their own projects. The management style is informal and participatory. The informality of their working relationships is important to them.

Retreats for all the staff are held in the country for several weekends during the year. They are designed to create a common ground 'to get all the noses in one direction' to share knowledge, encourage efficiency, and enhance stability. An informal culture is at the heart of their business, a way of creating a common knowledge.

Green and environmental issues are part of their living and thinking at work.

Impact of the organisation on the workplace

IMSA are planning a new headquarters to reflect their concerns with green issues. They have been working with the architect Alberts and Van Hout (renowned for their design of the headquarters of the NMB Postbank in Amsterdam) on a concept for an office building that will consume zero energy.

The main problem for IMSA at the moment is that their current premises are split across two buildings in Amsterdam, one of which is an old house. They would like a new headquarters to integrate nature, environmental conservation and ergonomic efficiency. A new building should help to transform the organisation, to develop a higher calibre of staff. Their staff need to be able to work on a variety of projects in the same space. A new building should reflect their own environmental concepts.

IMSA would like to use their proposed office building to prove that a better workplace can improve working relationships, productivity and motivation. 'Companies are tired of regular management buildings, offering the same boring service with full electric lights in the middle of the day'.

In planning a new building, however, IMSA have discovered that although an ecological concept is fundamental to their organisation, it is by no means clear how this translates into the architecture of the office. It is not obvious what sound ecological building practices are: too often architects select 'natural' building materials assuming they are ecologically sound to use. There is no clear knowledge or guidance on these issues. For example, designers need to know how to balance the energy costs of buildings in use against the energy costs that are involved in the production of building materials.

Proposals for a green building

The new office is planned to be located outside Amsterdam in a rural area. The building will be in the forest, designed to be partly underground, with grass roofs, on one level with sun terraces alongside glazed walls. A passive solar energy policy should be able to reduce energy consumption to 10% of that of a conventional office building. The building mass will be used for cooling. Recycled concrete materials will be used for the walls, the roof will be covered with copper. A solar attic will capture solar energy for storage in cells. Solar heat will be supplemented by heat pumps or by a small high efficiency burner. Only local task lighting should be required during daylight hours.

The idea of a green building for IMSA obviously goes beyond environmental design considerations, it is essential to the meaning of the working culture of the organisation.

MEPC plc, London, England

Company	MEPC plc	Case study workplace, architect	MEPC headquarters, designed by TTSP Architects
Sector	Property	Location	11/12 St James Square, London SW1Y 4LB
Country	United Kingdom	Area	6,875 sqm (74,000 sqft)
Number of staff	894	Type of project	Speculative development fitted out for use by MEPC, includes older Grade II listed town house
Number of staff in case study workplace	150	Use of information technology	Provision for one terminal for all staff

Source: DEGW and Building Research Establishment

The organisation

MEPC are involved in international property investment, development and dealing, and are the second largest property company in the United Kingdom.

Figure 11.32
MEPC Headquarters. (Source: David Rogers and David Jones)

MEPC are responding to the organisational pressures of a slump in the values of the property market, the need to increase the level of use of information technology, and the fact that they had outgrown their previous premises.

Impact of the organisation on the workplace

MEPC needed to be located in Mayfair, central London. The building that was selected in this area had been developed speculatively and incorporated an older structure, it was not at first appraisal an ideal building for their use.

The programme for fitting out the building had to resolve several key problems: providing the right level of density of use of space; the optimum arrangement of departmental groups; encourage an increased level of team working; maximise the access to daylight for staff working in the office; and focus on how technology might be used to free up the way staff worked. Particular issues had to be addressed: to what extent should local control of the working environment be provided, and how should the issues of status and space planning be solved?

The building provides floors of 8000 sqft (743 sqm), MEPC would have preferred more

Figure 11.33
Plan of typical floor.
(Source: DEGW and
Building Research
Establishment)

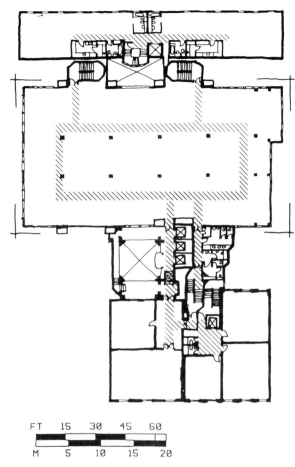

```
FT   15   30   45   60
M     5   10   15   20
```

Figure 11.34
Interior of offices.
(Source: MEPC)

Figure 11.35
Layout of typical
working area.
(Source: DEGW and
Building Research
Establishment)

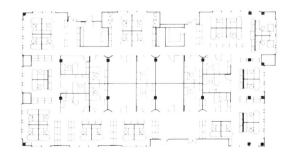

varied floor sizes to suit differing sizes of working groups (Figure 11.33). They would also have preferred a narrower depth of floor: their preferred depth is about 12 metres from window to window or from window to the building core. Such a shallow depth of floor can provide for very high levels of daylight and gives everyone the opportunity to have aspect out of the building. From MEPC's point of view it may even be preferable to provide a narrow depth of floor even where this may compromise the energy performance of the building, especially in urban locations where the building is competing with other buildings on greenfield sites which can more easily provide high levels of daylight.

Information technology

The issue of information technology was solved straightforwardly. As the databases for information technology are improved, senior managers and directors in the company will increasingly use terminals on the desk. This will result in some bypassing of junior management, and assist in slimming the organisation. The whole building has therefore been provided with a local area network and there is a terminal and printer on every desk. Some managers now have laptop computers as well. A raised floor is installed throughout the building, accommodating twisted pair wiring for horizontal distribution. Fibre optic cables are installed in the vertical risers.

Status and image: internal offices for senior staff

The building is intended to provide high quality space, but to avoid gimmicks. A dining room serving healthy food is provided for staff, but sport or gymnasium facilities have not been provided. The issue of status has been solved in an interesting way: the most junior staff who work in open plan areas have been provided with workstations on the perimeter of the building immediately adjacent to the windows (Figure 11.34). Such staff are more likely to be in the office all of the time. Senior managers and directors are provided with enclosed offices in the interior of the building. Moreover, in order to encourage more team working, the total proportion of open versus enclosed space has been increased significantly. In MEPC's previous offices about seventy per cent of the floor area was enclosed offices, in the new building about seventy per cent of the floor area is open plan. The overall average of space occupied per person is about 13.5 sqm.

A high level of local control of temperature and lighting has been provided. Each enclosed office and every group of four or five people are provided with local controls.

A healthy building

MEPC have been careful to ensure that the building is healthy and avoids the risk of sick building syndrome. The air quality and building materials have been rigorously tested. MEPC have established an Environmental Concern Committee that is studying the impact of green issues on office development. There was concern over installing full air conditioning, but it was recognised that on a polluted and noisy urban site it was difficult to avoid.

Olivetti Information Services Research (OIS), Bari, Italy

Company	Olivetti Information Services	Case study workplace, architect	Olivetti Research Centre, designed by DEGW and Studio De Lucchi
Sector	Software products and services	Location	Bari, Italy
Country	Italy	Area	13,000 sqm (139,935 sqft)
Number of staff	5,500 in Olivetti group	Type of project	New building to be completed in 1993
Number of staff in case study workplace	550	Use of information technology	One terminal for each staff

Source: DEGW and Building Research Establishment

The organisation

Olivetti Information Services Group is involved in the development of information technology, software services and products, and consulting work. The Information Services Group arose as a result of the decentralisation of the Olivetti Group into operating units relating to industry, finance, and public authority markets.

The Group is a matrix organisation, part of a holding company. Project managers report across a network of relationships within the Group and to their clients. They must be able to frequently change their targets in response to rapidly changing markets. Project groups change frequently.

The critical problem for the organisation has been its distribution of activities over several locations. Their research is financed in the South of Italy, but their users and clients are often in the North of Italy or elsewhere. The provision of excellent electronic means of communication is therefore a necessity.

Information technology as the repository of work

A project leader works typically with twenty to thirty people and support staff. They are task leaders undertaking work packages. The management style is more democratic than the typical Italian organisation, an effect of the information technology tools that enable people to work uncoupled from their colleagues. In this sense information technology has become 'the repository of work' through the use of shared data and programmes, and standard tools and shared documentation. The technology has allowed Olivetti to manage with less layers of management and has promoted more flexible working patterns. All of their staff use information technology.

Impact of the organisation on the workplace

The speed of change of the organisation has to be reflected in the design of the workplace. It must be possible to re-configure the workplace and re-allocate space easily. The workplace should in a sense operate independently of changing project assignments, allowing work to continue irrespective of any particular location within the office. It is the optimum use of information technology that can make this kind of working possible. The workplace must support the use of this technology by enabling connectivity (through the raised floors) and allowing for flexible access to the cabling.

An oasis for information technology

The new Research Centre for Olivetti Information Services Group at Bari has been designed

Figure 11.36
*Plan of typical floor.
(Source: DEGW and
Building Research
Establishment)*

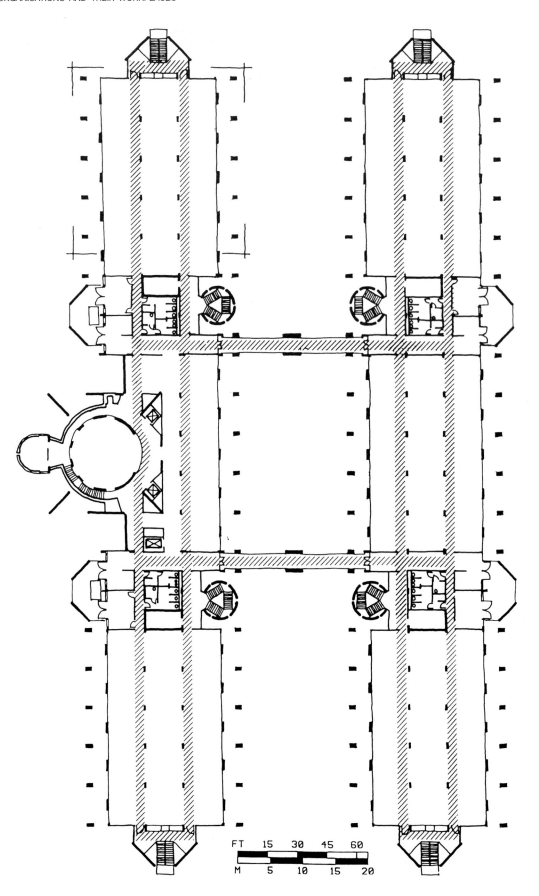

to be able to respond to a high level of organisational flexibility. The building has been partly funded by the Italian government and is located in the rural south of the country. The isolation of its location and the intensity of the climate led the architects to design the building as a green oasis in an arid landscape. Gardens and cloister-like spaces between wings of the building are intended to shelter the building from the sun and to reinforce an image of the place as a refuge for the creation of ideas.

A site of 120,000 sqm (1,291,711 sqft) was procured in an agricultural area near the motorway. Landscaping of the site to screen its presence from roads and to soften the harsh environment has been carefully considered. The planning structure of the building allows for each wing of the building to accommodate working groups of up to thirty people (amounting to ninety people on each of the building's three floors) (Figure 11.36). Each working floor of the building 3000 sqm (32,292 sqft) is therefore subdivided into six wings of about 500 sqm (5,382 sqft). Each wing may further be subdivided into working spaces on the perimeter of the floor with support or laboratory spaces zoned for the interior of the wing (the central zone may also be used for additional working space if so required) (Figure 11.37). Each working space on the floor is designed to have an equivalent footprint so that it is easy to re-configure the space for changing project requirements.

A mixed mode servicing strategy

The interior zone of each wing is designed to be more highly serviced than the perimeter spaces, as it is in these zones that more equipment or laboratory functions will be located. In the central zone of the floor there is a raised floor containing all the services, including air conditioning. The whole building has been designed with a passive energy policy. Even though the building will accommodate very high levels of information technology and is located in the hot southern climate it is not fully air conditioned. A mixed mode servicing strategy has been developed that allows for more intensive levels of artificial servicing to be used on an as-needed basis. The mass of the building, shading louvres, and natural ventilation are all used to keep the building cool.

Figure 11.37
Layout of typical working area. (Source: DEGW and Building Research Establishment)

PA Consulting Group, London, England

Company	PA Consulting Group	Case study workplace architect	PA Consulting Group headquarters, designed by Arup Associates, space planning by DEGW.
Sector	Management consulting	Location	123 Buckingham Palace Road, London SW1 9SR
Country	England	Area	9,290 sqm (100,000 sqft)
Number of staff	1,750 consultants worldwide	Type of project	Leased space in speculative office development
Number of staff in case study workplace	12–1,300 staff	Use of information technology	One terminal per staff is provided for those permanently in the office, for consultants technology is provided as required.

Source: DEGW and Building Research Establishment

The organisation

PA Consulting Group is a consultancy in management, computers, telecommunications, technology and personnel services, managing complex change and creating business advantage. They have clients in industry, commerce and government.

PA Consulting Group grew out of one building in Knightsbridge, London in 1986, and evolved into an organisation with six main skill groups occupying several buildings by the end of the 1980s. The organisation needed to re-group its activities into one building which had to be located in central London for access to their clients and to maintain their market presence. This was an expensive decision and one that pushed the organisation to seek ways of maximising the value of its high cost premises. It has led towards sophisticated policies for the management of the space of the office over time, increasing the amount of sharing of workstations, and thereby intensifying the utilisation of the office asset.

As PA Consulting Group grew it was concerned to move away from a simple pyramidal hierarchy towards six skill-based groups with their own executive structures. Formal ranks of status were dispensed with.

The impact of the organisation on the workplace

PA Consulting Group occupies several floors of the office building designed by Arup Associates. The building provides large floors wrapped around an atrium, in the centre of which lifts provide access to the floors from bridge structures.

The purpose of the new headquarters is to bring together the various divisions of the organisation, to better serve multi-disciplinary projects, and to increase communication. The building must be able to respond to the need for flexibility, it was this consideration that led PA Consulting Group away from an initial intention to provide both enclosed and open office space towards a more radical solution in which only open plan space has been designed.

The decision to go towards a completely open plan office was driven by the need to achieve easy re-grouping of staff and activities

Figure 11.38
*Plan of typical floor.
(Source: DEGW and
Building Research
Establishment)*

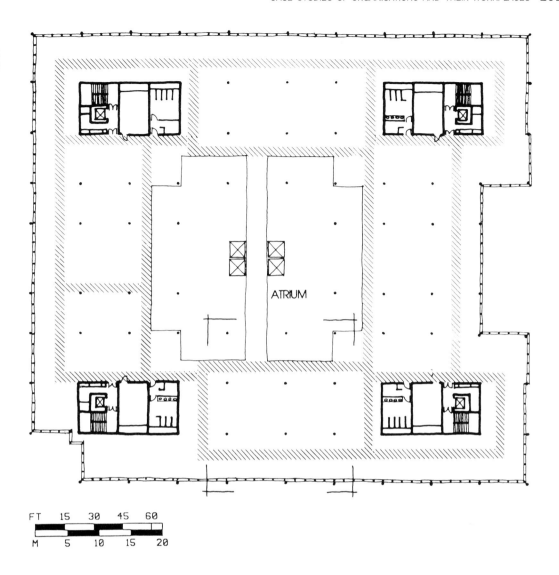

and to maximise the utilisation of the available space. This was further enhanced by the evolution of the office design to maximise the use of space over time. A series of workstation types have been designed expressly for staff who are in the office for varying amounts of their working time. A total of 850 workstations have been provided for 1200 staff.

Tailoring the workstation to the user

Three types of workstations have been provided that correspond to the amount of time different kinds of staff are expected to be working in the office. The first type is for staff who are expected to be in the office 100% of the time, this would be used by secretaries and admin-

istrators for example. These workstations are larger than others and more generously provided with dedicated storage space. A second type of workstation has been provided for staff who are expected to be in the office about 75% of the time, this might include senior managers, for example. These workstations have less area and less dedicated storage capacity. A third workstation type is provided for consultants who spend much of their working time outside the office (Figure 11.40). None of these desks is dedicated to individuals and they provide no permanent storage capacity. They are intended always to be shared by consultants on an as-needed basis and are provided with wired access panels for the connection of terminals as required.

Figure 11.39
*Office interior.
(Source: DEGW and
Building Research
Establishment)*

Figure 11.40
*Consultant's
workstation. (Source:
DEGW and Building
Research
Establishment)*

Figure 11.41
*Quieter spaces in
corner of the plan.
(Source: DEGW and
Building Research
Establishment)*

Figure 11.42
*Layout of typical
working area.
(Source: DEGW and
Building Research
Establishment)*

ATRIUM

The shared workstation type is provided for only a proportion of the total number of consultants, based on the assumption that at any one time only a small number of the consultants will be working in the office.

The design of workstations has also taken into consideration the need to provide some amount of visual and acoustic privacy: the desks provide lateral views towards the daylight from atrium or window, but are more highly screened from one side to the other in the facing direction. The screens are designed to be sound absorbent.

The move to an entirely open plan office coincided with the introduction of clean desk policies to facilitate the sharing of desks and with a no smoking rule which applies everywhere except in one dedicated smoking/meeting room on each floor. There was resistance to the total open plan concept when it was first raised, as the experience of open plan in their previous offices had not been good.

Zoning of floor space to manage working in open plan space

The floor plan has been carefully zoned for groups. More private, quieter spaces (including meeting rooms and areas) are provided in the building corners and on the perimeter away from the busy circulation routes (Figure 11.41). The open plan group areas wrap around the atrium allowing for groups of staff to spread between one area and the next if necessary.

The depth of the building from atrium to the perimeter is 35 metres, but with open planning there is always at least a view of daylight obtained throughout the space. The large floor areas are found to be suitable for the size of working groups.

The operational effectiveness of the office is enhanced by the high provision of several different kinds of meeting areas: there are informal meeting places by the atrium and alongside desks (Figure 11.43), and more formal meeting rooms for clients or presentations.

The zoning of the floor is continued through to the lighting system which allows the user to select the lighting level and zone of lighting to be switched on. This is useful for consultants who need to work in the building at any time of the day or night.

Figure 11.43
*Informal meeting
spaces.
(Source: DEGW and
Building Research
Establishment)*

Information technology and telecommunications

The sharing of workstations by consultants who may come in and out of the office at very varied times of the day or week places great demands on telephone and communication systems. PA Consulting Group have installed an advanced telephone system that allows extension num-

bers to be easily changed, user programming of the telephone, call forwarding and follow-me functions. All of the terminals and workstations are wired onto a central data network which also assists in the flexibility of patterns of use of space over time. Consultants may also use fax machines and laptop computers in their homes.

Security and access

There is a ground floor reception at the building entrance from where visitors are directed up in lifts to PA Consulting Group's own reception floor. Staff gain access from other floor levels by using a swipe card. Consultants to the organisation are provided with access cards that have encoded 'sell-by' dates, so that they will no longer operate after a specified date. At the reception desk computer terminals provide information in several languages and allow the visitor to register. Separate zones of the building are designated for client access. The building may be used twenty-four hours a day, a requirement for the consultants.

Intensifying the use of space over time

PA Consulting Group have succeeded in bringing their organisation together in a building that is designed to be used in a highly intensive and cost effective manner. The planning and zoning of space, and the design of furniture, as well as the management of the facility, have been integrated together to maximise the value gained from an expensive central city location and contribute to improved organisational performance.

Policy Studies Institute, London, England

Company	Policy Studies Institute	Case study workplace, architect	100 Park Village East, designed by Jestico + Whiles
Sector	Non-profit organisation	Location	100 Park Village East, London NW1
Country	England	Area	1,951 sqm (21,000 sqft)
Number of staff	40 staff and researchers	Type of project	Rehabilitated office space
Number of staff in case study workplace	40	Use of information technology	1 terminal per each staff (20 terminals are networked)

Source: DEGW and Building Research Establishment

The organisation

The Policy Studies Institute is an independent research organisation studying economic, industrial, and social policy, and the workings of political institutions. Research is undertaken in project areas organised by subject. There are 35 professionals and 7 administrative and management staff. The impact of information technology has eliminated the role of secretaries, as such. The funding of research is less centralised, many new projects are funded individually, and there is a faster through put of projects.

The organisation has been changing significantly, moving from what was described as a 'medieval barony' to a new structure and form of hierarchy in which the Director controls a management team including the group heads of research teams. A particular research group may handle as many as twenty projects. Within the teams there is a great deal of autonomy for the direction of research. If 'productivity' can be measured for such a kind of work then it is simply the output and cost of producing research reports.

Figure 11.44
Plan of typical floor. (Source: DEGW and Building Research Establishment)

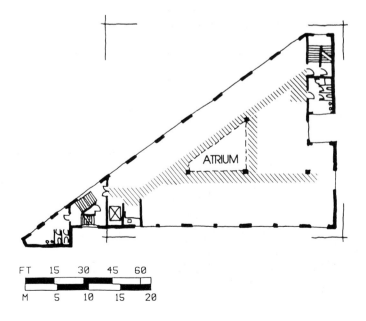

Impact of the organisation on the workplace

The Policy Studies Institute wanted office space that is suitable for doing research in, that would allow good communications within the building and a clear sense of identity for the organisation. The brief was for a lot of enclosed rooms supported by a library, informal meeting areas, and a larger conference facility. All the offices had to be adequately provided with information technology. They supported an energy efficiency as goal for the building, both because it was in tune with their values and because it would make economic sense. The offices have been created by refurbishing an existing older office building, the refurbishment was designed by Jestico + Whiles.

Low cost energy efficient refurbishment

The five storey office building was purchased by the Policy Studies Institute. The key problem was to reconcile their highly cellular office space requirements with the problem of the windowless space in the centre of the triangular shaped building while avoiding expensive air conditioning.

An atrium was introduced through the central space for the top three floors, to bring light and air to the centre of the building (Figure 11.46). This achieved a greater area of perimeter for positioning cellular offices and avoided the need for air conditioning. This solution enabled many rooms in the building to be naturally ventilated, supported by mechanical ventilation to the atrium and to support areas on the lower floors. Windows were replaced and upgraded with double glazing. Roof insulation was improved. The result is an energy efficient building, using only 193 kWh/sqm of heated floor area with very low electrical and lighting costs. The building has been used as a case study of energy efficiency in offices by the Best Practice Programme of the Department of Energy.

Enclosed offices for research work

The pattern of research work is such that small enclosed offices are still thought to be the most useful way of organising office space for concentrated thoughtful activity (Figure 11.47). But now individual academic cells are accompanied by new forms of technology and by greater freedom in the location of work. The Policy Studies Institute provided more desks and enclosed offices in their building than they have staff (by about fifteen per cent), the additional spaces are used for shared and special equipment and for particular projects on an as needed basis. Many research staff work part of the time at home, this has been encouraged. The traditional role of secretary has disappeared as all researchers word process their own documents. One floor of the office

Figure 11.45
Policy Studies Institute.
(Source: Jestico + Whiles)

Figure 11.46
The atrium.
(Source: Jestico + Whiles)

Figure 11.47
Layout of typical office floor. (Source: DEGW and Building Research Establishment)

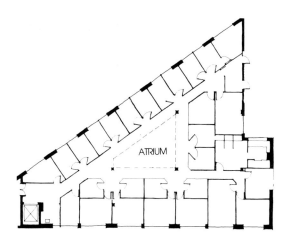

ATRIUM

is wired up for mainframe computer connections for some of the larger scale social survey analysis that is required, but most writing is done on personal computers. Many staff request computers for working at home.

The typical floor of the office is about 4000 sqft (371 sqm) on which every staff member has their own room (although junior researchers share space). All the offices have access to natural light and there are some larger spaces for administration and publishing (desk top). The atrium through the centre of the building helps to create a sense of communication between the offices and gives identity to the space.

Spie Batignolles, Cergy Pontoise, France

Company	Spie Batignolles	Case study workplace, architect	Headquarters for the group, designed by Saubot and Jullien
Sector	Construction	Location	Parc St. Christophe, Cergy Pontoise
Country	France	Area	60,000 sqm (645,856 sqft)
Number of staff	39,000	Type of project	Collection of new buildings in owner occupied business park
Number of staff in case study workplace	3,200	Use of information technology	I terminal for every 3 staff

Source: DEGW and Building Research Establishment

The organisation

Spie Batignolles is a large construction company. The company has recently created a new divisional grouping of its three main units in order to better co-ordinate regional and international activities. This has involved grouping within the same branches the *sousmetiers* or subsidiary activities under the same direction.

The organisation is composed of many different companies and it was decided to try and develop a more centralised and unified culture. A balance between centralisation and decentralisation is being developed. Spie Batignolles are also trying to reduce levels of hierarchy and to be more participatory. The key problem is to improve the flow of information up from the bottom of the company.

The work of the organisation is project based so there is a need to be able to create temporary project structures oriented to the results or goals of each job. This requires the layout of the workplace to be flexible and easy to change.

Impact of the organisation on the workplace

The president of Spie Batignolles decided to bring together the thirteen subsidiary companies onto one site to create a higher level of synergy of operations and communications. The development of a business park for their own headquarters was also an opportunity to project a higher image of the company (Figure 11.49). The site at Cergy Pontoise was also accessible to most of their staff who tended to live in the North and West of Paris which is accessible by the RER trains and local highways. There were in addition financial advantages in relocating all of their business operations to a new town development area.

The Parc St Christophe in Cergy is a 94 acre campus style development entirely occupied by the headquarters activities of the construction group. 3200 staff work in 18 buildings on the site. The subsidiary divisions of the company each occupy equivalent and identical small groups of buildings that are known as 'poles' which represent a particular area or kind of

Figure 11.48
Site plan of Parc St Christophe.
(Source: DEGW and Building Research Establishment)

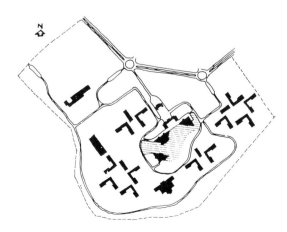

work. Each pole has its own reception entrance that is distinct from the overall reception and security gate for the park as a whole. Independent of the poles are a series of central support and amenity buildings (Figure 11.49), including three cafeteria buildings and a central meeting and conference facility. The central meeting facility can accommodate meetings of up to three hundred people.

The buildings are placed in a landscaped park linked by pathways across lakes and grassed areas.

A generic building type

What is perhaps most significant about the development is the way in which the buildings for the units of the organisation were conceptualised as though they were being briefed for the speculative office market: all the office buildings are virtually *batiments blancs*, that is office buildings that could have been occupied by almost any user (Figure 11.50). The buildings are in this sense generic buildings, designed to be used and easily subdivided for use, by many kinds of organisations (Figure 11.51). If Spie Batignolles were to vacate part or all of one of the poles on the park, another organisation could easily take over the space. Each

Figure 11.49
Amenity buildings. (Source: DEGW and Building Research Establishment)

Figure 11.50
Typical office building. (Source: DEGW and Building Research Establishment)

Figure 11.51
Plan of typical floor. (Source: DEGW and Building Research Establishment)

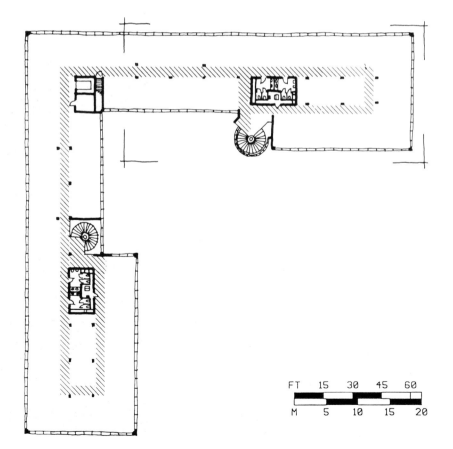

Figure 11.52
Layout of typical floor.
(Source: DEGW and Building Research Establishment)

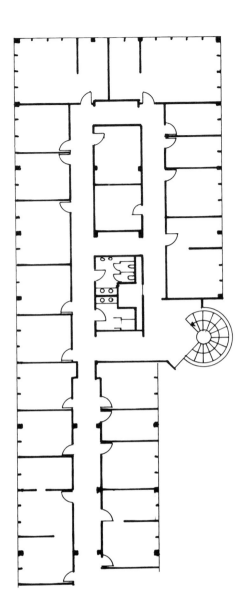

Low-tech, intelligent offices

The offices are shared and convey a low-tech feeling although they are highly served by information technology in what are described as intelligent buildings. The grid of the building provides for offices of three different sizes to fit between two and six people (with two, three or four of the standard window bays). Because projects change frequently Spie Batignolles have designed the office partitions to be demountable, they are often being refitted to suit the changing needs of multi-disciplinary groups and teams.

Offices are provided with high levels of daylight and opening windows and are usually without raised floors for cabling (Figure 11.53). Cabling is distributed to desks through central power poles from the ceiling that also provide a position for uplighters above the desks. Each desk is also provided with a task light. The workstations with fixed or mobile pedestals were provided by Steelcase Strafor, staff and their families were invited to an open day to review the products of three furniture manufacturers.

Figure 11.53
Office interior, opening windows.
(Source: DEGW and Building Research Establishment)

floor, or half floor, of each building is designed to be separated from the rest.

The basic office building is in the form of two identical wings at right angles to each other, with four storeys, ranging across two depths, either 12 metres or 18 metres. The narrower part of the building allows for two rows of enclosed offices on either side of a circulation route, the traditional way in which Spie Batignolles accommodates all of its staff (Figure 11.52). In the wider zones of the building there is space for a central zone for support spaces or equipment. All of the data and cable patching rooms are carefully designed to allow access by different users in parts of the building.

The emphasis is on individual control of lighting and ventilation during working hours. The buildings are served with a building automation system (*Gestion Technique Centralisée*) that allows for heating and lighting controls at any point on the grid of the building. In their previous offices staff did not like using air conditioning and in their new location it was felt to be unnecessary. It was thought to be important that staff could easily control their own environment.

The individual office buildings have local meeting rooms and managers' offices are provided with meeting tables as well. In parts of each building where larger meetings may take place or where heavy use of equipment use occurs the area is more highly served with raised floors and air conditioning.

The data and power infrastructure for the site was planned to allow for a tenfold increase in future data handling capacity. It is expected that terminal use will increase to one for every staff in the near future.

The security system for the large site makes use of reprogrammable smart cards for access control to different buildings and parts of the site.

Volvo Car Corporation, Goteberg, Sweden

Company	Volvo Car Corporation	Case study workplace, architect	PVH headquarters Volvo Car Group, designed by Lund and Valentin.
Sector	Manufacturing	Location	Goteberg
Country	Sweden	Area	33,000 sqm (340,000 sq ft)
Number of staff	34,000	Type of project	New built owner occupied 1988
Number of staff in case study workplace	900	Use of information technology	65% of staff have terminals

Source: DEGW and Building Research Establishment

The organisation

Volvo Car Corporation has evolved its organisation in similar ways to its well known methods of producing cars by using small working groups. This has been reflected in the planning and design of their new headquarters completed in 1988.

Figure 11.54
Volvo Car Group Headquarters. (Source: DEGW and Building Research Establishment)

Figure 11.55
Reception area. (Source: DEGW and Building Research Establishment)

The Car Group has been re-thinking the relative merits of centralisation and decentralisation: marketing has been centralised away from Goteberg to Brussels, for example. There has been somewhat of a return to centralisation over the last decade, enabling a stronger focus by departments on particular skills and thereby reducing the numbers of people employed.

The Car Group has found that the introduction of smaller working groups has enabled a reduction of levels of hierarchy, although there are thought to be still too many levels in the pyramid. The managerial style is very democratic. Staff are encouraged to take decisions and even to make mistakes if necessary to learn.

Information technology is being used extensively to link the headquarters with construction and manufacturing departments. There are 300 units of CADCAM systems in the Car Group, 200 in Construction, 60 in Manufacturing and 40 in the headquarters offices. The systems are linked to plants at Goteberg and elsewhere in Sweden. The systems are also linked through to their suppliers so that drawings can be communicated electronically.

The impact of the organisation on the workplace

The greenfield site for the new headquarters is 15 kilometres from the town centre of Goteberg, at the centre of the large Volvo owned complex of buildings and plant. The new headquarters was designed for 900 staff and has

Figure 11.56
*Plan of typical floor.
(Source: DEGW and
Building Research
Establishment)*

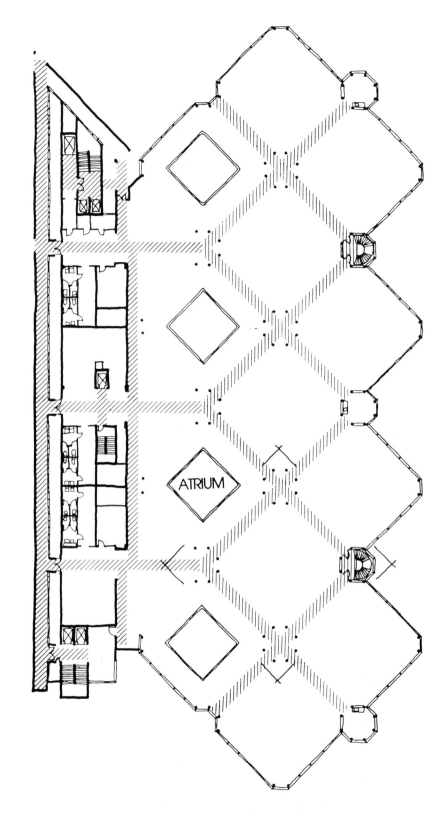

ATRIUM

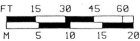

been based on planning a good working environment of the typical working group of between six and ten people. Car parking for the facility was designed in decks underground to preserve more of the landscape.

The main building entrance is a large atrium of 12 metres height, showing displays of Volvo's products and leading up to the large restaurant area. Swipe cards allow access to other parts of the building which is clearly signposted.

Move from totally open space to group areas

The history of office design for Volvo is a story of radical changes in an approach to space planning of the workplace to match the needs of the organisation. In the 1970s Volvo's offices were designed on very large entirely open plan floors (one floor was 8000 sqm (86,114 sqft) accommodating 725 people). The new offices have reversed the trend of totally open space by

providing group open areas for between fifteen and eighteen people (Figure 11.56). The move to group areas rather than total open plan reflects the organisational approach to create smaller working groups that achieve higher levels of self-management. Volvo have found that the group open plan bays work very well in terms of communication, privacy, and controlling the problems of disturbance that were experienced in the totally open plan solutions.

Nine working group areas of 15 metres by 15 metres have been created on large floor plates of 3500 sqm on a diagonal grid. The 15 metre bay is a useful structural dimension to work with in concrete. It is intended that each bay can be occupied by two smaller working groups (two groups of up to ten people) or could be occupied by one larger group. The point of access to each group bay is at the corner in one of either two positions, this allows for the possibility of connecting two bays together where that would be useful for a department.

Volvo prefer larger floorplates to bring together large departmental groups and avoid the use of stairs. The group bays are interspersed with atriums that bring light into the deeper space and are the sites of very large scale sculptures that rise up through the building. The atrium forms the focus of three bays. At the rear of the building are the main building cores, central support spaces and major circulation routes. Conference rooms are arranged adjacent to the four atriums. The size of the floors is such that there are staff as far as 20 metres from windows, but so far there have not been any complaints (on the other hand 60% of staff are at or very near windows).

Moving people not desks

The group areas are designed so that every workstation is identical and is provided with a large area of work surface. The footprint of each workstation is always the same and allows Volvo to move people around the office without ever having to change the configuration of furniture (Figure 11.59). There are low partitions between the desks at the perimeter of each bay providing a sense of group community and privacy. Within each bay small informal meeting areas are provided. A full scale mock up of the new group space was set up before the building was completed and was available for review and

Figure 11.57
Plan of typical working group area. (Source: DEGW and Building Research Establishment)

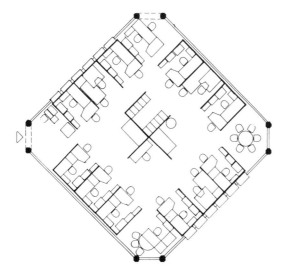

Figure 11.58
Group working area. (Source: DEGW and Building Research Establishment)

comment for eighteen months. The mock up led to a reduction in the size of the bay. The group areas are considered very productive and well-liked. Between 1989–90 Volvo moved 500 people through the office without any difficulty.

Generous space standards and amenities

Compared to United Kingdom office buildings, the space standards at the Volvo Car Group are generous, amounting to around 35 sqm per person (gross external area), it is expected this will reduce eventually to 30 sqm per person when the building is fully occupied. The staff are provided with excellent and unusual amenities as well: large scale works of art, planting throughout the work and support areas, a small library for staff use, an excellent cafeteria, and a small shop for groceries and gifts and a bank cash machine.

Along the front of the building are a series of small glass walled bays in which staff congregate to have a break and make tea or coffee (Figure 11.60). One such bay would serve up to three of the larger working group areas.

Highly serviced but energy efficient office space

A high level of power is provided, both clean and supported by back-up generators. Cables are carried overhead and dropped down to partitions in the group areas and down one central pole in each group area. (Cables are not allowed into the desk in Sweden). There is therefore no requirement for a raised floor which has enabled the building to be lower than otherwise, a considerable advantage for a site which had severe restrictions on building height.

Downlighting to 500 lux standard is provided from fluorescent fittings. Individuals can switch on and off their local light fittings and move them along a track to reposition the source. (Apparently staff do not often move the light source). There are also task lights at every desk.

The high level of use of information technology has created a heavy heat load from equipment, as well as from people and lighting. The high level of insulation of the building has resulted in the surprising requirement for no heating in the winter, and the need for air conditioning all the year round. A minimal electrical heating source is available for exceptionally cold periods of weather, but has rarely been used.

Figure 11.59
Typical desk worksurface area. (Source: DEGW and Building Research Establishment)

Figure 11.60
Coffee and tea point. (Source: DEGW and Building Research Establishment)

12 Initiatives for the Responsible Workplace

Introduction

The trend papers and the case studies have provided the source material for ten areas targeted for intervention by user organisations and their consultants and suppliers wishing to drive down occupancy costs and at the same time to use office space more effectively. These targets range from those with the most immediate scope for action, to those requiring more fundamental and longer term changes of strategy. All of the interventions are intended to provide makers and users of Responsible Workplaces with ways of adding value and minimising costs. The target areas are:

- facilities management
- furniture and settings
- layout: openness and enclosure
- services and the internal environment
- building skin
- building shell
- recycling and re-use
- building intelligence
- procurement and tenure
- location and the city

At each of these levels significant changes and opportunities are identified. A series of initiatives and approaches are outlined for each target area which are intended to be concrete, relevant, and timely and above all relevant for those involved in the design, use and management of workplaces. Almost all the interventions outlined fall into the short and medium term (the next five years). For each area of initiative we have not attempted to suggest each and every possible new trend, development or idea for a product or service. Instead we have focused on what we believe to be the most significant. Some initiatives are neither surprising nor radical; they simply refocus attention on getting the most out of the least in ways that are also environmentally responsible. Many ideas overlap and recur across the fields, suggesting the powerful relevance of these proposals. For each initiative we state:

- *The significance of the opportunity*: how does this area of intervention offer solutions which maximise value and minimise costs?

- The aspects most important to *focus* on for product and service development. There are the most important new ideas or issues to contend with in approaching new or improved products and services.

- Ideas for new *products and services*. The ideas are presented in terms of whether actions or research should be undertaken in the short (next three years), medium (three to five years) or longer term (more than five years).

- *Measurements* to identify things users or suppliers need to know to understand needs, performance, and success; particular regulatory pressures where relevant; and measures that relate the initiative to the wider community of professional knowledge.

- *Sources and precedents* from the trend papers and case studies which provide arguments, evidence, or examples of ways in which these initiatives have already been considered or implemented.

Sources and precedents

Trend Papers

Bruce Lloyd,
Chapter 4

William Bordass,
Chapter 7

Adrian Leaman and Iain Borden,
Chapter 2

Andrew Laing,
Chapter 3

Case Studies

Digital Equipment Corporation, Finland.
Suppliers included within the workplace to better serve users.

Volvo Car Corporation, Sweden.
Churn managed through semi-enclosed areas for working groups using standard workstation footprints.

Dent Lee Witte plc, UK.
Management of shared space for non-hierarchical consultancy facilitated by careful furniture selection.

Glaxo Pharmaceuticals UK, Ltd.
Cultural change drove redefinition of workplace to enable less hierarchy and more communication.

PA Consulting Group, UK.
Maximising use of expensive central city space by designing shared workstations to suit the amount of time staff are in the office.

FACILITIES MANAGEMENT

Significance of opportunity

Facilities management should move from merely minimising costs to using knowledge of how the workplace can be used innovatively to support organisational effectiveness. Cost minimisation should be value adding, maximising the effective management of the workplace building through time. More facilities decisions need to both reduce costs and enhance employee effectiveness.

Focus

- Understand the effectiveness of the use of the workplace for the organisation

- Maximise utilisation of space over time

- Use information technology to support multiple work settings within and/or outside the office for individual and/or shared use

- More and better post occupancy evaluation and user feedback.

Measurements

- Costs in use and accounting procedures to enable valid cross building comparisons

- Occupancy costs as % of turnover; asset utilisation (revenue/sqft/capita).
  - occupancy of space through time
  - costs of churn
  - work time spent in non-office locations.
  - staff satisfaction surveys
  - environmental costs and benefits at the workplace.

- Comprehensive accessible databases

NEW PRODUCTS AND SERVICES	TIMESCALE		
	Short	Medium	Long
• Leasing as opposed to ownership for more workplace facilities such as furniture.	✔		
• Improved performance specification and contract management with suppliers.	✔		
• Software to support users' own space planning and building management			
• Management of access and security of wide range of core and peripheral workers working in various places and settings.	✔		
• Information technology and telecommunications services to manage shared space and mobile work (phone routing, network systems)	✔		
• Contract out tactical facility management.	✔		
• Energy management, recycling, green supply policies.	✔		
• Use BREEAM 'New Offices' to assess environmental performance of the building	✔		
• Measurement of FM performance in relation to organisational success.	✔		

Source: DEGW and Building Research Establishment

Sources and precedents

Trend Papers

Alan Flatman, Chapter 5

George Atkinson, Chapter 10

Case Studies

ITN, UK. Designed own furniture using cheap materials for quick and easy changes to support group working

Dent Lee Witte, Plc, UK; Spie Batignolles, France; Volvo Car Corporation, Sweden. Staff involvement in furniture selection.

Dent Lee Witte Plc, and PA Consulting Group, UK. Furniture designed to support shared space use.

Digital Equipment Corporation, Finland. Furniture supports diverse shared work settings supported by high levels of networked information technology.

FURNITURE AND SETTINGS

Significance of opportunity

The settings of the workplace are highly adaptive to changing organisational requirements. They are also the least constrained in terms of procurement and the one with potentially the fastest turnover in the life-cycle of workplace components. Furniture is a highly accessible way to add value to workplace performance, of doing the most with the least.

Focus

- More away from focus on the workstation for the full-time individual
- Flexible work settings for groups, projects, teams, and shared space over time
- Furniture to support varied, intensive, and developing use of information technology (including 'Groupware', the software for interactive group work)
- Storage – new needs for mobility and redesign in relation to information technology

- User inputs: selection processes; users' knowledge and experience for feedback; furniture as part of post-occupancy evaluation (see Facilities management)
- Definition of corporate image and culture
- Use of furniture and setting design to bridge between the base building specification and users' needs: creating the most effective space to suit the work process
- Increased environmental and regulatory pressures

Measurements

- Tools to create typologies of work patterns related to furniture requirements: methods of envisioning the design brief for the work process.
- Measures of the extent to which furniture can support both simultaneous as well as sequential work tasks.
- Compliance with regulatory requirements.

NEW PRODUCTS AND SERVICES	TIMESCALE		
	Short	Medium	Long
• Equipment to support group, project, team work	✔		
• Support different users over time (shared desks, hot desking, mobile work), provide temporary personalisation and easy abandonment	✔		
• Settings for different kinds of tasks (multiple settings)	✔		
• Visual and acoustic privacy in open areas	✔		
• Storage: mobility, local versus group, and integration with electronic storage			
• Furniture to allow individual environmental control	✔		
• Higher ergonomic standards	✔		
• Furniture products linked to facility management:			
– Users planning space through software, envisioning the work process		✔	
– Tools to plan and manage shared space, facilities, and mobile communications		✔	
– Furniture to handle mobile information technology and communications equipment	✔	✔	
• Design products to respond to users' concerns about: airborne pollution, durability, recycling, non-toxicity, and energy efficiency	✔		
• Information technology and communications which support personal mobility and are not workstation based		✔	

Source: DEGW and Building Research Establishment

Case Studies

PA Consulting Group, UK. Entirely open offices, but zoned to allow quieter areas.

Greenpeace, UK. Small group open areas for campaign teams.

MEPC, UK. Enclosed offices in internal space with glass fronts, open plan space with aspect.

IBM, UK. Use of temporarily unoccupied managers offices for quiet work and meetings by other staff.

Edding, Germany. Combi office allows individual privacy and group work.

Dent Lee Witte, plc UK. In open plan shared desking office, flaps on desks may be turned up to indicate a need for privacy.

Digital Equipment Corporation, Finland. Mobile phones allow workers to seek privacy in open plan shared space office: individuals walk to a quiet place to talk privately.

LAYOUT: OPENNESS AND ENCLOSURE

Significance of opportunity

Layout must balance the push to cellularisation (led by Germany and Scandinavia) against the pressures to minimise costs and add value through higher density interactive work patterns in open plan settings. The traditional opposition of open versus enclosed space should be challenged by more creative definitions of types of space and patterns of use. (Few organisations can afford the Combi-office which provides both cellular and group space for users).

Open areas should be designed and managed to allow both quiet and reflective work and the use of shared and group space. Smaller more highly defined open areas for small groups may be preferable. Enclosed space should be allocated less by status and ownership by individuals and more by recognising shared spaces for particular tasks may require enclosure. Very small personalised highly controllable enclosed spaces for individual work are one direction of change.

The use of information technology to support mobile working within the office allows entirely new ways of planning space.

Focus

Design the right balance between maximising communication and space for quiet and reflective work; between group, team and project work, and confidential or individual work; and between group areas and individual access to daylight, aspect and ventilation.

Measurements

- Measure occupancy of space over time
- Evaluate how far work tasks can become mobile
- Evaluate degree to which information technology networks can support new layouts and patterns of work

NEW PRODUCTS AND SERVICES	TIMESCALE		
	Short	Medium	Long
• Planning models of open layout to provide areas of high interaction and areas for quiet work	✔		
• Planning models of open space for different work styles facilitated by mobility of work across shared spaces	✔		
• Designs for cellular space for increased electronic communication and sharing through time	✔		
• Partitions and furniture designed for more acoustic and visual privacy	✔		
• Networked file servers and reduction of paper based communication supports mobility: influence office planning concepts	✔		
• Products to allow use of other non-office locations for work (at home, at clients)		✔	
• Information technology and communication tools to support mobile and varied work locations	✔		
• Avoid sick building syndrome with careful layout design, ventilation, lighting, and user controllability.	✔		

Source: DEGW and Building Research Establishment

SERVICES AND THE INTERNAL ENVIRONMENT

Significance of opportunity

The demands of information technology on the internal environment are expected to decline as equipment becomes more robust, more energy efficient and emits less heat. Many users have made clear their preference to avoid air conditioning and to control their own environment. The design of base building shells should avoid wherever possible an imposed requirement for full air conditioning.

Naturally serviced workplaces, which maximise natural ventilation and make use of the building design and fabric to cool the interior, can still support highly intensive information technology work. Mixed mode buildings, designed for the local installation of air conditioning only in zones where it is really necessary, can maximise natural servicing strategies while allowing for high levels of servicing if required. The distributed servicing of the building for heating, ventilation, and air conditioning allows for independent local controls. These can be supported by linked central systems serving decentralised equipment.

Focus

- Design robust buildings that provide passive environmental control, minimum energy consumption, minimum throwaway elements, capable of accommodating more intensive services in local areas

- Think of services as having short, medium, and long term elements

- Develop ad hoc approaches to services within a rigorous strategic framework

- Avoid duplication of servicing voids at both floor and ceiling. Save volume, materials

- Integrate information technology and services

Measurements

- Measure true energy requirements for equipment under typical use patterns (avoid over specification)

- Environmental impact assessments and audits of buildings, eg BREEAM

- Carbon emissions from energy use

- User satisfaction

NEW PRODUCTS AND SERVICES	TIMESCALE		
	Short	Medium	Long
• Systems to add functions to a base building servicing provision	✔		
• Control and management and zoning of services through simple and user friendly building intelligence (see *Building intelligence*)	✔		
• Mixed mode services: products and strategies (both natural ventilation and air conditioning)	✔		
• Use BREEAM 'New Offices' to assess environmental performance of the building	✔		
• Improved distribution and zoning efficiency (individual components and integrated systems)	✔		
• Better site planning and building massing to protect against noise pollution (avoid air conditioning)	✔		
• Ways of extracting unwanted heat at source with stand alone equipment	✔		
• Structured cabling and convergence of communications standards to reduce amount of cables.	✔		
• Single, universal, long life cables for voice and data.	✔		
• Advanced communications and information technology increasingly personal rather than workstation based (see also *Location and the city* and *Furniture and settings*)		✔	
• ISDN networks will facilitate more homeworking.			✔

Source: DEGW and Building Research Establishment

Sources and precedents

Trend Papers

William Bordass,
Chapter 7

Simon Hodgkinson,
Chapter 8

George Atkinson
Chapter 10

Case Studies

Greenpeace, UK.
Big double glazed
windows, low
emissivity glass,
openable.

Edding, Germany.
Natural light in Combi
offices.

AWK, Germany.
Windows part of
economic energy
policy.

*Olivetti, Information
Services Group, Italy.*
Mixed mode
servicing, zoned for
opening windows in
part.

BUILDING SKIN

Significance of opportunity

The building skin should be considered as integral to the way buildings perform and are managed, no longer simply as a sealing of the building from the external environment. The skin, although independent of building shell, should complement robust simple building designs that maximise the use of natural forces and enhance overall building performance. It should be altered to suit changing needs in a way that is not extravagant or wasteful of materials and energy. (See also *Building intelligence*).

The window element is particularly significant, providing:

- aspect

- natural light

- natural ventilation

- personalised control

- staff well being

all of which will be of increasing importance for users. (See also *Re-use and recycling*).

Focus

New balance between:

Maximising aspect and daylight:	Minimising overheating and glare
Individual's preference for shallow space:	Depth of space required for group work and support space
Depth and configuration for natural ventilation:	Flexibility of use of space
Operable windows with individual control	Glare and comfort problems, avoidance of draughts, noise and disturbance

Need to thermally balance the heat loads of the building across the floor plate through the use of multi-zoned servicing systems with local services and controls (see Building services).

Measurements

- Environmental targets, labelling, energy use, audits

- Window to floor area ratio – balance of aspect and energy use

- Statutory requirements for distance of workstation to windows (Germany)

- Design and product guides (Green)

- Cradle to grave impacts of materials

- User satisfaction – individual control

- Capacity to change to adapt to changing external and internal circumstances

- Performance as a filter, intermediary between inside and outside

NEW PRODUCTS AND SERVICES	TIMESCALE		
	Short	Medium	Long
• Openable, more energy efficient windows, more user control	✔		
- windows for mixed mode buildings – night ventilation (automatic?)	✔		
- windows that avoid draughts	✔		
• Devices to reduce glare	✔		
• Lightweight cladding, easily dismantled, easily re-used and recycled – uncoupled from shell		✔	
• Cladding: climate sensitive passive environmental control, minimum energy consumption and throwaway elements, able to accommodate intensive services if required. (See *Building intelligence*).		✔	
• Combination of best existing products/technologies	✔		
• New materials which respond to changing environmental conditions	✔		
• Use of building intelligence to allow building to respond to internal and external environmental change	✔		

Source: DEGW and Building Research Establishment

BUILDING SHELL

Significance of opportunity

The shell is the building element with the longest life span. The critical area of opportunity will be maximising the simplicity, flexibility, and relative cheapness of building shells to allow the most inventive, individual and highly tailored adaptation to users' needs both initially and through time, in the least resource hungry manner. The rationalisation of the building shell (in design and construction) has to be balanced by diversity in how it can be adapted, fitted out, serviced, and used over time. The distribution of building cores should be designed to provide accessible distribution of environmental servicing, power and cabling.

Focus

Simplicity

Simpler more robust building shells and configurations will allow the greatest degree of modification and adaptation to change.

Flexibility

The building shell and configuration should minimise the constraints imposed upon im-mediate and successive users in terms of types of work settings, servicing, and capacity for re-use.

Low cost

Expenditure on services, fit out and settings is more valuable if tailored to the specific and changing needs of users, rather than pre-determined by high levels of expenditure on the shell.

Measurements

Relationship between depth of space and floor to floor height. The sectional floor to floor height of the structure is critical in providing future capacity of the building to absorb technology and servicing elements. The depth of space from building to perimeter to core elements (or from glass to glass) will be critical in providing access to daylight, views and the outside environment. The move away from fully-sealed air conditioned buildings may lead to pressure to reduce sectional height. This should be avoided as flexibility for local servicing requirements will need to be retained. In addition, natural ventilation will be more effective, and the space more aesthetically pleasing, if greater volume of space is provided.

Cradle to grave impacts (materials).
Product guidelines.

NEW PRODUCTS AND SERVICES	TIMESCALE		
	Short	Medium	Long
• Simpler, cheaper more robust shells with inherent capacity for change	✔		
• Design of narrower depth space carefully to avoid raised floors and air conditioning, while minimising solar and lighting heat gains with effective ventilation (see also *Building skin*)	✔		
• Lightweight, standard component shells, easily dismantled, easily recycled		✔	
• Shell and core buildings that are generously proportioned to support longterm changes in use	✔		
• Shell configurations (depths and floor to floor heights) which do not predetermine high levels of artificial environmental services around 15m glass to glass depth, 7.5m glass to core)	✔		

Source: DEGW and Building Research Establishment

Sources and precedents

Trend Papers

Simon Hodgkinson,
Chapter 8

William Bordass
Chapter 7

Case Studies

IMSA, Netherlands.
Recycled materials
and furniture
proposed to be used
for new building.

*Spie Batignolles,
France.*
Re-use of moveable
partitions to
reconfigure cellular
space (avoids
frequent construction
of new partitions as
the organisation
moves staff).

Volvo, Sweden.
Simple desk
configuration allows
frequent churn and
re-use without re-
designing or
replacing
workstations.

Greenpeace, UK.
Re-use of old furniture
in new headquarters.
(See also *Furniture*).

RECYCLING AND RE-USE

Significance of opportunity

Elements within buildings as well as entire buildings can be designed for recycling and re-use.

Cables are now 're-used' in structured wiring, and partitions are often moved. There is scope to re-use a wider range of products, both within existing buildings or at other sites.

Focus

- Distinguish between low value elements unlikely to be re-usable (such as sand, cement), and those higher value or robust items that will survive and merit re-use (such as bricks, long life services elements)

- The throwaway attitude to the fit-out and interior architecture of buildings may be challenged as green pressures will encourage higher expectations for re-use and recycling.

(See also *Procurement and Tenure*)

- The junctions of systems are the critical enabling points of re-usability. They should therefore be robust and based on common dimensional standards

Measurements

- Need to develop more knowledge on real life cycle energy costs of building and interiors materials and components. These include: initial costs; energy costs; operation and maintenance costs; labour; material and other embodied costs. Labelling systems for products to compare life cycle energy costs would enhance the ability to evaluate which elements or materials should be designed for recycling or re-use.

- Existing labelling systems for buildings (such as BREEAM) could evolve to incorporate comparative measures of potential for recycling for re-use of building materials and components.

- Product suppliers for interior components such as partitions, ceilings, furniture, lighting fixtures, air conditioning and other equipment may be under pressure to supply information on recyclability and re-usability of components.

NEW PRODUCTS AND SERVICES	TIMESCALE		
	Short	Medium	Long
• Dimensional co-ordination of products	✔		
• Services: Especially junctions to be standardised – such as partition to ceiling, cable patching.	✔		
• Furniture: Re-use, refurnishing of components. Leasing, provision of quality guarantees on re-use.	✔		
• Skins: Inner and outer layers – inner to be interchangeable.	✔		
• Insulation: Bagged for handling, cleanliness – becomes re-usable.	✔		
• Component systems more standardised for re-use.		✔	
• Improve junctions between different manufacturers' products for example, the three pin plug.		✔	
• Adaptive re-use of buildings (infrastructure)	✔		

Source: DEGW and Building Research Establishment

BUILDING INTELLIGENCE

Significance of opportunity

Building intelligence assists users to manage, control and use their workplace in a more effective, economical, and less resource hungry manner. The value of intelligence is not in providing technology as such, but in providing technology appropriate to the requirements of use over time. Intelligence should not pre-suppose highly specified and highly serviced workplaces where these are not needed. The critical step is in moving from prescriptive to responsive intelligence.

Focus

- Apply high technology systems to make better use of simple building elements (technology as caretaker)

- Avoid under utilisation of intelligence – over specification

- Develop robust intelligence for alternative scenarios and uncertainty of patterns of use over time

- Use concept of buildings as open ended systems over their whole life

- Review capacity of building shell to absorb technologies of intelligence over the long term, independent of current needs of particular user

- Differentiate between the intelligence used to support the business, to plan the space, and to manage the building

Measurements

- Capacity of buildings to accommodate intelligence (the capacity of the building shell, the needs of the particular user)

- Profiles of organisations' patterns of demand for levels of intelligence: assessment of appropriateness of intelligence for managing the business, the space and the building

- Measures of efficiency of intelligence in reducing operational costs (energy consumption, maintenance, reconfiguration of space) versus the effectiveness of intelligence in supporting overall quality of organisational performance

NEW PRODUCTS AND SERVICES	TIMESCALE		
	Short	Medium	Long
Cabling			
• Standard universal communication networks for all devices		✔	
• Accommodate range of cable networks flexibly and systematically	✔		
Electronic building and energy management (BEMS)			
• From dedicated single purpose devices to programmable multi-functions	✔		
• From central systems to distributed networks with local plant control.	✔		
From prescriptive to responsive building management			
• Building energy management systems that are user friendly and integrated to management.	✔		
• Lighting and ventilation adjust automatically to context of use (light, people)	✔		
• Intelligent access control, smart cards	✔		
• Plant to allow for variety of user control and command.	✔		
Adaptive facades			
• Passive, mechanical and electrical systems of facade controls	✔		
• Automatic control of light and heat transmission of facade using electronic systems		✔	
Automation and communication			
• Applications to support group working.		✔	
• Advanced electronic mail and video conferencing.		✔	
• Personal rather than workstation based communication.		✔	

Source: DEGW and Building Research Establishment

Sources and precedents

Trend Papers

Adrian Leaman and Iain Borden,
Chapter 2

Case Studies

IBM, UK.
Lease with rentalised fit-out.

Spie Batignolles, France.
Created own campus of buildings with simple speculative building types.

PROCUREMENT AND TENURE

Significance of opportunity

Procurement policies should be designed to encourage the design of new buildings with the capacity to accommodate change and facilitate the optimal re-use of existing buildings. A closer match between tenant and user requirements and the procurement of buildings is required. Procurement methods need to evolve to be closer to organisational requirements. Think of buildings as plant rather than real estate.

Focus

Respond to organisational change

- Provide smaller more flexible spaces for downsizing organisations

- Information technology and intelligence may challenge the idea of the building only as 'hardware', the building will be conceptualised as a total facility combining hardware and software for effective business operations

- Provide shorter more flexible leases (especially in the UK)

- Encourage more user feedback on the design and management of the building

- Developers and facility managers to provide international standards of service to follow international user needs across Europe

- Avoid boom and bust property cycle by closer relationships with users: for example more joint venture relationships between developers and occupiers for development.

Depreciation

- Depreciation for buildings should be broken down into the constituent parts of the building (e.g. shell, services, furniture) to more accurately reflect useful life of the components.

Capital investment

- Organisations should invest capital to support working patterns instead of directing investment at buildings (what does it take to get the job done?)

More choice

- The providers of workplaces should respond to the increasing number and sophistication of demands from end-users by offering a wider range of choices

Measurements

- Range of task types/working patterns which can be accommodated at a site

- Revenue/person/area

NEW PRODUCTS AND SERVICES	TIMESCALE		
	Short	Medium	Long
• Revise the valuation process to reflect environmental life–cycle costs.		✔	
• Shorter leases – suit different users with different time horizons	✔		
• Value land separate from buildings			
• Use BREEAM 'New Offices' to assess environmental performance of the building	✔		✔
• More options to rentalise fit out	✔		
• Owner occupied buildings to be designed to be adaptable for other users	✔		
• Developers to provide leased space that is more highly adaptive to user requirements	✔		
• Developers provide 'after-sales' services for tenants, develop longer term relationships as building managers, more joint ventures with occupiers.	✔		
• Developers to compete on **services** provision as well as space.	✔		
• Consortia of component suppliers design, build and manage buildings		✔	✔
• Expect new players who are integrators supplying range of services to optimise the relationship between the user and the building (adding value of intelligence across and between sites and buildings)			

Source: DEGW and Building Research Establishment

Sources and precedents

Trend Papers

Bruce Lloyd,
Chapter 4

Andrew Harrison,
Chapter 6

Alan Flatman,
Chapter 5

Brian McDougall,
Chapter 9

Case Studies

Spie Batignolles, France.
Greenfield campus of main office buildings, small downtown satellite office for client meetings only.

PA Consulting Group, UK.
High density use of shared space in expensive central office critical for prestige and client contact.

Dent Lee Witte plc, UK.
Desk sharing by consultants in high amenity office on river frontage.

LOCATION AND THE CITY

Significance of opportunity

Organisations can add value to their performance and minimise costs by taking greater advantage of the relative costs and benefits of different locations for workplaces. Evaluation of costs and benefits of location will increasingly include environmental issues, as these become of increasing concern to consumers and staff.

Focus

Closer match organisation: location

The costs and benefits of central and peripheral locations (downtown sites versus suburban or greenfield sites) should be more vigorously matched against the profile of organisational requirements, especially in relation to the characteristics of changing employment and work practices. Can long distance commuting be avoided by more home working? Can the site of the office be positioned better in relation to public transport? Is the pattern of energy use understood? What are the costs of pollution and of widespread car use?

Maximise value of central expensive sites

Products, services, and management tools which can maximise organisational effectiveness in expensive central sites either alone or in conjunction with working in other locations should be examined more rigorously. For example, shared space strategies can maximise the use of expensive downtown sites especially when combined with homeworking or working at other sites.

Redevelop and re-use damaged environments

The avoidance of greenfield sites for new development by re-using older damaged built environments will be seen as environmentally beneficial. Make the best use of existing infrastructure.

Measurements

- Frequency of internal and client meetings to establish need for central urban locations

- Need for network of face to face contacts

- Degree of reliance on central urban resources

- Capacity of information technology and communications systems to overcome locational ties

- Capacity of public transport services to substitute for private car use

- Amenity values to users of urban versus suburban or rural environments

- Evaluate scope for range of locations to serve different needs, central, peripheral work centres, homeworking

NEW PRODUCTS AND SERVICES	TIMESCALE		
	Short	Medium	Long
• Design workplace for changing work and events through time in central expensive locations	✔		
• Generic individual workspaces suitable for a range of activities for different people over time in central locations (desk sharing).	✔		
• Smaller buildings sited in various locations to maximise locational advantages.	✔		
• Access to advanced cable infrastructures provided by developers/network suppliers.		✔	
• Communication substitutes for transport such as information technology and homeworking.		✔	
• Higher density development of existing urban centres rather than business parks in greenfield sites (brown site developments).			✔
• Innovative uses of existing structures and infrastructures		✔	
• New kinds of city and patterns of use: living, leisure, work		✔	

Source: DEGW and Building Research Establishment

Selected publications

Selected DEGW publications

John Worthington and Allan Konya, *Fitting out the Workplace*, Architectural Press, 1988

Francis Duffy and Alex Henney, *The Changing City*, Bulstrode Press, 1989

Thomas Beuker, John Worthington and Takashi Murai, *The Human Office*, CSK Japan, 1990

The Responsive Office, Steelcase Strafor/Polymath, 1990

Walter Kleeman, *Interior Design of the Electronic Office*, Van Nostrand Reinhold, 1991

Frederique de Gravelaine, *Guide de l'Aménagement de Bureaux*, Editions du Moniteur, 1991

The Intelligent Building in Europe, Executive Summary, DEGW London, 1992

Francis Duffy, *The Changing Workplace*, Phaidon, 1992

Intelligent Buildings: Designing and Managing the IT Infrastructure, CSC Index, RIBA Publications, 1992

Selected Building Research Establishment publications

BR86   *Environmental design manual – summer conditions in naturally-ventilated offices. 1988. £18*

BR95   *Better briefing means better buildings. 1987. £10*

BR96   *Fire safety in buildings. 1986. £15*

BR97   *Building regulation and health. 1986. E10*

BR102   *Electromagnetic compatibility requirements for microelectronics in building services: a proposed standard. 1987. £24*

BR115   *Low-water-use washdown WCs. 1987. £10*

BR125   *Unvented domestic hot-water systems. 1988. £15*

BR126   *Domestic heat pumps: performance and economics. 1988. £20*

BR127   *Psychological aspects of informative fire warning systems. 1988. £8*

BR129   *Daylight as a passive solar energy option: an assessment of its potential in non-domestic buildings. 1988. £18*

BR143   *Thermal insulation: avoiding risks. 1989. £10*

BR150   *Building Regulations: conservation of fuel and power – the 'energy target' method of compliance for dwellings. 1989. £10*

BR170   *Energy use in buildings and carbon dioxide emissions. 1990. £25*

BR175   *Electric heating in highly-insulated buildings – experiences from the BRE Low Energy Office. 1990. £25*

BR177   *The Construction Products Directive of the European Communities. Draft Interpretative Document – Protection against noise. 1990. £12.50*

BR179   *The Construction Products Directive of the European Communities. Draft Interpretative Document – Energy economy and heat retention. 1990. £12.50*

BR180 *The Construction Products Directive of the European Communities. Draft Interpretative Document Hygiene, health and the environment. 1990.* £12.50

BR181 *The Construction Products Directive of the European Communities. Draft Interpretative Document – Mechanical resistance and stability. 1990.* £12.50

BR182 *The Construction Products Directive of the European Communities. Draft Interpretative Document – Safety in use. 1990.* £12.50

BR183 BREEAM Version 1/90. *An environmental assessment for office designs. 1990.* £15

BR192 *Process integration in building services. 1991.* £25

BR206 *Electromagnetic fields: a review of the evidence for effects on health. 1991.* £20

BR209 *Site layout planning for daylight and sunlight. 1991.* £35

BR220 *Domestic energy fact file. 1992.* £18
SO7 *Handbook of hardwoods. 1982.* £20
SO39 *A handbook of softwoods. 1988.* £8

BRE publications

As well as reports and books, BRE publishes four series of leaflets: *Digests*, which are concise, state-of-the-art reviews of building technology; *Good Building Guides*, which give well illustrated practical guidance on good building design and construction; *Defect Action Sheets*, which describe concisely common faults in housebuilding; and *Information Papers* which summarise the latest research results and describe how to apply them. The leaflets are available singly at prices from £3.50 to £4.50, and also on annual subscription: details of all publications from BRE Bookshop, Building Research Establishment, Garston, Watford, WD2 7JR, *Telephone* 0923 894040, *Fax* 0923 662010.

Index